WRATH OR REST

Saints in the Hands of an Angry God

An Exegetical Primer on
Eternal Security and the Judgment of God
in the Book of Hebrews

By R. Mark Musser, M. Div.

Also by R. Mark Musser
Nazi Oaks: The Green Sacrifice of the Judeo-
Christian Worldview in the Holocaust

ACKNOWLEDGEMENTS

I would like to dedicate this book to Pastor Paul Breckel, a fellow soldier in the cause of Christ, for giving me the idea about the title of the book.

I must thank Jim Myers, my colleague on the mission field in Belarus and Ukraine, for encouraging me to write this book and for his critique.

I also would like to thank my wife, Caren, David Breckel, and Tom Elliott for all of their assistance and support in the writing of this work.

My biggest thanks must go to Dr. Duane Dunham of Western Seminary whose classes and doctoral dissertation gave me a love for the warning passages in the book of Hebrews that stands behind much of the inspiration of this book.

Wrath or Rest was written in Kiev, Ukraine. It is a compilation of my lectures taught several times in various seminaries, Bible colleges, and institutes there, including a small seminary in Al-Maty, Kazakhstan.

Endorsements & Reader Comments

"I am very grateful to Mark for his lengthy labor in providing this excellent work. It is unique and greatly needed. The book of Hebrews has been at the crossroads of a heated debate between Calvinists and Arminians for a very long time. The Calvinists warn that only those who persevere until the end prove themselves to be the true Christian, whereas the Arminians warn that those who fail to persevere will lose their salvation. In "Wrath or Rest," Mark clearly shows a third alternative using sound exegetical evidence found throughout the book of Hebrews on how God can severely warn the saints without endangering the certainty of their salvation. This work is a serious challenge to both the Calvinist and the Arminian positions – a must read."

- Dr. Earl Radmacher, Distinguished Professor of Systematic Theology and President Emeritus of Western Seminary in Portland, Oregon.

"'Wrath or Rest' can be recommended to both Christians and unbelievers alike – to Christians because it puts the book of Hebrews into its proper context in biblical doctrine and might shake them out of their hidebound lethargy; to unbelievers because it will show them what the Christian faith is all about."

– Mike Gray of St. Karnick's The American Culture

"An excellent exposition of the middle ground between Arminianism and Calvinism. Musser offers the best explanation of the difficult and seemingly conflicting positions in Soteriology found in the Scriptures. A must read not just for pastors and teacher, but for any serious student of the Word!"

– Sergei Chervichidze

"Wrath or Rest has been one of the most helpful teachings on the book of Hebrews we have come across."

– Daniel & Stephanie Ice

"Having been fascinated with Hebrews for a long time, I found 'Wrath or Rest' an outstanding treatise – very enlightening and edifying."

– Duncan Allen

CONTENTS

- Hebrews 4:11 -
Therefore let us be diligent to enter that rest,
so that no one will fall,
through following the same example of disobedience!

CHAPTER ONE

PRELIMINARY ISSUES

Interpretive Difficulties

The epistle to the Hebrews is one of the most demanding books in all of the Word of God to understand and interpret. Even more difficult is to apply the great truths of this magnificent book into daily Christian living, severe warnings and all. In the modern church relatively little is taught concerning the practical significance of the Melchizedekian Priesthood of Christ from the epistle of Hebrews, and the average pastor usually ignores the infamous warning passages. Yet the author of Hebrews, in spite of the great difficulties and perplexities of the epistle, and while recognizing the spiritual dullness of his readers (5:11-14), concludes that he has written to them only briefly (13:22). Moreover, to read all 13 chapters of this epistle out loud to a congregation would have taken at least 50 minutes, perhaps considerably longer, depending on how long the reader would pause in between phrases and sentences.[1] Thus, the so-called 'brevity' of this epistle and the rich content which permeates the entire book, are a silent rebuke to the modern tendency within Christian circles which disparages anything doctrinal or lengthy, and shows that the mental capacity of the average worshiper in the 1st century was anything but simple or naive.

---

[1]   Clough, Charley. *Hebrews*, Sermon Tape Series, Lubbock Bible Church (Lubbock, 1973).

Hebrews is a most unique book in the New Testament, and this has created any number of unique problems for the Bible student. Most notable in the book of Hebrews are the five infamous warning passages (2:1-4; 3:7-4:13; 5:11-6:8; 10:26-31; 12:12-29), and the Melchizedekian high priesthood of Christ (5:1-10:18). Both the warnings and the emphasis upon the high priestly Order of Melchizedek are unique in comparison to other New Testament documents. The warnings are untypically severe, and the doctrinal explanation of the Melchizedekian Priesthood of Christ is a foreign subject to the average Bible student. Much of the book of Hebrews therefore is highly unusual.

Even more untypical in relation to the rest of the New Testament is that there is no consensus as to who the author is and who the audience is. This has left the reader with some critical problems which can only be tentatively resolved:

> Hebrews is a delight for the person who enjoys puzzles. Its form is unusual, its setting in life is uncertain, and its argument unfamiliar. It invites engagement in the task of defining the undefined. Undefined are the identity of the writer, his conceptual background, the character and location of the community addressed, the circumstances and date of composition, the setting in life, the nature of the crisis to which the document is a response, the literary genre, and the purpose and plan of the work. Although these undefined issues continue to be addressed and debated vigorously, no real consensus has been reached.[2]

Thus the book of Hebrews is an outstanding problematic book with regard to historical setting.

Calvinism vs. Arminianism

Much more difficult is that Hebrews is a major theological battleground between Calvinism and Arminianism, and the doctrine of the Perseverance of the Saints is the primary theological bone of contention. The perseverance of the saints teaches that all genuine Christians will not fall away from the faith into apostasy, but persevere until the final

---

[2] Lane, William, *Hebrews* (Dallas, Texas: Word Publishers, 1991), 2 volumes, p xlvii.

hour so as to maintain their eternal salvation. However, the book of Hebrews warns the readers in passage after passage about falling away into apostasy (2:1-4; 3:12; 4:11; 6:1-6; 10:26-31; 12:25-29). Is it therefore possible for a Christian to commit apostasy? Indeed, the warning passages seem to indicate this tragic possibility. This therefore creates a very serious tension on the doctrine of perseverance in particular. On the one hand, this doctrine teaches that all genuine Christians will finally persevere in their faith. On the other hand, the book of Hebrews warns the readers about their lack of perseverance throughout the book (3:6, 14; 4:14; 6:11-12; 10:23, 35-36). Furthermore, the historical failure of the Exodus generation to persevere in their faith is used as the illustrative basis for its warnings (11:29; 3:7-4:11). By faith, after having been redeemed out of Egypt, the Exodus generation crossed the Red Sea (Ex 14:31; Heb 11:29) with "the greatest army in the world snapping at their heels."[3] However, they later failed to persevere in their faith to reach the promised land of rest, and this heinous failure is used as an example to avoid at all costs (2:1-4; 3:7-4:11; 10:28; 12:25-29). Thus a long cherished doctrine in the Calvinistic tradition stands on very tenuous grounds in the book of Hebrews. More to the point, a very rigid stance on the doctrine of the perseverance of the saints will crumble under the weight of the exegetical evidence found in Hebrews. The Arminian position that the perseverance of the saints is not guaranteed, that a Christian can fall away from the faith, is actually on much stronger ground here. Look at the historical failure of the Exodus generation. Look at all the warnings in Hebrews based on this historical failure. Moreover, how is it even possible to warn someone if the outcome has already been guaranteed? Answers to these sticky problems have been ingenious on the part of many a Calvinist on this point. Needless to say, these answers have not honestly satisfied the exegetical evidence found in Hebrews.

Even more acute for the Calvinist is that if the Hebrew readers fall into the judgment of which the author warns them, this will have a direct impact on their ability to persevere. The Exodus generation was *forbidden* by God to enter rest. In other words the Exodus generation was forbidden by God to *persevere* into the promised land, and this terrible failure is then held before the Hebrew readers as a most serious warning to them

---

3   Dunham, Duane. *A Doctoral Dissertation on the Hebrew Warning Passages* written for Grace Theological Seminary.

(2:2-3; 4:11; 10:28-29; 12:25). There came a time when God said enough was enough, and He literally stopped them dead in their tracks in the desert (Num 14; Heb 3:7-4:11). The same thing may also happen to the Hebrew readers (4:1-3; 6:1-3). *If God permits* (6:1-3) therefore places a big wrinkle in the whole perseverance approach. In other words, if these warnings are real genuine warnings aimed at real Christians (which the Arminian strongly holds), then the doctrine of the perseverance of the saints cannot remain unscathed. In some real sense, they will not be able to persevere, and this by the edict of God.

On the other hand, if we assume that the Arminian position is correct, and that these warnings can really be experienced by genuine believers, then this seems to indicate that a believer can lose his salvation. The failure to enter the promised land, the failure to inherit rest, is often associated with entering heaven. As such, since the Exodus generation failed to enter rest, they lost their salvation. This however, contradicts many other passages which teach that salvation is eternally secure, not only in Hebrews, but in many other passages as well (Heb 7:25; 10:10-14; John 6:35-40; 10:27-29; Rom 8:1, 31-39; Eph 1:13-14, 2:8-9, 4:30; Col 2:10-15). A salvation which can be lost is a contradiction in terms, and so the Calvinist properly maintains that a Christian cannot lose his salvation. But then how is Hebrews to be understood? If a saint falls into God's judgment can it still be considered that he persevered so as to maintain his eternal salvation? Or has he indeed lost his eternal salvation? Thus the Calvinist and the Arminian find themselves at a most serious crossroads which neither side can really resolve.

In order to avoid the conclusion that a Christian can lose his salvation, many strong Calvinists assume that the Hebrews congregation to whom the author is writing is a mixed crowd of unbelievers and believers, i.e., the unbelievers being those who will fall into the judgment and the believers being those who heed the judgments and thus continue to persevere. Thus the ability to persevere tells us who the real Christian is and who is not. The problem with this view is that Hebrews nowhere mentions that the congregation is mixed, but actually everywhere assumes exactly the opposite, that they are in fact all believers. Trying to maintain the security of the believer is certainly an honest and sincere motivation, but to resort to the doctrine of perseverance of the saints here in Hebrews in order to maintain it does not help resolve the problem, but actually confuses the issues further. In the end, this theological thrust actually clouds rather obvious passages which indicate the addressees in Hebrews are real believers, and that they can indeed fall into judgment. In the end, the doctrine of the inevitable perseverance of the saints relegates serious warning passages, originally intended for believers to unbelievers. This is unacceptable.

This problem becomes especially acute in Hebrews 6:4-6. In 6:4-5, the author explicitly uses five[4] very expressive phrases to indicate clearly that the addressees are indeed real Christians,[5] and then adds in 6:6 that these same ones are also in danger of falling away or apostasizing,[6] and this will inevitably lead into judgment (6:7-8). But since the Calvinist already knows ahead of time that all saints inevitably persevere and therefore cannot fall away, the five expressive phrases which indicate very strongly that the addressees are real believers, are outright denied. The out of place doctrine of a *nominal faith* then creeps in (of which the author mentions nothing) to replace the straightforward emphasis that the addressees are indeed real Christians. The forced exegesis of many a Calvinist on this point in order to maintain their theological system is not as notorious as it should be.[7] Furthermore, it is not a coincidence that every time a strong Calvinist comes across a serious warning passage in the New Testament (1 Cor 6:9-10; Gal 5:19-21; Eph 5:5; Heb 2:1-4; 3:6-4:13; 5:11-6:8; 10:26-39; 12:12-29), the doctrine of a *mixed congregation* conveniently shows up to rescue their sacred cow, i.e., the perseverance

---

[4]   Four participles are used to express five different phrases which describe the readers conversion experience.

[5]   Hebrews 6:4-5 ... For in the case of those who have been **once enlightened** and have **tasted of the heavenly gift** and have been made **partakers of the Holy Spirit**, and have **tasted the good Word of God** and the **powers of the age to come.** Not a few try to maintain here that **taste** means only to **sip**, meaning that some of the Hebrew readers have fallen short of a genuine conversion. The problem here is that Hebrews 2:9 expressly says that Jesus **tasted death** for every man. The cross was more than a sip, but a full genuine experience.

[6]   This last participle *falling away* grammatically agrees with the previous four participles which describes their spiritual conversion experience. This grammatical agreement becomes even more significant in that one article controls all five participles in 6:4-6. This means that those who once became Christians (6:4-5) are also the very same ones who are about to fall away (6:6).

[7]   Dillow, Jody, _Reign of the Servant Kings_ (Hayesville, NC: Schoettle Publishing Company, 1992) This book is an excellent critique of both the Arminian and Calvinistic positions showing their inherent weaknesses when they exegete warning passages.

of the saints.[8] The doctrine of perseverance precludes ahead of time that a Christian cannot fall into judgment since they always inevitably persevere. The strong Calvinist therefore is left gasping for words trying to grope with the warning passages in Hebrews, whereas the Arminian can interpret them rather straightforwardly as they ought to be.

If a Christian cannot fall into judgment, then why do we find warning passages directed against them? Strong Calvinists say that the warnings are for a mixed congregation of believers and unbelievers, and that the judgment itself is for the nominal Christian, and not for the real persevering believer. This answer is unsatisfying. For all practical purposes, it is therefore impossible to warn a real Christian in such a scenario. This creates a further problem which is very difficult to comprehend. Why would an author of Scripture spill so much ink over illusory Christians? Recognizing this, some Calvinists have even resorted to the hypothetical theory in Hebrews 6. The apostasy and ensuing judgment is hypothetical, "the writer is *merely* describing what would be the case if the elect were to fall away (an impossibility)."[9] First of all, the word 'merely' does not belong in such a serious warning passage. Secondly, to make such a serious warning passage hypothetical is no less difficult to comprehend. Again, why would the author spill so much ink over a hypothetical warning? The strong Calvinist argues that warnings are used to *ensure* that a believer will not fall away or apostasize. In other words, serious warnings are used in Scripture to guarantee the doctrine of the perseverance of the saints! As such, serious warning passages originally intended to warn real Christians about falling into apostasy and judgment have *merely* become the instrument by which the doctrine of perseverance of the saints is guaranteed! This is circular reasoning

---

[8]   It is rather refreshing to read Dr. Dunham's doctoral dissertation on the Hebrew Warning Passages written in the 1960's for Grace Theological Seminary. He is a strict five point Calvinist, and yet he allows the text of Hebrews to speak to him rather than dictate with theology in advance what difficult verses mean. He acknowledges that the warnings in Hebrews are intended for real believers, but he also tries to show that the apostasy in Hebrews does not mean a total repudiation of the faith, that the primary question at hand is not perseverance but sanctification, and that the judgments in Hebrews are not Hell but divine discipline. In this way, he is able to maintain the doctrine of the Perseverance of the Saints without resorting to forced exegesis. This is a much more even-handed approach which is far truer to the text of Hebrews. The problem here, however, is that after Dr. Dunham is done, the *Perseverance of the Saints* has still taken a serious blow, and does not look as pretty as it once did.

[9]   Erickson, Millard. *Christian Theology* (Baker Book House: Grand Rapids, Michigan, 1983), p. 993.

and does not satisfy the exegetical problems in the book of Hebrews. It has the look of clean theology, but cannot cope with the tragedies of everyday life.

This answer that warnings ensure perseverance in real Christians may still in fact be a possible theological answer, theoretically speaking, but not here in Hebrews. Calvinistic theology has determined exegesis far too much here. Rather than accept the obvious fact that the doctrine of perseverance has some serious weaknesses when it comes to interpreting warning passages, the language of Scripture is watered down to accommodate its theology.

The primary problem is that passage after passage in the book of Hebrews identifies, assumes, and presupposes that the addressees were real Christians who are about to fall into judgment. Unbelievers cannot drift away from something which they have never possessed in the first place (2:4). Unbelievers are never considered to be holy brethren (3:1), nor partakers of the heavenly calling (3:1). Neither can they hold fast a confidence firm until the end which they have never had to begin with (3:6). An unbeliever cannot become dull of hearing (5:11) since he is already spiritually dead. Neither is he able to partake of spiritual milk (5:13), let alone solid spiritual food (5:14). He simply cannot be exhorted to mature spiritually since this is not even a remote possibility for him (5:14). Likewise, he cannot be told to go beyond the basics of the Christian faith (6:1). An unbeliever cannot be called 'once'[10] enlightened (6:4), not to mention a partaker of the Holy Spirit (6:4). He has never tasted the heavenly gift, nor the powers of the age to come (6:4). An unbeliever cannot be considered a beloved one (6:9), and certainly no one can be convinced of better things for him in the future (6:9). God will reward no unbeliever for his good works (6:10; 10:35), precisely because he has never been sanctified once for all through the blood of the covenant (10:10-14, 29). Not only this, but the author includes himself when he warns his recipients (2:1,3; 3:6; 3:14; 4:1; 6:1-3; 10:26; 12:25). Is it possible for an outstanding Christian leader who is even an author of Scripture, let alone the average layman, to commit apostasy? The author of the book of Hebrews affirmatively says yes. He simply assumes throughout the letter, warnings, sins and all, that the recipients are believers.

---

[10]   "Once" here means 'once for all' as it directly parallels the once for all sacrifice of Christ mentioned later on in Hebrews 9-10.

Final Apostasy & Hell

Because of the terrible nature of the sin and the untypical severity of the warnings, many have presumed that the sin being committed in Hebrews is final apostasy so as to lose salvation, and that the judgments against this sin are the fires of hell. However, these two fundamental presumptions will not bear up under the pressure of the overall context of Hebrews. In spite of the fact that these two unexamined presuppositions have never been proven, they have silently dictated the course of this theological controversy without proper warrant. With even greater, if not ironic interest, is that both sides have general agreement over these two unproven assumptions. Here is one place where both sides agree, and yet what they agree on actually stands on very tenuous grounds.

While both the Calvinist and the Arminian tend to agree that Hebrews is warning the readers about final apostasy and hell, they disagree sharply as to who will be judged by the warnings. Since the Calvinist believes that a Christian cannot lose his salvation, and that all real Christians will persevere, the judgments that we find in the book of Hebrews cannot be addressed to real Christians. In other words, since all real Christians persevere, those who heed the warnings in Hebrews are real Christians, but those who do not heed the warnings are considered nominal Christians precisely because they did not persevere. The Arminian on the other hand, simply asserts that all the people in the congregation in the book of Hebrews are real Christians, but those who do not persevere will lose their salvation. The rather interesting fact here is that even though both of their viewpoints are opposite one another in theory, in the end, they both agree on one thing: the judgments we see in Hebrews will be meted out to the unsaved. As such, in practice they come up with the same conclusion.[11] This is very suggestive in that when the Calvinist deals with the sinning Christian, he is much more Arminian than he himself is willing to admit.[12]

---

[11]   Dillow, p. 383.

[12]   This most interesting combination has been witnessed in Ukraine on the mission field. John MacArthur, a famous Bible teacher in America who strongly emphasizes Calvinistic views on the perseverance of the saints, is actually very popular among many Arminians in Ukraine who regularly warn their members every Sunday that God will throw them into hell if they commit certain sins. Compared to Eternal Security, John MacArthur's teaching is actually very religiously correct among many an Arminian throughout the former Soviet Union. This should cause many a Calvinist to pause

With regard to the first assumption that apostasy means final apostasy so as to lose salvation, both the Calvinist and the Arminian seem to be thinking here in a rather confused way that there is a sin which Jesus has not died for: apostasy. If someone commits apostasy, this is the unpardonable sin for both systems. Hence not a few commentators begin talking about the unpardonable sin and loss of salvation in 10:26-31. Of course the strong Calvinist says that someone who commits apostasy cannot be a real Christian. But regardless, he still thinks in a rather fuzzy way that apostasy is some kind of unpardonable sin. Hence he rules out the possibility that someone who commits such an act can be a Christian. In his mind, apostasy is so heinous that it cannot be forgiven, and so therefore, according to his doctrine on the perseverance of the saints, such a person was not saved in the first place. For either system, apostasy is therefore beyond the scope of the cross.

The great problem here is that the meaning of apostasy has not been investigated properly in the book of Hebrews, nor even in the Bible in general for that matter. Both Calvinists and Arminians tend to have a very rigid view on the meaning of apostasy, a rigidity which neither the book of Hebrews, nor the Bible supports. What is for certain in the book of Hebrews is that the apostasy being warned of cannot be the unpardonable sin. The historical example of the Exodus generation clearly teaches that apostasy was committed in the desert more than once, and these apostates were later and rather quickly forgiven by God (Ex 32; Num 14). And if apostasy was forgiven under the austerity of the Old Covenant, then nothing less can be expected under the grace of the New Covenant. Hence as heinously as the Exodus generation performed, they did not commit the unpardonable sin. Likewise, as heinously as the Hebrew readers were beginning to act, they are not being threatened with the unpardonable sin. Those who have been once for all sanctified by the cross, i.e., eternal security, will still experience the fiery judgments of God if they continue to sin willfully (10:10-29), but this is never stated to be the unpardonable sin, much less loss of salvation. The fact is that both the Calvinists and the Arminians have a notion of apostasy based on Roman Catholic ecclesiastical tradition, not upon the biblical evidence.[13] **Sola Scriptura** has somehow been lost along the way

---

about his views on salvation. Are they really that radically different? The answer is no.

13   Dunham, *A Survey of Biblical Apostasy.*

in understanding the nature of biblical apostasy. Worse is that a very dubious source with notorious historical practices is actually the basis for their views on apostasy.

With regard to the second assumption both the Calvinists and Arminians are somehow assuming that there is only one way for God to punish His people: to throw them into hell. This is an extreme view in light of Hebrews and the Scriptures in general. In spite of the fact that immediately before the author of Hebrews severely warns his readers in 12:25-29 for the last time in the book, he reminds them, "for those whom the Lord *loves* He disciplines, and He scourges every son whom He *receives* (12:6)." Needless to say, this is not the kind of teaching which threatens people with eternal hellfire. Moreover, 1 Corinthians 11:28-32 mentions three specific categories of divine discipline which are clearly distinguished from condemnation into hell: physical death, weakness and sickness. These verses actually teach that God may even kill a Christian, or inflict sicknesses or weaknesses upon him for his sins. Paul then adds in verse 32 that God metes out this discipline so they will *not* be condemned with the world. Thus divine discipline of sinning Christians and the doctrine of hell are mutually exclusive categories. The book of Hebrews speaks of yet another category of divine discipline worse than death: to live out in a desert like a refugee for 40 years without a home and without rest, experiencing the wrath of God in the process. The Exodus generation was actually better off in Egypt than in the wilderness, but because of their lack of faithful perseverance, God sentenced them to die out in the wilderness through a period of 40 long wasted years. However, this judgment cannot be associated with hellfire. Moses and Aaron also endured this fiery judgment. They too were forbidden the rest inheritance in Canaan because of their own unbelief (Num 20:8-20). Yet the assumption is that both of them were certainly saved. Furthermore, if Moses and Aaron can endure divine judgment, then so can the Hebrew readers, not to mention the modern church. In short, as severe as they are, the fiery judgments in Hebrews are not qualified with hellish overtones, and they unquestionably occur within a salvation context. The warnings and judgments in the book of Hebrews are thus specifically designed for wayward believers. As such, the book of Hebrews is talking about a special type of judgment for Christians, not the more general judgment of hell designed for unbelievers.

While Hebrews does clearly teach that all saints are required to persevere (3:6; 3:14; 6:11-12; 10:23; 10:35-39; 12:1-15), nowhere does it say that this process is inevitable. In fact the warning passages clearly indicate otherwise. The reason why the Hebrews readers are about to fall into judgment is precisely because of their lack of perseverance (3:6; 3:14; 6:11-12; 10:23; 10:35-39). One of the primary thrusts of the book of Hebrews is the certainty of divine judgment if God's people continue to sin willfully, not the inevitable perseverance of the saints, nor an irremediable apostasy that leads to hellfire.[14] While perseverance in good works are not the condition of salvation, they are most certainly commanded as a consequence of salvation. However, the requirement to do good works and the fulfillment to do them are two different operations. The former is a divine command demanding the personal responsibility of the latter, and no preconceived theology can ensure that any Christian will finally and inevitably do the right thing. Commands are notoriously abused by the free will of many a person, even in the Bible.

Somewhat curiously, Calvinists strongly believe in a doctrine called Unconditional Election, meaning that God elects ahead of time those who will believe. Yet when they come to discussing salvation, i.e., who is really saved, this doctrine is no longer taken seriously, and is replaced by the perseverance of the saints, which by definition is highly conditional. In order to persevere you must fulfill divine commands. Thus in the Calvinistic system, unconditional election is actually not unconditional at all, but conditionally based upon the ultimate perseverance of the saints. Only those who persevere until the end have been unconditionally elected. This is a theological tautology.

The fact of the matter is that unconditional election fits in far better with the doctrine of eternal security than the perseverance of the saints. Eternal security teaches unconditionally that no Christian can lose his salvation under any circumstances, not even the sin of apostasy. While this may not sound pretty, it is still far more consistent with the meaning of the doctrine of Unconditional Election. The problem was that the Roman Catholics strongly opposed the teaching on Unconditional Election during the Reformation. They cried out that this would lead to licentiousness and irresponsible behavior. Since people knew that they were already saved, they could live any way they wanted to without

---

14   Dunham, *The Nature of the Sin Which Occasioned the Warnings*.

eternal consequences. Hence, in order to address this accusation, Calvin taught the doctrine of the perseverance of the saints. People who do not persevere in faith and good works were never saved in the first place.[15] In this way, the grace of God has been rescued from human distortion, thus satisfying the Catholic charge. The problem here, however, was that this was done not so much on an exegetical level consistent with biblical teaching as it was for political purposes, i.e., to satisfy the complaints of the Roman Catholics,   "When one was in the midst of a debate which was ripping apart the fabric of Western Europe, one needed powerful arguments like this (perseverance of the saints) in his arsenal."[16] The perseverance of the saints made Calvin's case airtight against Catholic criticisms,[17] but this airtight case goes beyond the biblical evidence. The Bible is much more realistic on this subject than clean Calvinistic theology.

In spite of the fact that Calvinists believe in the total depravity of man, their doctrine of the perseverance of the saints is an overly optimistic view which has great difficulty explaining the failures and sins of God's people. The fact of the matter is that the law of sin operates much more automatically than the law of the Spirit of life. To walk in the Spirit requires the fulfillment of a supernatural command (Gal 5:16), whereas to walk in sin does not. Sin automatically happens with few hindrances. Walking in the Spirit requires continual vigilance and diligence on the part of the believer. In fact, it is a present imperative requiring continual fulfillment so as to avoid fulfilling the desire of the sin nature. When the command is not fulfilled, sin is an automatic result. This is precisely why Paul commands the Galatians to walk in the Spirit so that they will not carry out the desires of the sin nature. To walk in the Spirit thus requires constant vigilance precisely because the sin nature will reside within the body until death. Walking in the Spirit is a responsibility of the believer to fulfill at all times as he depends on the power of God to do so (Gal 5:16). This and only this can stop the *practice* of sin in the life of the believer. Furthermore, this is no automatic process. Nor is it guaranteed.   Walking in the Spirit is not some kind of divine guarantee, but is an explicit command of Scripture. One

---

[15]   This may certainly be true in many cases, but not all.
[16]   Dillow, p. 9.
[17]   Ibid.

must swim upstream against the current of the world, the flesh and the devil, and there are many dangers along the way, including the sin of apostasy. The Calvinist somehow has this rather peculiar idea that all Christians will automatically be winners, that they will all walk in the Spirit on a consistent basis, and this view is vigorously maintained in spite of biblical evidence which suggests otherwise, let alone the tragic realities of everyday life. A theology which cannot explain tragic failure is a theology which has removed itself from the blood, sweat and tears of real biblical living. The doctrine of the perseverance of the saints has all too often been presented in an unrealistic manner which does violence to the language of Scripture. This doctrine is certainly the ideal for any Christian, and God does demand it at all costs, but real life, even biblical real life, is still very often much more muddy than the average Calvinist will want to admit.

The fact is that Christians will continue to sin in spite of the doctrine of the perseverance of the saints and they will also continue to sin even under the Arminian threat of loss of salvation. No system of theology can prevent the practice of sin or even apostasy without the personal application of divine principles into the life of the believer. Sin and apostasy are biblical realities which can be committed by real people in the Bible and also in everyday life. A much more realistic, yet less rigid view on sin and apostasy must therefore be accommodated for in both theological systems. The Calvinist must admit that Christians can commit apostasy and experience the judgments of God being warned of. The Arminian must admit that the loss of salvation is not a spiritual club which the author of Hebrews is using to exhort his readers. Both of these views are wrong in the book of Hebrews because they have faulty concepts of apostasy and divine discipline.

Enter Eternal Security

Over the last several decades there has been a growing schism between the doctrines of the perseverance of the saints and eternal security in evangelical circles. In days gone by a strong line of demarcation between these two doctrines was usually absent. Most generally theologians and scholars assumed that they were one in the same doctrine. While some theologians may have used the words 'eternal security', they meant 'perseverance of the saints'.[18] On the other hand, some theologians may have used the word 'perseverance', but meant 'eternal security'.[19] Even in seminary, students are asked to write a doctrinal statement on the perseverance of the saints and/or eternal security. However, there is a distinction between these doctrines which is now becoming more apparent among theologians of different persuasions. The fact is that eternal security, though demanding perseverance consistent with God's commands, does not teach that all saints will inevitably persevere. The one who has eternal security has the personal responsibility to persevere. Hence, with real responsibility comes the real possibility of failure. Hence also the tragic examples that are found in the Bible, and the many warnings, especially the ones we find in Hebrews. However, unlike the perseverance of the saints, which tends to cast doubt on the whole salvation issue since no one can really know for sure whether or not he is saved until the end, eternal security teaches absolutely that no Christian can lose his salvation.

Furthermore, the Christian can know this at the point of salvation, not by looking at his own progressive works, but by looking at the cross and the eternal promises of God which a holy God cannot fail to keep. This however, does not mean that everything will be rosy. On the contrary, if a believer does not persevere in his faith, then God will mete out divine discipline and judgment to that believer, which is not loss of salvation. In other words, eternal security teaches that a saint must either persevere in his faith, or suffer divine discipline and judgment. More serious is that this divine discipline also entails loss of eternal rewards or inheritance. While all saints certainly have an unconditional eternal inheritance with God which is not based on works and therefore cannot be taken away (Rom 4:13-16; Gal 3:18; Eph 1:13-14), it is also true that connected with the same inheritance, there are highly conditional eternal rewards, which can only be inherited by works, and therefore can be lost through disobedience (Heb 3:18-4:3; 6:11-12; 12:14-17). This is the biblical answer to the Catholic charge of licentiousness. What will happen to those who are Christians and yet sin willfully after their salvation? The book of Hebrews answers that question – wrath or rest – judgment or reward.

---

[18]   Pink, Arthur. *Eternal Security*. (Guardian Press: Grand Rapids, Michigan, 1974).
[19]   Chafer, Lewis Sperry. *Systematic Theology*. 4 volumes.

Contrary to popular opinion, the doctrine of eternal security can exegetically explain most of the difficulties that are found in Hebrews far better than either the Calvinist viewpoint or the Arminian viewpoint. Eternal security can easily teach the passages in Hebrews which indicate that a saint is eternally secure (7:25-28; 10:10-14; 10:29; 12:24). It can also accommodate the tragic reality of failure and apostasy in the life of the saint precisely because it does not assume ahead of time that all Christians will be winners, and therefore has a stronger understanding of eternal rewards, not to mention sin and divine discipline which will be meted out to any disobedient behavior on the part of God's people. Eternal security also has its own spiritual club so to warn the saints, i.e., loss of eternal reward or inheritance. However, this forfeiture of eternal inheritance is distinct from losing salvation. In this way, it is possible to warn saints very severely without questioning their eternal salvation. Moreover, this seems to be exactly what the Bible presents as Christian doctrine throughout the New Testament. There are many passages which teach that a Christian cannot lose salvation (John 6:35-39; 10:27-29; Rom 8:31-39; Eph 2:8-9; Col 2:9-15; Heb 10:10-14). There are many other passages which teach that a Christian can lose his inheritance reward (1 Cor 3:10-15; 6:9-10; 9:24-10:13; Gal 5:19-21; Eph 5:5; Col 3:23-25; Heb 3-4; 2 John 8). Though saved once for all, perseverance or divine discipline, inheritance or disinheritance, are still the only options available for a Christian. Moreover, either way ensures the holy integrity of the grace of God.

The strong Calvinist must face the fact that the author of Hebrews is either warning his readers about hellfire, or divine discipline, but is not discussing the inevitable perseverance of the saints. The only other option is that the Calvinist can modify his view on perseverance to the point that it can take into account the sin of apostasy being committed by genuine believers. In other words, perhaps at issue in the book of Hebrews is not perseverance, but sanctification.[20] For example, though the Exodus generation failed in the spiritual life by committing apostasy and therefore were forbidden to finish their course and take possession of their inheritance, they still persevered in the sense that they followed the glory cloud, and continued to worship at the tabernacle. Their apostasy was therefore not a total repudiation of ancient Judaism. In this way

---

[20]   This is the view of Dunham.

the doctrine of the perseverance of the saints can be maintained without resorting to forced exegesis. However, when most think of perseverance, the Exodus generation is not what normally comes to mind. This view is therefore a significant departure from how this doctrine is normally understood. Nevertheless, though this may not be a pretty view of perseverance, it is still a far more realistic, accurate picture of the book of Hebrews, and much more consistent with the biblical evidence.

There is no question that eternal security is a dangerous grace teaching which can easily be distorted by many. However, safe teachings on salvation which are politically acceptable are no less dangerous for the simple reason that the message has been modified to satisfy the complaints of people. Paul was accused more than once of teaching antinomian doctrines which promote sin (Acts 21:21; Rom 3:8; 6:1; Gal 2:17). What's more, if this complaint is not ever experienced by a Gospel preacher, then maybe he should reconsider the message that he is preaching. Being so pre-occupied with the possible dangers of sin and corruption, he may not be teaching the good news of the gospel after all, but some other gospel which somehow guarantees that God's grace cannot be taken advantage of by people. What is so often overlooked in this whole debate is that any doctrine of Scripture can easily be distorted by people. If the Jews distorted the Old Covenent Law to their own destruction, then any doctrine is potentially hazardous, and cannot provide any guarantee of distortion, including the perseverance of the saints. If the Law can be misunderstood and misapplied, then so can eternal security, perseverance, or any other doctrine of Scripture for that matter.

It therefore goes without saying that the law-free Gospel message of grace and eternal security *is* a very dangerous message to preach. It is dangerous to give any sinner grace. However danger does not mean that the message is not true. Freedom, danger, and testing is largely what life is all about. Freedom, danger and testing began in the Garden of Eden, and still continues today even in a world completely corrupted by sin. It was dangerous for God to give Adam and Eve free will, but God still gave it. The results were humanly catastrophic. In the same way, it is dangerous for God to give sinners grace, but He still gives it. The fact of the matter is that God, in His inscrutable sovereignty, has offered to the human race a law-free Gospel full of risks which can be distorted by sinful human beings. However, just because people distort it does not mean that the message is not true, or that God is to blame, or that somehow He loses His holiness when people abuse His blessings. Throughout history, the natural inclination of people, sometimes even great believers, is to take great blessings from God and distort them to their own destruction. King Solomon may be the best example of all of this. However, the problem here is not with God's blessing, but with the recipient. The responsibility lies with the unthankful recipient who distorted the blessing, not upon the holy gracious God who gives the blessing. Divine blessings are inherently dangerous, especially in a world of sin and death, let alone in the Garden of Eden.

In short, the Gospel of eternal security is a dangerous doctrine to teach. Nevertheless, even though people can and do take advantage of grace of God, they will do so at their own expense. The book of Hebrews has serious warnings for any who willfully sin against God's free grace. Take a good hard look at what happened to the Exodus generation. The book of Hebrews is the most systematic explanation of what happens to God's people who continue to sin willfully after the point of salvation. Not only will God severely discipline such a saint in this life, but this will also have eternal repercussions with regard to spiritual inheritance in the eschatological kingdom of God. God will impartially judge such saints with holy severity consistent with his righteous character. Eternal security is therefore not an easy-free doctrine made up by soft Christians with some kind of anti-nomian bent to them as many complain. The book of Hebrews demonstrates how eternal security was never intended to lull the saints into a false sense of security. Grace is not leniency. This is one of the great themes of Hebrews.

Authorship & His Historical Situation

The verdict is still out as to who wrote the epistle of Hebrews. There is much deliberation on the subject, not a little supposition, but no dogmatic assertions can be made. The most popular answers given to this intriguing question have been Paul, Barnabas, Luke, Clement, Apollos and Silas. These suggestions are all conjecture however. What we do know for certain is that Timothy could not have written the epistle (13:23). Moreover, the author can neither be one of the original 12 apostles. In 2:3 the author categorically asserts his relationship to Jesus and the original apostles. There he mentions that the Gospel message was *first spoken though the Lord by those who heard*, i.e., the apostles. He then adds the phrase, "it was confirmed *to us*." The *'us'* unmistakably distinguishes the author from both Jesus and the original apostles. As such, Martin Luther's suggestion of Apollos as the author is as good as any, and Silas is not a bad suggestion either since Paul includes his name in a few of his own letters (1 Thess 1:1; 2 Thess 1:1). Dogmatic assertions however, simply cannot be made. Whatever the case may be the author of Hebrews was an excellent writer. It is by far the most polished Greek found anywhere in the New Testament, and it very often approaches Classical Greek.

In any case, the author appears to be in a delicate situation with civil authorities. At the conclusion of the letter, he specifically asks the Hebrew congregation to pray for him (13:18). He then mentions that he and his companions are convinced that they have acted honorably in all things with a good conscience. This suggests that he and his friends were under some kind of civil or public scrutiny. It seems that they are defending themselves against some accusation, and they are convinced that they have done nothing wrong. In the following verse, he then urges them again to pray for him and his companions so that he may be restored to them sooner (13:19). The exact circumstances here are not given, but it is apparent that the author is in trouble with authorities of some kind, and that this has hampered his ongoing relationship with the Hebrew congregation. He then is aware of the fact that Timothy has been released from prison (13:23), and so if Timothy comes to see the author soon, they will both come to visit the Hebrew congregation together. Whatever the case may be, there is a sense of persecution in the air (12:4).

We know of no situation in which Timothy was ever in prison with the apostle Paul. This suggests that since Timothy was in prison at the time of the writing of Hebrews, the apostle Paul is most probably dead (2 Tim 4:6), having been recently executed by the Roman Emperor Nero, perhaps as early as 64-65 AD as some hold, or later in 67-68 AD as others suggest. Prior to this, Paul had been arrested in Troas, whereupon he ultimately landed in Rome, most probably because of trumped up charges of imperial treason. Paul thus requests Timothy, who was in Ephesus at the time (2 Tim 1:16-18; 4:19), to "make every effort" to come to him soon (2 Tim 4:9), and that when he comes, "bring the cloak which I left at Troas with Carpus, and the books, especially the parchments (2 Tim 4:13)." Paul was thus forced to abruptly leave his things with Carpus in Troas, and the best reason for this abrupt departure would be his arrest. Later, of course, Timothy undoubtedly passed through Troas from Ephesus, bringing Paul's things with him to Rome. It is also more than likely that it was sometime after Timothy's arrival in Rome that he was arrested because of his close association with Paul. At this time it was very dangerous to be associated with Paul, even in a place like Troas (2 Tim 1:15), let alone in Rome itself. This would also pinpoint the writing of Hebrews between 64-69 AD. All of this, however, is of course conjecture, but it is good reasoned conjecture.

In any case, the author considers himself a student of the original apostolic witness (2:4), and the Pauline circle could have very well been his primary apostolic contact. At the time of the writing of Hebrews he is at home within the Pauline circle, not only doctrinally, but also in personal fellowship as he knows Paul's protege Timothy (13:23). Not unlike his Christian brother Timothy, the author also appears to be someone who exercises authority over more than one church, writing as he does from a different location to another. He has great pastoral concern for his readers as he personally knew them and their history. Yet this personal intimacy with them does not cloud the judgment of the writer. The Word of God must be heeded at all costs.

A Word of Exhortation

The book of Hebrews is aptly described by the author himself as a "word of exhortation (13:22)." This is the best way to understand the book, i.e., the way the author himself understood it. Strictly speaking, Hebrews is not a letter or an epistle like that of the apostle Paul or Peter. Peter explicitly calls the writings of Paul *letters* (2 Ptr 3:15-16), not to mention **Scriptures**. The author of Hebrews however, does not identify himself, nor his audience, and does not write in typical letter form. Then in the conclusion he calls his writing a " word of exhortation." Much has been made of the fact that Hebrews reads much more like an actual sermon which was publicly delivered than a letter. The sermonic nature of the argument, the use of rhetoric, and the conversational[21] tone of the letter (2:5; 5:11; 6:9; 8:1; 9:5; 11:32) seems to strongly indicate that the book of Hebrews was intended to be a written public sermon to be read out loud to the congregation. The writer cannot be with his readers in person, so he writes to them. However, he does not write them a typical letter, but rather gives to them a sermon. Nonetheless, in spite of its strong sermonic nature, Hebrews still ends with a greeting, and so therefore cannot be completely contrasted with a letter.[22]

What is true however is that the book of Hebrews may reflect what sermons were actually like in the first century early church. When Paul delivered a public sermon to a synagogue in Pisidian Antioch on his first missionary journey (Acts 13:14-41), it was called a "word of exhortation (13:15)." After the reading of the Law and the Prophets, the synagogue leaders asked Paul and Barnabas if they had any "word of exhortation for the people." To this invitation, Paul delivered a stirring sermon to the synagogue on Old Testament history and prophecy. The crux of his message was that the promised Old Testament Messiah was crucified by the Jerusalem leaders, but has been raised from the dead (13:16-37). Before finishing his sermon, Paul exhorts the synagogue to believe in Jesus Christ for the forgiveness of sins (13:38-39), and then concludes with an ultimatum that they need to "take heed" lest they personally experience the judgments written by the Old Testament prophets (13:40-41). That Paul's sermon was a "word of exhortation" there can be no doubt, and while his content may have been expressly distinct, this style of public address was typical in synagogues throughout the Roman Empire. Instruction and exhortation were basic to the whole Jewish synagogue system, and this was continued and reinforced in the early church. It is no coincidence that after Paul urged Timothy to give attention to the public reading of Scripture, he also urged him to exhort and teach (1 Tim 4:13). Thus the author of Hebrews uses a very common method of instruction and exhortation in the early church to encourage and warn his audience. The peculiar difference is that the author of Hebrews seems to have written a sermon in the form of a letter, rather than publicly

---

[21]   Lane, William. _Hebrews_, (Word Publishers: Dallas, Texas, 1991), 2 volumes, pp. lxxiv-lxxxv.

[22]   Kistemaker, Simon J. _Hebrews_, (Grand Rapids, Michigan: Baker Book House, 1984), p.4.

deliver a sermon to them in person. Further distinct is that this homily became inscripturated into the New Testament.

Both Paul's sermon and the book of Hebrews are replete with explanations, exposition, instruction, and hortatory admonitions, not to mention much Bible history and prophecy, encouraging and/or warning their audiences of the necessity to respond properly to the Word of God. Thus a strict, technical definition for the **word of exhortation** will be difficult to substantiate. A "word of exhortation" appears to engulf all of the necessary elements of what is today called a "sermon" and it covers both evangelism and edification. In the book of Acts, Paul was evangelizing a Jewish synagogue. In the book of Hebrews, the author is pushing his audience toward spiritual edification.

In the book of Hebrews, the strong interrelationship between doctrine and practice is one of the cardinal characteristics of what the author meant by a "word of exhortation." The author believed very strongly that there is a strong correlation between apostolic doctrine and practice. To the author, apostolic doctrine is both practical and personal, and the reason why is stated uniquely in Hebrews 4. There, apostolic doctrine, i.e., the Word of God, is considered to be **alive** and **active** (4:12). Moreover, this living, active Word is quickly identified as God Himself in the following verse (4:13). That the author views the Word of God as divinely animate there can be no question. To divide therefore, God's written word (1:5-13; 2:11-13; 3:7-11; 4:3; 5:5-7; 8:8-12; 10:5-7; 10:15-17; 13:22) from the living word (4:14), is a foreign thought not entertained by the author of Hebrews. Indeed, the author uses without discrimination the Old Testament written word, the spoken word of the Son (1:1-2), the apostolic word (2:1-4), the 'heard' apostolic word (2:1-4), the living and active word who is God Himself (4:12-13), and the New Testament written word (13:22), interchangeably. In short, the Word of God, whether spoken, heard, written or read **is** " alive and active and sharper than any two-edged sword, and piercing as far as the division of the soul and spirit, of both joints and marrow, and able to judge the thoughts and intentions of the heart. And there is no creature hidden from **His** sight, but all things are open and laid bare to the eyes of **Him** with whom we have to do (4:12-13)." This being so, the Word of God is to have a living and active role in the life of the believer.

Moreover, if this life-changing role of the Word of God has been arrested in the believer, in the context of Hebrews this the author calls drifting (2:1), unbelief (3:12), apostasy from the living God (3:12), hardness of heart (3:13), deceit (3:13), sin (3:13), disobedience (3:18; 4:11), and falling away (6:6). Thus, to neglect careful attention to the Word of God, whether spoken, heard, written or read, is tantamount to apostasy from the *living* God (3:12). In short, the author of Hebrews has a very high view of the Word of God. He is absolutely convinced of its personal nature and practicality no matter how spiritual or invisible the doctrinal principles may be. That the struggle of faith is later treated in great length (11:1-40) should surprise no one. It would not be wrong to conclude that the Hebrew word of exhortation could be simplified as an exhortation to believe God (3:1-4:16; 10:22-23; 10:35-39; 11:1-40). The superiority of Christianity is an invisible reality which can only be explained by the "word." It cannot be seen, touched, felt, or smelled by the senses. The only way to appropriate its blessings therefore is by this irritating method called faith, something which the Hebrew readers were growing weary of (12:1-13).

Since the basic assumption of the author is that the Word of God is living and active, it is sometimes difficult to tell where doctrine stops, and where the exhortation begins, and vice versa. This has resulted in any number of suggested outlines of the book of Hebrews given by various scholars. A dogmatically drawn outline of the book of Hebrews would perhaps be a presumptuous endeavor, but anyone who labors to draw one up is quickly struck by the fact that the author continually goes back and forth between doctrine and practice:

DOCTRINE	*PRACTICE*
1:1-14 – *Jesus is Superior to Angels*	2:1-4 – *The Danger of Drifting*
2:5-3:6 – *Jesus is Lord over the World and Moses*	3:7-4:16 – *The Danger of Unbelief*
5:1-11 – *Jesus' High Priesthood is Perfect*	5:12-6:20 – *The Danger of Spiritual Dullness*
7:1-10:18 – *Melchizedek and the New Covenant*	10:19-39 – *Warning to Practice Christ's Priesthood*
11:1-40 – *Hall of fame of faith*	12:1-13:25 – *Divine Discipline and Morality*

[23]

---

[23]   This table has been modified from an article by John Niemala, *No More Sacrifice* in *Chafer Theological Seminary Journal* (Volume 4.4 – October 1998 and Volume 5.1,

This helps to illustrate what the author of Hebrews meant by a '**word of exhortation**' in 13:22. It refers to the entire preceding book of Hebrews itself,[24] which shows no artificial distinction between theology proper and practical theology. By definition, apostolic doctrine *is* practical. In the book of Hebrews, the doctrines of Revelation, Christology, Eschatology, Substitution, Sanctification, and the Ascension are all followed by practical exhortations which the readers need to apply into their daily lives by faith.

The Recipients: Their Identity & Previous History

Even though a specific group of people is not identified anywhere in the letter, much can be gleaned from the book of Hebrews to give a rough and ready sketch of their history and their current status. The generic title, "To the Hebrews," goes back to the end of the 2nd century if not before,[25] and therefore is only generally helpful. However, by looking over the entire letter, the book of Hebrews seems to have been written to Hellenistic Jewish Christians either in a local synagogue or in a local house church, the latter perhaps more likely. That they were Hellenists and not native to Jerusalem is supported by the fact that they were well familiar with the Greek Old Testament, the Septuagint. The sacred writer Hebrews quotes time and time again the Greek Septuagint. That they were Jews is supported by the fact that the author constantly appeals to the authority of the Old Testament. He specifically wants to show that the necessary advancement into the New Testament revelation of the Son is actually supported and taught in many places throughout the Old Testament Scriptures:

> ... his insistence that the Old Covenant has been antiquated is expressed with a moral earnestness and driven home repeatedly in a manner which would be pointless if his readers were not especially disposed to live under that covenant, but which would be very much to the point if they were still trying to live under it, or imagined that, having passed beyond it, they could revert

---

Jan-Mar 1999; Fountain Valley, CA), and also from a doctoral dissertation completed by Duane Dunham titled, *Hebrews Warning Passages*.

[24] Bruce, F.F. *The Book of Hebrews*, (Grand Rapids, Michigan: William B. Eerdmans Publishing, 1990), p. 389.

[25] Ibid., p.3.

to it. Again, our author's appeal to the Old Testament scriptures reflects his confidence that his readers, even if their loyalty to the Gospel is wearing thin, will recognize their authority. This they would indeed do if they were Jews; they had recognized the authority of those scriptures before they became Christians, and if they relapsed from Christianity into Judaism they would continue to recognize their authority. Converts to Christianity from paganism, on the other hand, adopted the Old Testament as their sacred book along with the Christian faith; if they were tempted to give up their Christian faith, the Old Testament would go along with it.[26]

Furthermore, the reference to " instructions about washings (6:2)," also strongly suggests that the addressees were Jewish in origin. These are Jewish ceremonial washings, which more than likely are related to the Levitical priesthood, which the Gentiles would not have necessarily followed. The washings here are clearly plural, referring to many. This makes Christian baptism highly unlikely. All of this evidence supports the contention that the addressees were a group of Jewish Hellenistic Christians.

The group does not have to be a small one, nor a narrow conservative one as some have suggested. The greeting at the end of the book seems to allow for a somewhat sizeable audience, "Greet *all* of your leaders and *all* the saints. *Those from Italy* greet you. Grace be with you *all* (13:24-25)." The reference to *all* the leadership seems to imply a somewhat sizable group of people, and the fact that they were well-known outside of their own community by another group, i.e., *those from Italy*, reinforces this. How many people were in the local congregation is of course impossible to say, but it is not necessarily an exceptionally small one.

Although no dogmatic assertions can be made as to the exact destination of the letter, the phrase *those from Italy*, seems to imply that the letter was written to a group of people in Italy, most probably Rome. The picture conveyed by this phrase is that author sends a greeting from a group of Italian people residing where the author is currently staying. Since they were originally from the same Italian city, they knew their

---

[26]   Ibid., p.6.

compatriots well, and had an express interest in their well-being, and so they send the recipients of the letter their greeting:

> The ambiguity of the formulation "Those from Italy greet you" (13:24b) is well known. The fact remains, nevertheless, that in the sole parallel to **apo thj Italiaj** provided by the New Testament the phrase clearly means "from Italy" in the sense of outside the Italian peninsula (Acts 18:2). The expression is used to in reference to Acquila and Priscilla who were currently in Corinth. They had sailed "from Italy" when Claudius issued a decree expelling Jews from Rome. In Acts 18:2 "Italy" denotes "Rome." This may be the most natural way of reading Heb 13:24b as well. In the closing lines of Hebrews, the writer conveys to the members of the house church in or near Rome the greetings of Italian Christians who are currently away from their homeland.[27]

In Acts chapter 18, Acquila and Priscilla recently came to Corinth *from Italy* (18:2). The following phrase then states the reason why they went to Corinth from Italy, "because Claudius had commanded all the Jews to leave *Rome* (18:2)." This establishes a one to one relationship between *Italy* and *Rome*. If Acts 18:2 and Hebrews 13:24b are parallel phrases, and if "from Italy' means outside the Italian peninsula, then it is more than likely that the epistle of Hebrews was written to a congregation in Rome. While there are certainly other plausible explanations for the phrase "those from Italy," this seems to be the best one. This is further reinforced in Acts 27 when Paul's journey to Rome is characterized as a journey to *Italy* (Acts 26:32-27:6).

The expulsion of the Jews from Rome in Acts 18:2 by Claudius, sometime between 49 and 51 A.D., also fits in very well within the context of Hebrews. Hebrews 10:32-34 states," but remember the former days, when after being enlightened, you endured a great conflict of sufferings, partly, by being made a public spectacle through reproaches and tribulations, and partly by becoming sharers with those so treated. For you showed sympathy to the prisoners, and accepted joyfully the seizure of your property, knowing that you have for yourselves a better possession and an abiding one." In addition to this, the Latin author Seutonius wrote

---

[27]   Lane, p. lviii.

in 120 A.D. in the *Lives of the Caesars*, that the Jews were expelled from Rome over disturbances concerning *Chrestus*. While *Chrestus* would be a misspelling, this is undoubtedly a reference to Christ. It would be difficult to substantiate that in 50 A.D. the Jews rioted over a *Chrestus* different from Jesus Christ. That there were Jewish riots over Christianity in Rome in 50 A.D. is the best explanation for Seutonius' reference. This not only fits in well with Acts 18:2, but also accords very well with the previous chapters (Acts 14-17) where Paul endured not a few Jewish riots over his law-free Gospel message about the Christ in Galatia and Macedonia. The situation in Rome would have differed little among the Jewish population.

The controversy over Christianity among the Jews became so fierce that the Emperor Claudius was forced to expel them from Rome, which included the likes of Aquila and Prisca, who were undoubtedly Jewish Christians. It is also very possible that the recipients of the letter to the Hebrews also endured the sufferings of this same expulsion together with Acquila and Priscilla. How many were expelled is of course difficult to say, except that generally speaking, the Jews were certainly expelled from Rome. Many also later returned after the situation calmed down, among them Aquila and Prisca, whom Paul greeted in his epistle to the Romans written in the mid 50's. By 60 AD, Paul was speaking with Jews who lived in Rome (Acts 28:17-31). So while it may be true that not all the Jews were necessarily expelled, and that many of them later returned, they still did lose their property and some were imprisoned in Claudius' persecution.

Correspondingly, that the writer of Hebrews reminds his readers that they have "not yet resisted to the point of shedding blood (12:4)." In 50 A.D., there was an expulsion, not martyrdom. Moreover, Claudius' expulsion would also match the time frame when the author reminds his readers about their previous sufferings. Some time has passed since those days. The apostolic era is beginning to wane (2:1-4), the readers have had sufficient time to advance beyond the basics (5:12), and Timothy has just been released from prison (13:23). All of this seems to indicate that Hebrews could not have been written before the 60's A.D. Again, the dates of 64-69 AD before the fall of Jerusalem[28] is perhaps the best

---

[28]   Interestingly Kistemaker (p.14) argues that the consistent reference to the wilderness tabernacle throughout the book of Hebrews assumes the temple has already been destroyed. Most commentators hold that Hebrews was written just before the fall of

date for the writing of Hebrews, and the writer's reference to the former days of suffering some years earlier would match Claudius edict rather well. Whatever the case may be, the recipients of the letter to the Hebrews experienced something like Claudius' expulsion, and the author reminds them of their former perseverance to encourage them once more in the face of opposition.

Much has been made of the Greek present tense in 13:10, "We have an altar, from which *those who are serving* the tabernacle have no right to eat." It has been asserted here that this verse indicates that the temple services are still in operation, and that this means Hebrews must have been written before 70 A.D. when the temple was destroyed by the Romans. Although this certainly is a possible interpretation, it is not convincing. In Hebrews, the author is specifically talking about the tabernacle, not the temple. The Greek present tense is also very often used in Scripture to teach a general truth. In fact, the author never mentions the temple anywhere in the book of Hebrews. He is far more concerned in contrasting ancient and pure Old Testament religion with Christianity, than he is in contrasting Christianity with present Judaism. The author is dealing with fundamental theological issues and not necessarily with present practices in Jerusalem. The constant appeal to the Exodus generation throughout the epistle of Hebrews clearly contrasts the New Covenant and the Melchizedekian Priesthood with the untainted Old Covenant and Levitical priesthood. The sacred author shows no interest whatsoever in contrasting Christianity with Judaism, but strictly in contrasting Christianity with pure Old Testament religion.

Nonetheless, it would seem strange that if the temple had been destroyed, the author would not use this as ammunition for his cause to teach the Hebrew readers that it had indeed become obsolete. In fact, nothing is ever mentioned in the book of Hebrews about the fall of Jerusalem or the destruction of the temple, which occurred in 70 AD. This in and of itself suggests that Hebrews was written in the 60's.[29] In

---

Jerusalem because it would seem incredible that the author would not refer to this landmark event in light of his argument. Since Clement of Rome refers to Hebrews in the last decade of the first century, it seems unlikely that Hebrews was written after 85 A.D. Thus Hebrews was written sometime between 65 A.D. and 85 A.D.

[29] Robinson, A.T. *Redating the New Testament*. Robinson's primary thesis is that most of the New Testament must have been written before 70 A.D. because no letter ever mentions the destruction of Jerusalem. This assertion has not been seriously challenged since he wrote the book.

fact, Acts 21 provides an excellent historical background for the book of Hebrews as it shows what was going on in Jerusalem a dozen years before its destruction. In that chapter, James is leading the Jerusalem Church where many Jewish Christians are zealous for the Law. What's more is that they are still reverently observing the temple services (Acts 21:15-26). In fact, it is quite obvious that many Jewish Christians, including Paul himself, would come from all over the Roman Empire to worship at the Jerusalem temple (Acts 21:27-29). Thus it is not necessary that the readers in the book of Hebrews live in Jerusalem. There is no contradiction between being spiritually distracted by the Levitical worship system and living in Rome.

If the apostle Paul was executed in 64-65 AD by Nero sometime after the notorious fires of Rome wherein he blamed the Christians for starting them though he himself was the culprit, such a terrible persecution would severely try the hearts of Jewish Christians living in a local converted synagogue. They would certainly be tempted to leave their Christian associations, and go back to the safety net of Judaism. By Roman law, up until the outbreak of the Jewish war in 66 AD, the Jews were allowed to practice Judaism freely without hindrance. Thus when Nero began to separate out the Christians from the Jews for persecution in the mid 60's, this would afford ample temptation for the Jewish Christians in Rome to leave their Christian background in favor of more peaceable terms with the imperial government. Nero's present wife, a nationalistic Jewess who hated Christians, apparently made clear to Nero the distinction between Jews and Christians. Before this, Christians were placed under the umbrella of Judaism. This is readily seen in the earlier persecution of Jews in Rome under Claudius when both the Jews and Jewish Christians were forced to leave Rome (Acts 18:2), if not for the simple reason that at this time, many of the first converts to Christianity were actually Jews, and this created many problematic relational difficulties between them. Now however, and from this time forward, a marked difference between Jews and Christians becomes obvious to the Roman imperial government, and this rupture quickly became permanent after the destruction of Jerusalem in 70 AD.

The Basic Theme of Hebrews

It would not be an understatement to say that the entire book of Hebrews is a footnote to the opening paragraph. Hebrews 1:1-4 is the controlling theme of the entire book, and all of the major arguments found in the later chapters flow from this initial announcement. God spoke through His Son, and in the case of the Hebrew readers, this means that the Old Testament prophets, theophanies and miracles are no longer necessary, but in fact out of date, together with the entire Old Testament sacrificial worship system (5:1-10:18). Once the Son has come to speak, the Old Testament prophet is out of a job. No matter how important his job may have been in the previous times and in various ways, his role has been superseded by a superior office, i.e., the Sonship of Jesus Christ. It is simply not possible for any Old Testament prophet to succeed the Son.[30]

---

[30] This of course does not preclude the Apostolic ministry nor the ministry of the New Testament prophets found in the pages of the New Testament following the death and resurrection of Christ. The Apostles were historical eyewitnesses and official heralds to the Son (Acts 5:32; 1 Cor 15:3-9), and the New Testament prophets aided this apostolic ministry as they too could preach the 'very' word of God (Acts 13:1; 15:32; 1 Cor 12:28-37; Eph 2:20, 3:5, 4:11; 2 Ptr 3:2). Regardless of their critical role in the early church, however, their ministries too came to an end just as the Old Testament prophets did, and the reason for this is that their respective ministries are inextricably tied to the one-time death and resurrection event of Jesus Christ. Thus the apostolic era, which included the ministry of the New Testament prophets, is a one time historical event which cannot be repeated just like the death and resurrection of Jesus Christ. While many popularly hold today that New Testament prophets are still in existence, this is contradicted by evidence in the book of Ephesians. Ephesians 4:11 speaks of the apostles and prophets given to the church following the ascension of Jesus Christ to equip the saints for the work of the ministry. Before this, 3:5 asserts that the New Testament prophetic message is the same as the Apostolic message. There it states that the mystery of Christ has been revealed to the holy apostles **and** prophets which was never made known before to Old Testament generations. This makes Ephesians 2:20 very damaging to those who maintain that the gifts of either apostles and prophets are still in existence. There Paul states that the Church is built on the foundation of the apostles **and** prophets. A foundation can only be laid once. As Christ died once for all, the Apostolic era together with the apostolic office of the New Testament prophet, is also a once for all operation which cannot be repeated. Paul himself intimates the temporary nature of the apostolic gifts (1 Cor 13:9). A decade later Peter tells his readers to **remember** the words spoken **beforehand** by the apostles and prophets, and then roughly about the same time, Jude speaks of the 'faith once for all delivered to the saints (1:4).' Furthermore, the temporary nature of the apostolic ministry is clearly limited by the fact that they were **historical eyewitnesses** of the ministry of Jesus Christ. The onceness of the Christ event together with the onceness of the apostolic message is a dogmatic onceness which is seldom appreciated in today's modern liberal age, even among many modern Christian groups. Dogmatic assertion is no longer in vogue today, but Hebrews 1:1-4 still asserts that there are

God, who at various times and in various ways spoke in time past to the fathers by the prophets, 2 has in these last days spoken to us by *His* Son, whom He has appointed heir of all things, through whom also He made the worlds; 3 who being the brightness of *His* glory and the express image of His person, and upholding all things by the word of His power, when He had by Himself purged our sins, sat down at the right hand of the Majesty on high, 4 having become so much better than the angels, as He has by inheritance obtained a more excellent name than they (1:1-4).

Moreover, the reason why God has spoken finally in His Son is because Christ has died once for all, one of the primary themes throughout the book of Hebrews (7:27; 9:12; 9:23-28; 10:10-14). This has left an indelible mark on biblical history which cannot be reversed. The one time death, resurrection and ascension to heaven of Jesus Christ has fulfilled the Old Covenant and has inaugurated the beginning of the apocalyptic days of the New Testament worship system according to the Order of Melchizedek (7:1-9:28). It was this great fundamental change in God's time calendar that the Hebrew readers were ignoring. They were pining for the " good old days" without recognizing the fact that compared to New Testament revelation, the Old Covenant revelation was inferior. It was this longing for the old ways that caused them to neglect their so great salvation spoken to them through the word of the apostles (2:1-4).

Indeed the Old Testament Word of God mediated through angels (2:2) has been superseded by the Heir of all, the Creator-Savior who upholds all things by the word of His power, and who sat down on the right hand of majesty on high after having died on the cross for the sins of mankind (1:1-4). This Creator-Savior is none other than the Lord Jesus Christ who is superior to all the angels (1:5-14), who is both God and man at the same time (1:8-9; 2:14-17), and who will one day fulfill the final eschatological destiny of man to rule over all Creation (2:5-8).

---

no prophetic successors to the Son. There can be no improvements made upon the revelation of the Son until He comes back. Even though the New Testament apostles and prophets succeeded the Son in time, they are not successors by nature. They are good only insofar as they reflect the Son in all that He is, and all that He has done. Their message is inextricably tied to the historical person and work of Christ. In the words of Paul, Christ is the cornerstone, the most important part of the building, while the New Testament apostles and prophets are the foundation (2:20).

Considering this most superior source, this is precisely why the Hebrews should pay close attention to the word which they heard lest they drift away (2:1), and neglect so great a salvation (2:3). The Hebrews are about to fall into a judgment akin to the Exodus Generation (3:1-4:16), where God swore in His wrath that they would die in the wilderness without obtaining the promised rest of Canaan, even though He did save them out of Egypt (3:7-11). Like the Exodus generation, the Hebrews were on the verge of following the same example of apostasy and disobedience (3:12-4:3; 4:11; 6:4-6). To this the author asserts that they will not escape (2:3; 12:25), for the Word of God is alive and powerful and judges the thoughts and intentions of the heart with the fullest intimate penetration, and there is no creature who is hidden from His sight (4:12-13).

In the book of Hebrews, the sacred author uses two Old Testament examples of judgment, the Exodus generation near the beginning of the book (3:1-4:11), and Esau near the end of the book (12:15-17), to illustrate what is about to overtake his own readers if they continue in their disobedience. These two Old Testament examples are the illustrations, and Hebrews 2:1-4; 3:7-4:13; 6:1-6, 10:26-31 and 12:25-29 provide the New Testament explanation and application of these particular judgments to the situation at hand. The author of Hebrews severely warns his readers of a repeat performance of the Exodus generation and Esau, and of reaping the same bitter consequences of irreparable failure.

However, in the midst of these impending warnings, it is still no less true that the Hebrews not only have a Savior who died for their sins (1:3), but also a propitious and merciful high priest according to the Order of Melchizedek who sits at the right hand of majesty on high (2:17-18). He can still come to their aid in time of need, distress and temptation (4:14-16; 5:7-10). The Hebrews have a High Priest sitting in heaven who can give them spiritual strength to overcome their temptations right from the very throne of grace (1:3; 4:14-16). What's more is that this high priesthood is far superior to the Levitical priesthood since it is according to the Order of Melchizedek and not according to the order of Aaron (4:14-5:10; 7:1-28). The Order of Melchizedek issues forth from heaven, whereas the Aaronic-Levitical order is limited by its earthly boundaries. However, because of their unbelief (3:7-19), spiritual sloth and dullness, the Hebrews are not ready to accept these great spiritual truths (5:11-14). To their shame, they actually need to be taught the basics all over again

(5:12), and so they have a great need to grow up spiritually (5:11-6:2). However, God may not allow them to press on to spiritual maturity, but may judge them instead, leaving them behind in a spiritual wilderness without any hope of recovery (6:1-8).

The Hebrew readers, however, have not yet passed the point of no return. They are on the verge of crossing this line, but the opportunity for spiritual growth has not yet been taken away. *Today* is still open to them to sanctify Christ Jesus in their hearts. Hence, the sacred author presses the Hebrews onward and upward toward spiritual maturity, convinced of better things than judgment for them (6:9-20). As such, he begins a long section explaining how the high priestly Order of Melchizedek is designed for their spiritual encouragement, assurance and perseverance (7:1-10:18). Since the Exodus generation received the Old Covenant on the basis of the Levitical priesthood (7:11), so the Hebrews need to understand that they are recipients of the New Covenant based on the superior order of the Melchizedekian Priesthood of Christ. This being so, if the priesthood changes, then there must also be a change of covenants as well (7:12). The author then goes on to tell his Hebrew readers that since the death of Christ has fulfilled the penalty against sin under the Old Covenant (9:15), Jesus is now the mediator of the New Covenant on the basis of a most superior priesthood located in heaven itself, i.e., the Order of Melchizedek (8:1-9:23). That this Melchizedekian Priesthood is superior to the Old Testament priesthood is actually taught as a principle in the Old Testament from both Genesis 14 and Psalm 110. Here the author finally begins to explain what he meant by speaking of Christ having sat down on the right hand of majesty on high after having made purification for sins (1:3). This initial announcement in 1:3 thus becomes the major theological argument of the book in 5:1-10:18, and it is imperative that the Hebrews understand this most important spiritual reality.

Seen in this light, the messianic high priestly Order of Melchizedek at the right hand of God is thus used by the author to both severely warn and strongly encourage the congregation to whom the letter was addressed. The Order of Melchizedek is used as a warning against the readers precisely because they are ignoring this messianic priesthood in favor of the Old Testament Levitical priesthood. At the same time the Order of Melchizedek is also the basis for their spiritual growth and maturity. The sacred author wants his readers to recover from their spiritual sloth and avoid the judgments of the warnings, and so he also speaks in great detail about this new great heavenly order to show them that giving up the Old Covenant Levitical system is not a sin, but actually spiritual progress. The high priestly Order of Melchizedek offers believers resurrection life and power to assist them to overcome temptation and sin, and gives them the ability to endure and persevere during difficult times of testing. The immortal, indestructible life of their messianic priest is thus a great encouragement to them to continue to pursue their sanctification. In short, the Order of Melchizedek is a supernatural priesthood far above the fleshly Levitical priesthood. Nonetheless, to neglect it is to invite disaster and judgment. To use it is to advance spiritually into God's rest, a great spiritual reward. Wrath or rest, judgment or reward – this is the main thrust in the book of Hebrews, and the Order of Melchizedek is the basis for both thrusts (3:1-10:39).

While the principle is oft ignored that the Bible student is not to build crucial doctrines drawn from obscure passages of Scripture, the author of Hebrews seems to do just precisely that in emphasizing the high priestly Order of Melchizedek. In fact, the author makes very clear that the mysterious historical appearance of the king-priest Melchizedek in Genesis 14, together with its messianic application in Psalm 110, is a typological key which unlocks the apocalyptic relationship between the old and New Covenants, a very tall order indeed. From these two enigmatic passages of the Old Testament, the author of Hebrews builds his strong assertion that Christianity is far superior even to pure, ancient Old Testament religion, let alone Judaism. In the age of the New Testament in which God has spoken with final authority, God ministers to His people through the Melchizedekian Priesthood of Christ, not through the Levitical priesthood of the Old Covenant. This ministry issues forth from the **heavenly** holy of holies, not from the **earthly** tabernacle. Therefore, the difference between them is nothing short of the difference between heaven and earth (13:14), between resurrection life and fleshly impotence (7:1-25). As such, any spiritual sluggishness preoccupied with the latter in place of the former is an obstruction to Christian progress, and this in turn, invites the wrath of God. It is this spiritual preoccupation and sluggishness (5:11-14), nay unbelief (3:12), on the part of the congregation that the author attempts to correct, and the Order of Melchizedek is the antidote to the crisis.

With bitter irony, the epistle to the Hebrews reveals that one of the great spiritual tests for the Christian is to be tempted to be more impressed with the lesser rather than the greater. Because Christian people are everyday people, they often tend to have a very shallow appreciation for the majesty of God, and are simply much more comfortable in more palatable and less majestic surroundings. The epistle of Hebrews was written to correct this tendency: how can the mundane share in the holy and mysterious majesty of God? Even more important is how can the mundane share in the glory of God without compromising His holy majesty? This is precisely what the enigmatic high priestly Order of Melchizedek is all about. God eagerly desires to share with His people the unfamiliar, and in the epistle to the Hebrews, this means sharing the heavenly priesthood of the ascended Christ with His Church. In Hebrews 4:14, this is uniquely designated as the *throne of grace* in which," we may receive mercy and find grace to help in time of need." God is unique. Therefore, He wants to share with His own people His unique perfections. The problem is that this represents a tremendous challenge to the human heart, and is often viewed by God's own people as a threat, rather than a comfort.

The great crisis in the Christian life is that there is no one like God, yet God desires His creatures to reflect His glory. This is the crucible in which God's people are tested, and at a time when the readers of the book of Hebrews were succumbing to the tremendous peer pressure of apostasizing from Christian truth (3:12; 6:6; 10:29), the author exhorts them both by strong encouragement (6:9-20; 10:32-39; 12:1-13) and severe warning (2:1-4; 5:11-6:8; 10:26-31; 12:25-29) to move ahead spiritually to the uncharted territory in the heavenly holy of holies, inside the veil, near the right hand of God, according to the Order of Melchizedek (1:3; 4:14-16; 6:19-20; 10:19-25). This is to be the new spiritual environment of God's people (10:19-25), the spiritual air which they are to breath and depend on for their very lives (4:14-16). As a spiritual pioneer, Jesus has already blazed the trail so that others could follow. The readers of the book of Hebrews however, seem to be more at home in the charted territory of Judaism, than in the lofty heights of Christianity. The author thus exhorts them, "Hence let us go out to

Him outside the camp, bearing His reproach (13:13)." The readers need to put into spiritual practice the Order of Melchizedek rather than be preoccupied with the Levitical priesthood.

In short, the Hebrews did not know how to worship God under the New Testament worship system according to the Order of Melchizedek. They were preoccupied with the Old Covenant religious pomp full of repetitious physical show. As such they neglected the weightier matters concerning the sufficiency of the death of Christ, the new order of worship under the New Testament, and the crucial principle of faith which activates in the soul all of the heavenly realities that the author of the book of Hebrews writes about. The author was thus forcing them to make a decision between worship of God based on faith in the Word and worship of God based on the outward repetitious performance of Old Covenant religion. They could not have both at the same time, something which they were finding very difficult to accept.

Needless to say, these are serious issues which the child of God can ignore only at his peril. Thus the author implores his readers to endure his *word of exhortation* (13:22). The author recognizes that some will be repulsed by the serious import of the warnings, and so he graciously entreats them to listen up. Listening to God is perhaps the most difficult task in all of the Christian life, and this problem becomes especially acute in the modern liberal age when anything doctrinal or dogmatic is considered unloving, legalistic and restrictive. Even in the modern church, more weight is generally given to spiritual experiences which are highly subjective, rather than to the clear and plain teaching from the objective Word of God. When this happens, it can only mean that God's people are having a difficult time listening to the Word of God.

The Dispensational Relationship Between the Old & New Testaments

In spite of the fact that the author of Hebrews was an avid student of the Old Testament Greek Scriptures, he was still nonetheless convinced of the superior nature of New Testament revelation. While the book of Hebrews is replete with quotation after quotation from the Septuagint, this great reverence for the Old Testament has not precluded the author from accepting wholeheartedly the superior nature of Christianity. Indeed, the book of Hebrews uses many citations from the Old

Testament itself to prove the superiority of Christianity, and therefore to soften the contrast between them is a violation of the Old Testament Scriptures themselves. The author clearly understands that which is last is best (1:1-4). It is now impossible to go back to the Old Covenant without endangering one's spiritual life. Furthermore, accepting the higher authority of New Testament revelation is not an attack on the Old Covenant. The author clearly understands that setting aside the former commandment (7:18), making the Old Testament Law obsolete (8:13), and recognizing its inherent limitation as only a "shadow of good things to come and not the very form of things (10:1)," does not promote laxity or lawlessness. On the contrary, the author specifically states that it is worse to fall away under the authority of the New Testament than under the Old Testament (2:1-4; 10:26-31; 12:25-29). Trampling underfoot the Son of God is no misdemeanor (10:29-31). The author of the book of Hebrews is therefore a prime example of how one can have an extremely high view of the Old Testament, without trying to make the New Testament a repeat of the old one. Jesus Christ has died once for all (10:10-14). The effects of this one time sacrifice for sin are indelible and permanent (6:6; 7:12). Recognizing the 'betterness' of the New Testament is not a sin, but a natural progression of the unfolding eschatological plan of God.

As the author of Hebrews recognizes the importance of progressive revelation, he speaks of the applicability of the promised New Covenant of the Old Testament (Jer 31:31-34) in the New Testament church. Several times he assumes that the New Covenant is applicable to his own readers and that they are under its authority (7:22; 8:6-10; 9:15-16; 10:29; 12:24; 13:20). This of course is not to deny that the New Covenant has no relationship to the future of Israel, but it is to say that even though the New Covenant was originally given to the house of Israel, and therefore also specifically designed for a future Israel, there is still a limited application of the covenant in the New Testament church. While the author of Hebrews recognizes that the New Covenant is essentially Jewish in its origin and ultimate fulfillment (8:8-9; 12:22-24), he has no doubt that the same New Covenant applies to the New Testament church. Indeed it would be difficult to understand how the church, even though it is in the parenthetical mystery dispensation not prophesied in the Old Testament (Rom 16:25-26; Eph 3:3-11; Col 1:25-27), could be completely divorced from the covenant promises of the Old Testament. Paul makes very clear in Romans 11 that all Gentile blessing has a Jewish foundation (Rom 11:16-27). Even Jesus says that salvation is of the Jews (John 4:22), and categorically connects His death to the inauguration of the New Covenant (Matt 26:28-29; Mark 14:24; Luke 22:20). To this truth the author of Hebrews is completely consistent as he applies the authority of the New Covenant to his own readers, even though they belong in the mystery age of the church (10:29; 12:22-24; 13:20). Paul even says that he and others are, "servants of a *New Covenant*, not of the letter, but of the Spirit (2 Cor 3:6)." These kinds of verses are indeed hard to understand if the New Covenant has no application whatsoever in the church.

On the other hand there is no doubt that the Old Testament covenants are specifically designed for the nation of Israel (Micah 7:18-20; Jere 31:31-34; Rom 9:4; Eph 2:12). Moreover, through Israel, God has also promised that the blessings of these covenants will be poured out upon the Gentiles in the apocalyptic future, especially during the Millennium (Gen 12:1-3; Isa 11:6-10; Micah 4:1-4; Rom 11:12-15; Rev 20). What was not specifically prophesied in the Old Testament was that there would be a spiritual application of the New Covenant to the New Testament church before the finality of the all things in the future kingdom of God on the earth. There may have been a very general pronouncement of blessing in the Old Testament that was to be given over to the Gentiles in the apocalypse, but there was still never any specific prophecy which promised that there would be a New Testament church based on the death, resurrection, and ascension of Jesus, in which both Jews and Gentiles would share equally the unfathomable grace riches of Christ in the heavenly places (Eph 3:3-11; Col 1:25). These truths were certainly kept a mystery in the Old Testament. The mystery age of the church was simply not presented in the Old Testament in the terms that are revealed in the New Testament precisely because it was hidden. At the same time however, they cannot be completely divorced from the blessings of the Abrahamic Covenant, which is the basis not only for the New Covenant,[31] but also for every subsequent blessing connected

---

[31]   The Abrahamic Covenant is the basis for the following 3 other covenants found in the Old Testament. The land aspect of the promise of given to Abraham (Gen 12:1) is later expanded and becomes the Palestinian Covenant (Deut 30:1-8) where Moses prophesies that God will bring Israel back to the promised land in the Apocalyptic

to God's so great salvation history program, not to mention the Gospel itself (Gal 3:8-18, 26-29).

This is not to say, however that the New Covenant has been fulfilled or has been exhausted in the church. The fact of the matter is that very little of the New Covenant has been fulfilled in the church, if anything at all, especially when one considers the apocalyptic magnitude of what fulfillment of the New Covenant really entails. In short, the New Covenant demands the millennial kingdom of God on the earth in order to be fulfilled. As such, it is perhaps far better to say there is a limited application of the New Covenant to the church, rather than suggest that there is any real fulfillment of the New Covenant within the church. Jeremiah 31, i.e., the prophecy about the coming of the New Covenant to the house of Judah and Israel when they will be both back in the promised land, clearly goes far beyond anything that can be said of the New Testament church. Only an apocalyptic Israel can completely fulfill the New Covenant as prescribed by Jeremiah the prophet. The advance of the church is therefore not so much a New Covenant issue as it is a dispensational issue. Since the Jewish nation rejected the Messiah, and since only a regenerate Israel in the millennial kingdom can fulfill the New Covenant, the church has been given a provisional dispensation in the meantime by which it can enjoy an application of New Covenant privileges ahead of the time. The plan of God thus did not stop with Israel's rejection of the millennial kingdom, but continues on in the church until Israel gets its act together. While the Millennium has not yet come, it is still true that Christ died once for all, and His death will not be without effect with regard to the progressive changes in the overall plan of God, albeit only invisibly in the church for the time being.

The author of Hebrews thus says something most interesting at the end of the book, "but you have come to Mt. Zion and to the city of the living God, the heavenly Jerusalem ... (Heb 12:22)." First of all, the fact that the sacred author says that his readers have **already come to Mt. Zion**

---

future after they have been banished by the punishments of the Old Covenant. The seed aspect of the promise (Gen 15:4) is later expanded and becomes the Davidic Covenant in which the Messiah shall come forth from the house of David, and He will be given an apocalyptic dominion after Israel is delivered from all of her enemies, which will begin with the Millennium on the earth (2 Sam 7:8-16; Ps 89). The blessing aspect of the promise is later expanded and becomes the New Covenant (Jer 31:31-34) which will completely replace the Old Covenant given to Israel. The New Covenant will be universally given to all of the house of Judah and Israel in the Apocalyptic future when God will forgive her sins and give her the Holy Spirit (Rom 11:25-28).

shows that he understands that the New Testament church is a part of Mt. Zion, i.e., the heavenly Jerusalem, as he writes the letter. Secondly, in the Old Testament, Mt. Zion is often presented as the great messianic apocalyptic kingdom of God which is coming down from heaven to the earth in order to fulfill the Old Testament, i.e., the Abrahamic, Palestinian, Davidic, and the New Covenants respectively (Gen 12:1-4; Deut 30:1-9; Ps 89; Jer 31:31-34; Isa 9:1-7; 11:1-10; Micah 4:1-4; 7:14-20). This means the New Testament church, albeit a little early, has already arrived at Mt. Zion in heaven through the death, resurrection, and ascension of the Messiah. Hence, even though the promised Old Testament kingdom based upon the regenerating power of the Holy Spirit as prescribed in the New Covenant is still physically coming down upon the earth in the future, the church has been given the great privilege of enjoying the heavenly benefits of Mt. Zion right now. This is precisely what the sacred author of Hebrews has in mind when he speaks of the fact that his readers have already experienced the "the powers of the age to come (6:5)." They have come to know "the heavenly gift and have been made partakers of the Holy Spirit (6:4)" earlier than predicted or anticipated by the Old Testament. With this in mind, the church actually has a special designation within the heavenly Mt. Zion. They are called the "church of the firstborn having been enrolled in heaven (Heb 12:23)." This is in contrast to the Old Testament saints who are called the "spirits of the righteous made perfect (Heb 12:23)." Hence, since the church is called the *firstborn*, they not only have greater inheritance rights than Israel, but they get to enjoy these great spiritual benefits right now on the earth, even though Mt. Zion has yet to come to the earth in all of its visible millennial glory as prescribed in the Old Testament. Hence it can be said that the New Testament church has a heavenly application of the New Covenant blessings here and now ahead of schedule upon this sinful earth. As such, the New Testament church is not only already in existence, but also fully blessed, even though the New Covenant will not be fulfilled until Jesus Christ sets up the Jewish messianic kingdom upon the earth in the Millennium after the Second Advent (Rev 19:1-20:10).

Furthermore this dual role of limited application and fulfillment of the New Covenant to the church and to the future Israel can readily be seen by comparing 2 Corinthians 3 with Romans 11. In 2 Corinthians 3:6 Paul says that he and his companions are servants of the New

Covenant under the ministry of the Holy Spirit. This makes a limited application of the New Covenant blessing of the Holy Spirit be given over to the New Testament Church. However, Jeremiah 31, which had no appreciation or understanding of mystery dispensation of the church (Eph 3:1-11;Col 1:25-27; Rom 16:25-26), specifically applies the fulfillment of the New Covenant to the apocalyptic house of Israel. Not only is this completely consistent with the rest of the Old Testament, but is also expressly stated in Romans 11, not in so-called apocalyptic cryptic language, but in clear doctrine expressed by the apostle Paul himself. In Romans 11:25-28 Paul applies the fulfillment of the New Covenant to Israel's apocalyptic future without limitation. When this happens, at the outset of the Millennium, it will bless the entire world beyond anything that has ever been experienced at anytime before, even far beyond that of the church age (Rom 11:11-15). This does not mean that the people in the Millennium will be greater than the resurrected church age saints, since they will still be in the flesh, but it is to say that there is far more to the New Covenant than anything the church has ever experienced.

These Dispensational issues actually seem to be part and parcel of the whole problem for the sacred author. A cloud of Dispensational unbelief was hovering over his readers. His Jewish audience, well versed from the Old Testament concerning the future millennial reign of Messiah on the earth full of heavenly power and the Holy Spirit, were unimpressed with current situation of the New Testament church. The lack of the visible manifestation of the glory of God in the New Testament church was confusing to his Jewish audience, and misunderstood as a weakness. The church seemed far removed from the promised glories of the millennial temple as described in Ezekiel 40-48. Rather than see the New Testament church as a matter of great spiritual progress, the Jewish readers thus treated it with disdain, disappointed with its so-called meager results. Looking for the glories of the New Covenant in the Millennium, they had great reservations about the superiority of the church age over the Old Covenant, and so set a reverse course backward to the old religious system. To this low view of Christianity, the sacred author writes the book of Hebrews, desperately trying to show his Jewish audience that even though the Millennium has not yet come (Heb 6:5, 12:22) the church has gone beyond the rituals of the old dispensation to superior spiritual realities within heaven itself, i.e., the priesthood of Christ according to the Order of Melchizedek (5:1-7:28). As such, he uses strong arguments from the Old Testament (7:1-28) to persuade them that it is time to move onto to this higher spiritual ground away from the Old Covenent Law and priesthood.

The Aaronic-Levitical Priestly Order vs. the Order of Melchizedek

The house of Moses (3:2-5), more commonly known as the Old Covenant tabernacle, was an earthly replica of the heavenly house of God (Ex 25:40; Heb 8:5), over which Jesus Christ now rules as an eternal king-priest according to the Order of Melchizedek (1:3; 3:1-6; 7:13-17; 10:21). The Old Testament tabernacle was only a model of heaven, not the reality. It was a type of Christ portraying in ritual picture form what He would later do in messianic history. Thus the tabernacle was a prophetic picture of that great future messianic event that would save Israel from her sins.

The Mosaic house was a tent or tabernacle, administered by the Aaronic-Levitical priesthood, which the Exodus generation originally built in the desert according to strict Old Covenant instructions from God (Ex 25:1-40). This tabernacle was built, in contrast to pagan worship systems, for the express purpose that Israel could worship God acceptably under the authority of the Old Covenant. Having been freed from Egypt, the Jewish people now needed to learn how to nationally worship their most holy God in a way that would please Him in the promised land of rest, and it was the tabernacle, administered by Aaron and the Levites under the auspices of the Old Covenant, that would accomplish this single great purpose. God saved the Exodus generation out of Egypt by his grace, but then gave them the Old Covenent Law in the desert, consisting of the Ten Commandments, plus many other commands, and also the tabernacle worship system. Israel was then commanded to keep this covenant in order to worship God properly, and in so doing, receive great blessing from God in the promised-land.

Because the Jewish people were sinners and therefore could not perfectly observe the ethical side of the Old Covenent Law, the tabernacle worship system was designed and established. It was set up to show and teach how sin could be ritually cleansed until the coming of Messiah. The Old Covenant tabernacle arrangement was a temporary worship system, consisting of bloody ritual sacrifices which were to be continually offered until the final defeat of sin was accomplished by the Messiah in the expected apocalypse. While the tabernacle did demonstrate the way to God was through sacrificial death, it also taught that until the coming of Messiah, there were actually many barriers placed between God and the Jewish people because of their sin. Sin was a most serious problem separating the Jewish worshiper from God. Sin merited the wrath of God, and not even the ritual sacrifices of the Jewish worship system could remove the prescribed barriers. Nonetheless, the Old Covenant tabernacle worship system did allow people to approach God. Furthermore, it pictured in ritual form what the Messiah would later do historically on the cross, i.e., sacrifice Himself on behalf of sinners. The only way to satisfy God's holy wrath against sin was through the sacrificial death of the Messiah on the cross whereby He was judged for man's sin as a substitute. The messianic substitute will die instead of the worshiper, thus satisfying the holy demands of the Old Covenent Law.

The great problem, of course, was such a Messianic answer could not be fulfilled until the future. What would Israel do in the meantime? How could they approach God even though they were still sinners, and sin had not yet been purged? The answer to this question was the Old Covenant tabernacle worship system. Ritual atonement, consisting of bloody sacrificial animals, was to be practiced until the coming of Messiah who would later bring about a real purgation of sin. The God of the Old Covenant, realizing Israel's sin problem, therefore provided the Aaronic-tabernacle system of ritual sacrificial substitution in order to show the Jewish people how they might approach Him until the coming of the Messiah. God showed the Jewish worshipers their sins could be ritually cleansed through the mediation of prescribed sacrificial animals administered through the priesthood of Aaron and Levi until the coming of the Messiah. God would thus provide a temporary remedy to their sin problem through the Old Covenant worship system. The Jews could therefore look forward to the coming Messiah as they practiced the Old Covenant tabernacle worship system. Through the tabernacle worship system they could see the light at the end of the tunnel so to speak.

The God of the Old Covenant was a most holy God, literally hidden from the sight of Israel within the tabernacle, so that Israel would not be consumed by His wrath due to their many sins. There were three major barriers placed between God and the Jewish worshiper in the tabernacle, and each passed barrier represented increasing intimacy with God. The first barrier was an outdoor curtain that surrounded the tabernacle. This outdoor curtain separated the lay people from the Levitical priests. The layman could approach and worship God from the door of the curtain, but could not enter. He would bring his sacrificial offering[32] to the door of the tabernacle, and the Levitical priests would then administer the blood according to strict Old Covenant regulations prescribed in the book of Leviticus. The Levitical priests therefore were allowed within the outdoor curtain area where they administered the sacrificial blood on an altar placed not far from the entryway. They thus worshiped representatively on behalf of the lay people. The priests also had to offer sacrifices for themselves as well. The next barrier was the tabernacle itself, a tent consisting of two compartments. The first compartment was called the holy place where Levitical priests worshiped the Lord (9:6). This is where the lampstand, the table of shewbread, and the sacred bread was located (9:1-2). The second compartment, known as the holy of holies,[33] was forbidden for anyone to enter. There was a veil placed between the holy place and the holy of holies, and no one was allowed to pass through this veil, because this is where God Himself, in the form of the Shekinah glory cloud, dwelled. Thus there was a complete separation between God and all worshipers. Complete intimacy with God was strictly forbidden under this Old Covenant worship arrangement. Complete transparency with God was fatal.

There was, however, one exception to this rule. Once a year, upon the most holy of all worship days known as the Day of Atonement on the Old Covenant calendar, Aaron the high priest, in contrast to the Levitical priests, was allowed to enter the holy of holies. Having passed through the sacred veil, Aaron entered into the holy of holies in order to administer unique bloody rituals of cleansing sprinkled upon the mercy seat, which sat underneath the cherubim, but over the ark of the covenant (9:4-7). The mercy seat portrayed God's throne, wherein He ruled the universe being surrounded and covered by the cherubim.[34] Within the

---

32 Not all offerings were bloody, but usually they were. Some offerings were sacrificial meal offerings representing fellowship with God.

33 The holy of holies is called the holy place in Hebrews.

34 The cherubim was a statue of the angelic creatures who surround God's throne. There was no statue or image of God placed on the mercy seat however, thus fulfilling the

ark of the covenant was placed the tablets of the 10 commandments and Aaron's rod that budded. This whole ritual sacrificial scene therefore vividly portrayed to the Jewish people that their sins committed against the ten commandments could only be graciously forgiven from God's mercy throne through the shedding of blood (9:22). God thus provided a gracious way through sacrificial substitution to remedy the great barrier of sin that separated the Jews from Himself, graphically portrayed on the Day of Atonement. Here was the only time wherein Israel had direct contact with God. However, it was still true that this contact was only representative through the high priest. It was also a very brief encounter with God. In the final analysis, the barriers separating God from the Jewish worshipers actually remained intact (9:8). The exception to the rule did not provide a direct encounter with God. The Messiah had not yet died for their sins. The Day of Atonement could only portray the future reality of Christ on the cross. It was still not the real thing.

It is this Old Covenant tabernacle worship arrangement which sets the stage for the book of Hebrews and the great emphasis upon the Order of Melchizedek, a great New Covenant privilege, never before offered to the people of God, but given provisionally ahead of schedule to the New Testament church. The messianic priestly Order of Melchizedek provides the remedy to the great problem of the Old Covenant barriers placed between the worshiper and God. Rather than give pictures of mere ritualistic cleansing according to the order of Aaron and Levi, the Order of Melchizedek provides a real sacrifice, offered once for all on the cross by the Lord Jesus Christ, the great messianic king-priest who rules over the heavenly house of God (1:3; 10:21). This is the force of Hebrews 1:3, "when he made purification for sin, He sat down at the right hand of majesty on high." Hebrews 1:3 teaches that Christ made a real and final purification for sin, and that He took His throne as the eternal Melchizedekian king-priest after He finished his work on the cross. Thus what was portrayed in the rituals on the Day of Atonement, Christ did in reality on the cross and in His resurrection and ascension. Furthermore, He made purification for sin on the cross through the sacrifice of Himself, i.e. through his own blood, not through ritual blood (9:11-14). Having thus completed this great work of purgation, Christ

---

second commandment to make no images of God.

then sat down. This is the mercy seat portrayed within the earthly holy of holies, and pictures His ascension to heaven.

Thus Christ did something which no Aaronic high priest ever did. Having finished His sacrificial work, He sat down. Because Aaron offered only rituals, he could not administer a real purification for sin (10:1-14). As such, he could never finish his work. He thus must continue to offer up the same sacrifices year after year which can never take away sin. Aaron simply could never provide a real cleansing through mere repetitious rituals. However, the cross of Christ was no ritual. It was a real, decisive, once-for-all act of cleansing which makes the Old Covenant order of Aaron and Levi superfluous with regard to the purgation of sin.[35] Christ's priestly Order of Melchizedek thus replaces the Aaronic-Levitical Old Covenant tabernacle order of worship. With the work of purification from sin done, He sat down, thus fulfilling in reality as the Melchizedekian High Priest what the Aaronic-Levitical sacrifices of the Old Covenant could only portray.

With great interest the sacred author of Hebrews asserts that the veil in the tabernacle, which separates the holy place from the holy of holies, represents the sacrificial and fleshly body of Christ (10:19-20). His sacrificial body of death is thus the way into the heavenly holy of holies. As such, if people accept His sacrifice, i.e., if they believe that Christ died for their sins, that He made a perfect sacrifice for their sins (10:10-14), this will give them the right and privilege to enter into the heavenly holy of holies without limitation. All religious barriers are hence removed, much unlike the Old Covenant system, "This hope is sure and steadfast and one which *enters within the veil* where Jesus has entered as a forerunner for us, having become a high priest forever according to the Order of Melchizedek."

The Hebrew readers, therefore, have greater spiritual privileges than Aaron himself, "Therefore, brethren, since we have confidence to *enter the holy place* by the blood of Jesus, by a new and living way which He

---

[35]   This does not mean that ritual sacrifices were evil in and of themselves, but that they were largely misunderstood in Judaism and therefore misapplied. Though the apostles were the original founders of the church, the apostles did participate in the Jewish ritual system in Jerusalem without any hesitation or sense of contradiction, but they were armed with the proper theological interpretation behind the ritual sacrifices. Christian interpreters also need to keep in mind that ritual sacrifices will be resumed during the millennium. These will not be Old Covenant ritual sacrifices, but New Covenant ritual sacrifices.

inaugurated for us *through the veil*, that his His flesh, and since we have a great high priest over the house of God, *let us draw near*, having our hearts sprinkled … (10:19-22a)." Jesus now represents them in heaven at all times, not just briefly on the earth as Aaron the high priest did. Moreover, this is possible because Christ died perfectly for their sins, thus removing all defilement that earlier separated the two parties. They have potential access to God, via resurrection life, within the heavenly holy of holies at all times.

The Hebrew readers need to take advantage of the superior blessings that have been conferred upon them, "Since we have a great high priest who has passed through the heavens, Jesus the Son of God, let us hold fast our confession. For we do not have a high priest who cannot sympathize with our weaknesses, but One who has been tempted in all things as we, yet without sin. Therefore, let us draw near with confidence to the throne of grace, so that we may find grace to help in time of need (4:14-16)." The Hebrew readers therefore have a resurrected high priest and a supernatural priesthood in heaven which they can use to grow spiritually. They can have a resurrection intimacy with God within the heavenly holy of holies which will supernaturally transform their lives. This priestly intimacy with God was simply never offered to the Old Testament saint to help him overcome his sins and temptations. Neither Aaron or any Levite could confer upon any Old Testament worshiper resurrection life and power. They were limited by the earthly tabernacle, offering up rituals rather than true spiritual reality.

This is far better than anything the earthly Aaronic-Levitical model of the Old Covenant can provide. This is the great significance of the Order of Melchizedek. Because Christ made a perfect sacrifice for their sins, all the previous religious barriers have been removed. The Hebrew readers now have a new priesthood and New Covenant privileges which confers supernatural resurrection life to help them in times of sin and temptation. They therefore need to draw near to their heavenly high priest within the heavenly holy of holies in order to grow spiritually and become the obedient children that God designed them to be. Christ has finished His work on the cross and has sat down. This victory of rest within the heavenly holy of holies is now being offered to the Hebrew readers which they need to desperately use at all costs, or face the consequences of a sinful, wasted life.

General Outline of the Book of Hebrews

I.   God's final revelation through His Son is preeminently superior over all (1:1-2:18).
   A. Jesus is superior to the Old Testament prophets (1:1-4).
   B. Jesus is superior to all the angels (1:5-14).
   C. The Hebrews are warned against drifting from their so great salvation (2:1-18).

II. The Hebrews are warned not to repeat the unbelief of the Exodus generation (3:1-4:13).
   A. Jesus is superior to Moses (3:1-6).
   B. The Exodus generation judgment is used to warn the Hebrews (3:7-19).
   C. The Hebrews are warned to be reverently diligent to enter God's rest (4:1-13).

III. The Order of Melchizedek is superior to Old Testament Worship (4:14-10:18).
   A. In contrast to the Aaronic Priesthood the Melchizedekian is perfect (5:1-10).
   B. Their persistent immaturity is pushing them toward apostasy and judgment (5:11-6:8).
   C. God's faithfulness can be trusted for better results (6:9-20).
   D. The Melchizekian Priesthood of Christ is superior to the Levitical Priesthood (7:1-28).
   E. The high priesthood of Christ has inaugurated the New Covenant (8:1-10:18).

IV. The Hebrews are admonished to obey the glory of New Testament worship (10:19-13:25).
   A. The Hebrews are warned to practice the priesthood of Christ (10:19-39).
   B. The faith of Old Testament heroes are examples to follow (11:1-40).
   C. The example of Christ is a pattern to follow in the trials of adversity (12:1-17).
   D. The glory of Mt. Zion far surpasses the austerity of Mt. Sinai (12:18-29).
   E. The Hebrews are given general ethical admonitions (13:1-19).
   F. The benediction exhorts the Hebrews to bear the warnings of the book (13:20-25).

CHAPTER TWO

THE NATURE OF THE SPIRITUAL CRISIS

The Nature of the Apostasy

The apostasy in Hebrews is that the Jewish Christians are both in the process and on the verge of denying the final once for all *significance* of the cross (6:4-6; 10:1-31). Their view of the cross was not only deficient, but also quickly becoming apostate (6:6; 10:29). Worse, if they continue in this vein, there can be no spiritual recovery (2:3; 4:11; 6:1-8; 10:26-27). The fact that the Hebrew readers were disregarding the great value of the cross becomes readily apparent in the heart of the epistle when the author emphasizes again and again that Christ died finally and once for all (7:27; 9:12; 9:25-26; 9:28; 10:10; 10:12; 10:14; 10:18; 10:26). This is the main thrust of Hebrews, something which the readers were having great difficulty in accepting. While the Jewish Christians in the book of Hebrews may have certainly understood that Christ died for their sins, they did not grasp the final once for all significance of His death. They were perhaps so habituated to their old repetitive religious system that they could not see the great Christian glories which the final once for all cross was offering to them (4:14-10:25). This coupled against a tense climate of persecution (Heb 10:32-34; 12:4) pushed the Hebrew congregation Into their old previous background from which they were saved. Thus, while the Hebrew readers may not have outright denied the *fact* of the cross, they were certainly denying the eschatological *finality* of the cross. The problem was not over history but over meaning. The primary problem was over what the cross means, and in Hebrews the cross means the end not only of Judaism, but of Old Covenant religion in general (7:26-8:13). That the Old Covenant must yield to the spiritual progress of Christianity and the New Testament would be very difficult for any Jew to accept. They were thus denying the *results* of the cross. By remaining back in the camp of cherished Judaism (13:13), the Hebrew readers were treating the significance of the cross with contempt (10:29). To refuse to progress forward into Christianity is to act as if Jesus had done nothing. This was their sin and apostasy. It is in fact an act of high treason which the author of Hebrews calls, trampling underfoot the Son of God, regarding common the blood of the (*new*) covenant, and insulting to the Spirit of grace (10:29)." This in turn was having a negative effect on their ability to persevere in Christian teaching and supernatural worship.

In light of Jesus' one time sacrifice for sins which fulfills the entire Old Covenant (9:11-15), to stay within the confines of Judaism is treason (10:29). To align with the Old Covenant religion is the equivalent of aligning with a dead, obsolete sacrificial system which is powerless to cleanse one's sin (10:1-4). In short, to go back to this outdated system is tantamount to unbelief and **is** apostasy (13:13; 10:26-29; 6:4-6; 3:12). It is this problem that the author of Hebrews is trying desperately to correct, and so he emphasizes over and over again the cross constitutes a final, unrepeatable, apocalyptic change which is not only irreversible, but more importantly, can be ignored only at their peril:

> The aim of the writer then was to open up the true significance of Christ and His work, and thus to remove the scruples, hesitations and suspicions which haunted the mind of the Jewish Christian embarrassing his faith, lessening his enjoyment, and lowering his vitality. The Jew who accepted Jesus as the Christ had problems to solve and difficulties to overcome of which the Gentiles knew nothing. ...It is easy for those who look back upon it as an accomplished fact to see that there was no real breach of continuity between the old religion and the new; but that was not readily perceived by those whose life and experience were marked by

the turmoil and instability which accompanied the abandonment of old forms, the acceptance of new ideas, the building on other foundations. Brought up in a religion which he was persuaded was of Divine authority the Jew was now required to consider a large part of his belief and worship as antiquated. Accustomed to pride himself on a history marked at various stages by angelic visits, divine voices, and miraculous interventions, he is now invited to shift his faith from institutions and venerable customs to a Person …. Cherishing with extraordinary enthusiasm, as his exclusive heritage, the Temple with all its hallowed associations, its indwelling God, its altar, its august priesthood, its complete array of ordinances, he is yet haunted by the Christian new born instinct that there is an essential lacking in all these arrangement and that for him they are irrelevant and obsolete. A blight has suddenly fallen on what was brightest in his religion, a blight which he can neither dissipate nor perfectly justify.[36]

The exact circumstances that precipitated the spiritual crisis in Hebrews is not clearly stated, but it is rather apparent the readers were far more at home within the rich religious traditions of Judaism than with the starkness of the Christian cross. Some had even quit coming to church (10:25). They were ignoring or even perhaps resenting the great spiritual changes which the cross had brought about.

This lack of appreciation for the great value of the cross is first mentioned generally in chapter two when the author warns his readers about neglecting their *so great salvation* (2:3), but becomes far more specific in chapter ten when the author warns them about trampling underfoot the Son of God, regarding common the blood of the covenant, and insulting the Spirit of grace (10:29). The nature of their apostasy thus becomes much clearer as the author expands his argument against them, and this clarity climaxes in 10:25-29, the fourth warning of the book. In chapter two the author broadly warns them about spiritual drifting and neglect (2:1-3). In chapters three and four, the author compares the apostasy of the Exodus generation with the present spiritual condition of his own readers (3:7-19; 4:11). Just as the Exodus generation disbelieved,

36 Dods, *Hebrews*, from the Expositor's Greek New Testament (Eerdmans Publishing: Grand Rapids, Michigan, reprinted 1990), Volume 4, edited by W. Robertson Nicholl. p. 237.

fell away, and hardened their hearts against God (3:12-13), so also the Hebrew readers were about to follow suit (4:11). In other words, the desire to go back to the Old Covenant system is being compared with the apostate desire to return to Egypt (Num 14:3-4). Either way, the spiritual judgment is the same: Inheritance Rest will be denied to those who commit apostasy (4:11).

Falling away (3:12) here in the original Greek is the infinitve to *apostasize*. It is here where many commentators have presumed that this word being used here means final apostasy, i.e., loss of salvation. However, what we have here is a problem in which the theology of apostasy has developed far beyond the original usage of the word. Nowhere does the author say that this is final apostasy, and even the English translation itself *'falling away'* should guard against such an excessive interpretation. Here in 3:12, the word is being used in a much more general sense than the technical meaning of theological apostasy which is understood as "a deliberate repudiation and abandonment of the faith that one has professed."[37] This rigid definition is typical among both Calvinists and Arminians, but is wanting of biblical evidence. With great interest, the author who wrote the definition above cites Hebrews 3:12, and then notes that Judas Iscariot is the most notorious example of apostasy, and then goes from there to speak about the antichrist, the man of apostasy.

This comparison is completely false. First of all, Judas's act against Jesus was not so much an act of apostasy as it was an act of betrayal. Judas is never called an apostate in the Bible. But even if the word was used to describe Judas's act of betrayal, the fact remains that Judas was never saved (John 13:10-11) whereas the writer of Hebrews takes great pains to establish that his readers were indeed saved. Nor is 3:12 parallel to the Antichrist. The fact is that we are dealing with two very different contexts, and therefore two very different meanings of the word. Again, the writer of Hebrews is discussing the sins of the saints, not the apostasy of the antichrist. Moreover, this big difference can be readily seen when the context of Hebrews 3-4 is understood properly. In Hebrews 3-4, the entire context revolves around the Exodus generation. Therefore the apostasy is determined by the historicity of the Exodus generation, not by Judas or by the Antichrist. As such, the apostasy in 3:12 cannot

---

[37]   Whitlock, *Dictionary of Theology*. (Baker Book House: Grand Rapids, Michigan), edited by Walter Elwell, p. 70.

be compared to either Judas or the Antichrist precisely because God forgave the apostasy of the Exodus generation (Num 14; Neh 9:16-21; Ps 78:38-39), something He never did with Judas (Mark 14:21), nor will do with the Antichrist (2 Thess 1:6-9; Rev 19:20). No matter how one looks at this, the apostasy committed by the Exodus generation was forgiven. Likewise the apostasy being described in the book of Hebrews is also forgivable. Here we have a classic example of where theology has determined exegesis.

Generally speaking, in the infinitive construction, the word *apostasy* means to "stand off, to remove, to withdraw, to stand aloof, to depart." Moreover, the New Testament reflects this somewhat broad semantic range of meaning even though the word is not commonly used. Perhaps most interesting is that Luke 8:13 is very similar to Hebrews 3:12. There in the parable of the sower and the seed, the word is used to describe those who "fall away" in the midst of temptation because of lack of root. In short, *to apostasize* does not mean to commit final apostasy as many conclude. This inference goes far beyond the semantic use of the word even in the New Testament, let alone the Old Testament and pagan literature:

> As the term *apostasy* is used in the Old Testament, it refers not to a total repudiation of the entire system of Judaism, but a rebellion against some revealed aspect of the word of God .... Apostasy is usually understood to involve a voluntary and knowing act of turning away from the true doctrine of Scripture...it can be either formal or informal, individual or group, public or private, doctrinal or practical rebellion. The limitation of the sin to severing ecclesiastical ties is not sustained by a study of the usage of the various terms related in the Bible .... The conclusion which must be drawn is that when the term *apostasy* is used to describe the sins of the saints, it is not that which the theologians refer to the same term by *final apostasy*. True believers do commit acts of temporary rebellion against God, and they suffer the consequences. This may be called apostasy, but the consequences are not eternal loss of relationship with God .... When it was discovered that in pagan literature *apostasy* meant rebellion, this appeared to be the best general term to describe the sin in both the Old

Testament and the New Testament. It was discovered that the theological definitions tend to follow ecclesiastical precedent, (from Roman Catholicism) rather than the biblical demands from context and lexicography. The result is an understanding of the sin of apostasy more clearly defined and rigidly applied than the scope of the term could unquestionably support. To maintain that this sin of apostasy is utter and final rejection of true faith in God, resulting in loss of salvation, or proving that one never was saved is most difficult to prove from a study of the passages where the term appears.[38]

It is this general meaning of **apostasy** which is to be preferred in Hebrews 3:12. There is nothing in the context which demands a technical meaning for apostasy. In fact, the context clearly indicates otherwise. What the author means by apostasy is first illustrated by the Exodus generation, and then applied to the Hebrew readers in chapters six and ten.

As such, the author becomes more specific as to what this apostasy is in Hebrews 6. Perhaps better stated is that he applies the apostasy of the Exodus generation to the New Testament situation with his own readers in chapter six. Here he warns his readers that their spiritual conduct will be tantamount to re-crucifying Christ (6:1-6), *if they fall away after having been once for all saved*. And then finally in Hebrews 10, the charge of apostasy against the cross becomes much more intelligible. In the first half of the chapter the author emphasizes the final once for all nature of the cross some five times (10:4, 10, 12, 14, 18). After this he mentions again that there is no longer any more sacrifice for sins (10:26) before finally charging them with trampling underfoot the Son of God, regarding the **blood** of the cross as common, and insulting the Spirit of grace (10:29). These are the three most concrete expressions in the book of Hebrews which describe their apostasy. Furthermore, it is no coincidence that when the author uses these three expressions to warn his readers, this loaded charge comes at the end of a strong theological argument explaining the Melchizedekian Priesthood and the New Covenant, in which, more than a dozen times, it is mentioned or alluded to that Christ died once (6:4; 6:6; 7:27; 9:14; 9:25-26; 9:28; 10:4; 10:10;

---

[38]   Dunham, *A Survey of Biblical Apostasy*.

10:12; 10:14; 10:18; 10:26). There is thus a strong interrelationship between apostasy, the warning passages, the fact that Christ died once for all, and the eschatology of both priesthood and covenant relative to the New Testament church. In other words, the Hebrew readers are being warned precisely because they are rejecting the final once for all eschatological *significance* of Christ's death. They are refusing to acknowledge they are no longer under the authority of the Old Covenant but under the authority of the New Testament. This is their apostasy.

Regarding the blood of the covenant as common (10:29) is the most clear expression depicting the apostasy of the Hebrew readers. The phrase **the blood of the covenant** is a reference to the New Covenant which has been inaugurated through the cross of Christ (7:11-12; 8:3-13; 9:15-16; 13:20). The Hebrew readers are specifically said here to be treating it as if it were something common, as if it was something ceremonially unclean, as if it was nothing of distinguishing importance. This, of course, is exactly the opposite of treating the cross with a final once for all apocalyptic significance. It seems that the Hebrew readers refused to accept the fact that the sacrifice of Christ is fundamentally different and unique from all other sacrifices of the Old Testament. The fact that they are still preoccupied by the Old Covenant sacrificial system clearly shows that they have not given the cross its deserved predominant position (10:1-18; 13:9-10). The cross of Christ is an incomparable difference which can only bring about incomparable differences in God's great salvation history program (9:8-28). It was these eschatological differences which the Hebrew readers were ignoring, and the reason why was precisely because they treated the cross as if it was something normal, as if it was nothing unusual, but merely an extension of the Levitical sacrifices. Closely connected, this also disregards the gracious progressive provisions of the New Testament and/or Covenant. Hence the sacred writer speaks not just of contempt for the cross, but also of disregard for the New Covenant, when he says "blood of the covenant (10:29)." Because of their faulty view of the cross, they were very hesitant about placing themselves under the exclusive authority of the New Testament and/or Covenant.

To revert back to Judaism, favoring the Old Covenant sacrificial system over the Christian cross and New Covenant, is also to **trample underfoot the Son of God**. This expression is used by the author of

Hebrews to show the flagrant defiance and total disregard for the plan of God centered in the crosswork of the Son of God. To value a ritual sacrifice on a par with or above the death of the Son of God, is an act of supreme indignity, disdain, and disrespect for the greatest divine activity in all of human history. What's more, such a scornful act was about to be committed, not by practicing an outward heinous sin like adultery or murder, but simply by being religious, by reverting back or by continuing a system which at one time may have been perfectly legitimate in the plan of God.

The fact of the matter is that throughout her history, Israel abused the Old Testament sacrificial system in a variety of ways (1 Sam 13:7-11; 15:17-23; Ps 40:6-8; Isa 1:10-15; Hos 6:6-8; Amos 5:22-25; Mic 6:6-8), and the Hebrew readers are about to do the same, albeit in their own contemporary way. In the Old Testament there were strict guidelines as to when, how and why ritual sacrifices were to be offered. They most certainly could not be used as a literal smokescreen for their sins, nor could they slavishly be depended upon as if the material ritual itself could magically bring about fellowship with a holy God. In the case of the Hebrew readers, they are perhaps closer to the latter abuse than the former, but both of them are so closely connected that neither one of them can be ruled out. How exactly they are abusing the sacrificial system is difficult to determine, but one thing is certain: they are favoring the old system in total disrespect for the New Covenant priesthood of the Son of God. Moreover, this abuse of ritualism becomes especially acute in light of the progress of revelation, covenant and priesthood. Now, the Hebrew readers are not merely trampling the courts of the Jerusalem Temple as in the days of Isaiah (Isa 1:12), but trampling underfoot the Son of God, a much more serious offence, so serious that it is also equated with insulting the Spirit.

Insulting the Spirit of grace is the last description of their apostasy in 10:29. The gracious provision of the Holy Spirit, promised in the prophecy about the New Covenant and based on the cross of Christ, is also on the verge of being rejected. To rebuff the cross and the Son of God is also a most serious affront to the Holy Spirit. Indeed, to revert back to the old system reveals an anti-grace attitude which is an outrage to the ministry of the Holy Spirit. The Old Testament sacrificial system never did provide its worshipers with the gracious ministry of the Holy Spirit.

This direct access to God was simply forbidden in the Old Testament to the population at large, given temporarily to a few of the kings like Saul and David, and then perhaps to some of the prophets, judges and priests. However, the New Covenant promises the gracious ministry of the Holy Spirit upon all, and it is based on the death of Christ. The New Covenant priesthood therefore provides the ministry of the Holy Spirit (7:1-8:13), but again, this great spiritual progress was insolently being neglected by the Hebrew readers.

The once for all death of Christ has inaugurated a new apocalyptic priesthood and covenant which is fundamentally different from the Old Covenant and priesthood (7:26-9:28). Moreover, this change of priesthood and covenant has also brought about an entirely new way of worship inside the heavenly holy of holies never before available to any saint (6:19-20; 10:19-23). It was these brand new changes that the Hebrew readers were having misgivings about because it meant the abolition of their old way of life in Judaism under the Old Covenant. As good as it was in its own day, once Christ has died once for all, there is no turning back to the old system. The progress of revelation, priesthood and covenant cannot be reversed. God Himself will not repent on this most critical issue (Heb 7:21-22). The Hebrew readers wanted the Old Covenant, Judaism and the Christianity all at the same time. The author warns them that this is impossible, and the reason why is very clear: Christ died once for all.

This is why the author spends such an inordinate amount of time explaining the superiority of Christianity, something which the Hebrew readers were not convinced of. In chapter one, the author of Hebrews establishes that Christ is superior not only to the Old Testament prophets but also to all of the angels as well (1:1-14), and if Christ is superior to the angels, then He is God's final apocalyptic prophet. Moreover, if Christ is superior to angels, this also means that His revelation is superior to the Old Covenant revelation since it was mediated through angels (2:3). In chapter three, the author explains that Christ is superior to Moses. As such the house which Christ built is superior to the house which Moses built (3:1-6). In other words, the heavenly tabernacle is superior to the earthly tabernacle (3:1-6; 9:1-14). Closely related to this is the whole discussion of the Order of Melchizedek (5:1-10:25). The heavenly Melchizedekian Priesthood of Christ is far superior to the earthly priesthood of Aaron and Levi. This means that the Christian order of worship is also superior to the Old Covenant form of worship (6:19-20; 10:19-25). This continuous assertion that Christianity is superior in every way to Old Covenant religion thus reveals the problem: the Hebrew readers really do not believe it. Again, they do not believe in the superiority of Christianity because they do not believe in the superior nature of Christ's once for all sacrifice, which fulfills the Old Covenant and ushers in a brand new arrangement of priesthood, covenant, and worship.

This being so, the author explicitly warns his readers five times that they must hold fast to Christianity (3:1, 6, 14; 4:14; 10:23). Because they did not believe in the superiority of Christianity, this was having a direct negative impact on their ability to persevere and worship God. Thus their apostasy consists of refusing to persevere in the spiritual realities of Christianity, which in turn left much to be desired in their worship. The sacred writer therefore commands his readers to consider Jesus, the Apostle and High Priest of their confession, perhaps a good theme verse for the entire book of Hebrews (3:1). He then warns them to hold fast their confidence, hope, and assurance until the end (3:6, 14). Later he commands them to hold fast their confession (4:14), and then finally admonishes them to hold fast their confession of hope without wavering (10:23). This is also very suggestive in that failing to accept the once for all death of Christ leads to doubt, lack of assurance, hopelessness and wavering, the exact opposite of a life of faith and certainty. A poor understanding of the cross will hinder the saint's ability to persevere and worship God acceptably. More to the point, in each case listed above, these admonishments to persevere occur within contexts which are speaking about the old and New Covenant tabernacle worship and priesthood. The Hebrew readers are so much at home under the Old Covenant tabernacle worship system that they are neglecting all of the great privileges of the New Testament tabernacle worship system. In their unbelief and spiritual immaturity, they have not appreciated the great contrast between the earthly house which Moses built and the heavenly house which Christ built (3:1-6; 9:1-14).

In fact, the spiritual condition of the Hebrew readers is so bad that the author actually questions the genuine reality of their own worship, "now Moses was faithful in all His house as a servant, for a testimony of those things spoken later; but Christ was faithful as Son over His house

– *whose house we are, if we hold fast* our confidence and the boast of our hope firm until the end (3:5-6)." Here the author clearly teaches them that they are Christ's heavenly worship house only insofar as they persevere in the spiritual realities of the royal priesthood of Christ. They simply cannot function on a spiritual level acceptable to God by depending on the old worship system.   They may be holy brothers (3:1), but they are the house of Christ if and only if they persevere in the spiritual realities of the Order of Melchizedek. How can they possibly spiritually experience the Order of Melchizedek if they are preoccupied with the order of Aaron and Levi?

Even at the end of chapter four, the admonishment to hold fast their confession also takes place in the context of the priesthood of Christ:

> Therefore, since we have a *great high priest* who has passed through the heavens, Jesus, the Son of God, *let us hold fast our confession*. For we do not have a *high priest* who cannot sympathize with our weaknesses, but One who has been tempted in all things as we are, yet without sin. Therefore *let us draw near* with confidence to the throne of grace, so that we may receive mercy and find grace to help in time of need (4:14-16).

The parallel admonishment to hold fast in chapter ten brings together both the house of God from 3:1-6 and Christ's priesthood in 4:14-16, as well as a new way of worship within the heavenly holy of holies:

> Therefore, brethren, since we have confidence to enter the holy place by the blood of Jesus, by a new and living way which He inaugurated through the veil, that is His flesh, and since we have a *great high priest over the house of God, let us draw near* with a sincere heart in full assurance of faith, having our hearts sprinkled clean from an evil conscience and our bodies washed with pure water. *Let us hold fast our confession of our hope without wavering*, for He who promised is faithful (10:19-23).

Thus the requirement to persevere in the book of Hebrews is not a question of whether or not a Christian can lose his salvation, much less the doctrine of the perseverance of the saints where all real Christians will inevitably persevere, but with the *practical worship experience* of the priesthood of Christ in their lives. As such, the Hebrew readers are the house of God only insofar that they put into practice the priesthood of Christ (3:6). Without the priesthood of Christ, there can be no sanctification and spiritual growth, and without this there can be no genuine Christian worship experience in the life of a believer. Worse, judgment is certain in such a case. Without growing up in the royal priesthood of Christ, eternal rest inheritance can be forfeited. They therefore need to hold fast at all costs or suffer God's fiery judgment.

These passages show that the Hebrew readers are having a very difficult time accepting the new spiritual realities of Christian priesthood and worship. Like many other Jewish people, they were stumbling over the great significance of the cross which had changed the priesthood, covenant, and worship.

The Spiritual Condition of the Hebrew Readers

The congregation to whom the author was writing was clearly a Christian community in deep spiritual crisis, as the warning passage make so horrifically clear. However, the "danger which roused the writer to interpose was not such a definite and grave heresy as evoked the Epistle to the Galatians or that to the Colossians, nor such entangling heathen vices and difficult questions of casuistry as imperiled the Corinthian Church, but rather a gradual, almost unconscious admission of doubt which dulled hope and slackened energy."[39] The primary problem is that they were becoming spiritual drifters (2:1) in the face of adverse conditions (12:1-4). What's more, this spiritual drifting is directly related to the fact that they have not accepted the superiority of Christianity. If they do not believe that Christianity is superior to Old Covenant religion, then how can they possibly boast about it, much less persevere in it? Without majesty and glory, there is little reason or motivation to worship or even sacrifice oneself. Not recognizing the great glories of Christianity, they were drying up spiritually, being tempted to go back to the old system, full of religious pomp and show.

It is highly likely that the Jewish Christians in the book of Hebrews were becoming disillusioned by the lack of outward display which

---

[39]   Dods, p. 235.

characterized their earlier form of worship under Judaism. This would explain why the author consistently and forcefully emphasizes the superiority of the invisible Order of Melchizedek throughout the book of Hebrews. Even though this order was invisible, it is at once far superior because it originates from the heavenly holy of holies, not from the earthly tabernacle "made of hands (9:11, 24)." The fact that the Melchizedekian order is an invisible order places great stress on the faith of the worshiper, and this test of faith the Hebrews were growing weary of. The invisible spiritual atmosphere of the New Testament was taking its toll on the faith of the recipients. Moreover, since worship in the New Testament cannot be readily seen, the Jewish Christians may have well assumed that this new form of worship was slack,[40] if not boring. Worship in the New Testament was not as "fun" as it was under the Old Covenant.

As such, they had lost interest in the Word of God (2:1). They were neglecting their so great salvation (2:3). They were not listening to God's voice in the Scripture (3:7; 4:7). In fact, they were hardening their hearts against the Word of God (3:8, 13, 15). This precarious attitude toward New Testament doctrine has left the readers spiritually dull (5:11), untrained by the word of righteousness (5:13) and sluggish (5:14). They were going astray in their hearts (3:10). They were ignorant of God's ways (3:10). They were losing their Christian confidence, assurance and boldness (3:6, 14; 10:32-39). They were falling away from the living God (3:12), and falling into unbelief (10:32-39). Some had even quit coming to the assembly (10:25).[41] They were also disheartened (12:1-12), forgetful (12:5-6), sorrowful (12:11), weak (12:12), spiritually crooked (12:12), and in great need of spiritual healing (12:12). This spiritual immaturity (5:13), spiritual remoteness (10:22), wavering (10:23), shrinking back (10:38), and spiritual lethargy (12:7-13) was leading them toward the fire of God's judgment (2:1-4; 6:1-9; 10:26-31; 12:25-29). It is striking that several times in the letter, the author admonishes them to hold fast their confession of hope (3:1, 6, 14; 4:14; 10:23). This again suggests that they were struggling with their Christian confession of faith, all too ready to abandon it for the conveniences of Judaism. This deplorable spiritual condition, together with God's impending wrathful sentence, motivated the author to write

---

[40]   Dunham, *Hebrews 2:1-4, The Danger of Drifting.*

[41]   In light of this fact, it is very possible that these members who left the church could have very well committed this apostasy which the author is so sternly warning them about.

---

the book of Hebrews. At the same time, while the wrath being described in Hebrews, particularly in chapters 3-4, is historically rooted in God's disciplinary actions meted out against the Exodus generation for their apostasy (Psalm 78:21-39; 106:32-33; Heb 3:11; 4:3) that is then brought up to date into the New Testament Church (Heb 2:1-4; 12:25-29; 1 Cor 10:1-13), this is not to be equated with Paul's more theological use of the term in Romans and 1st Thessalonians to characterize ultimate judgement against unbelievers (Rom 2:5; 5:9; 1 Thess 1:10; 5:9). "Wrath" in Hebrews means "anger against sin" (Deut 9:6-24; Psalm 95:7) in a more general sense. In other words, "wrath" in Hebrews means divine discipline against the saints for apostate behavior, not final judgment against an unbelieving world that is depicted in the book of Revelation (Rev 15-19).

CHAPTER THREE

THE UNITY OF THE WARNING PASSAGES

Much confusion has resulted in the book of Hebrews for the simple reason that the warnings have been so often interpreted separately and independently of each another. Even sound exegetes who understand the critical importance of this issue, still fail to integrate the warning passages in Hebrews. The context of *all* the warning passages in Hebrews is often not properly used, and so the Bible student is left with conflicting and competing conclusions. Many will go to Hebrews 6 for example, a very difficult passage to be sure, and interpret it independently of all the others, and try to demonstrate that a Christian can lose his salvation. This is a poor method of interpretation. Hebrews 6 is a tough and enigmatic passage. The fact that it has been interpreted in so many different ways with few convincing cases is a strong testimony to its elusive character. It is not good procedure to take the most difficult and obscure passage to prove a theological position. When this is done, it actually shows the weakness of the theological position. A theological view based on difficult verses will quickly cave in under the pressure of many other passages which are clearer. It is amazing how clear passages of Scriptures are so often ignored in favor of obscure verses which are used to maintain a sacred theological cow. This actually shows the interpreter's insensitivity to the teaching of the Word of God. It is a maverick method of interpretation which cannot withstand the weight of sound biblical exegesis. Difficult passages can be made to say almost anything one wants them to say. This cannot be done so readily with more clear passages of Scripture. One of the most important principles of sound interpretation is to take the more clear passages first before moving onto the more difficult passages. This is a most important principle in the Hebrew warning passages. Hebrews 6:4-6 simply cannot be made to stand alone, but like every other passage in Scripture, must be interpreted in context.

There are *five* warning passages in Hebrews, not just one, and not just Hebrews 6, to help the Bible student understand what the readers are being warned of. These warnings simply cannot be interpreted separately, but as a unit. They go together. They complement one another. If all the warning passages are understood in Hebrews, then some of the obscurity of the more difficult passages is lessened. This also relieves all of the pressure that is placed on 6:4-6 to explain everything. The Old Testament examples of the Exodus generation and Esau already shed much light on the nature of the Hebrew warning passages. Furthermore, the warnings in Hebrews 6 and 10 are virtually identical, and the warning in chapter ten is actually more straightforward than in chapter six. All of the warnings therefore must be understood in light of each other, and this helps alleviate some of the difficulties in individual passages. Of course, individual passages must speak for themselves, but the entire context of all the warnings in Hebrews places parameters on what such texts mean. These parameters curtail excessive and peculiar interpretations often drawn from passages like 6:4-6 which are seldom really understood in the first place.

In 2:1-4 the Hebrew readers are on the verge of drifting away, not listening carefully to New Testament revelation of the Son of God as entailed in chapter one. The author warns with absolute certainty that they will not escape judgment if they drift off course. In 3:12, this drifting is leading them down the road of apostasy and unbelief, and is compared to the Exodus generation. If they continue in their apostasy and unbelief like the Exodus generation, they will be cut off from the house of God (3:6), lose their spiritual participation with Christ (3:14), and fail to enter God's rest (4:1-11). This is the judgment that they will not escape in 2:1-4. In chapters five and six, the reason for their drifting and unbelief, nay even potential apostasy, becomes clearer in that they are said to be entrenched in perpetual self-induced spiritual immaturity. This persistent spiritual lethargy is pushing them toward apostasy, or a falling away (6:6), which will bring about irreparable consequences (6:4-8). 10:26-31 then warns of a continuing in willful sin which will reap the fury of God's fire. In 12:12-29, with Esau's failure serving as another example, the Hebrew readers are about to refuse the New Testament revelation given to them by the Son, and this stubborn refusal will not escape the future eschatological heavenly earthquake. Moreover, it is significant to note that each subsequent warning gets a little more serious. The author starts out fairly mild in chapter two, but the issue becomes much more perilous in chapters three and four. In chapter six, the warning significantly heats up, and then in chapter ten it becomes downright frightening, and then finally in chapter 12 the Hebrew readers are about as close to the torch as anyone would ever want to get.

2:1-4 and 12:25-29 are virtually identical and serve as bookends to the other three warnings. They also tie in with the rest of the warnings, not only because of content, but also because of the strong allusions to Mt. Sinai and the Exodus generation. Both 2:1-4 and 12:25-29 warn the Hebrew readers they must pay careful attention to the Revelation of the Son (2:1; 12:25). Both passages warn they will not escape if they do not listen up (2:3; 12:25). The only difference is that 12:25-29 describes what they will not escape from, a future eschatological earthquake (12:26-27). Here the only essential difference is that the sacred writer is emphasizing the eschatological consequences of their sin. Whatever is not done in this life on an eternal spiritual basis will be shaken away. Both passages also refer back to Mt. Sinai and the Exodus generation (2:2-3; 12:25). In 2:2-3 the author reminds them of the consequences of breaking Law given at Mt. Sinai, "For if the word spoken through angels proved unalterable and every transgression and disobedience received a just penalty, how will we escape if we neglect a so great salvation." In 12:25, the author asserts, "For if those (the Exodus generation) did not escape when they refused Him who warned them on earth, much less will we escape who turn away from Him who warns from heaven." This reference to the Exodus generation ties in with the warning in chapters three and four, and even the warning in chapter ten makes reference to the judgment of the Law of Moses (10:28). This continual reference to the Exodus generation cannot be ignored. The Exodus generation therefore, their sin, their judgment, is exactly parallel to the Hebrew readers.

The only warning in Hebrews in which the Exodus generation is not alluded to is in chapter six. However, the issues are essentially the same. Hebrews 6 is actually the New Testament explanation and application of the Exodus generation failure to the present circumstances. After referring to the Exodus generation's dismal failure in 3:7-4:11, the author of Hebrews then begins to contrast the priesthood of Christ with the priesthood of Aaron (4:14-5:10), something which the Hebrew readers were refusing to acknowledge, steeped in the ways of the Old Covenant. They were not listening to New Testament truth as 2:1-4 and 12:25-29 makes so clear. Moreover, Aaron is yet again another reference to the Exodus generation. However, before the author goes on to further contrast Aaron's priesthood with Christ's priesthood in 6:9-10:18, he stops his flow of thought for yet another warning in 6:1-8. Nonetheless the echoes of the Exodus generation have not disappeared. The warning of Hebrews 6 is all wrapped up in the whole argument contrasting Aaron with Christ (4:14-7:28).

Hebrews 6:1-3 is a peculiar statement, "therefore leaving the elementary teachings about the Christ, let us press on to maturity, not again laying a foundation ... and this we will do, *if God permits.*" If God does not permit someone to press onto maturity, this is a judgment. Furthermore, it is a judgment exactly parallel to the Exodus generation. God did not **permit** the Exodus generation to enter His rest in the land of promise. He swore in His wrath they would never enter rest but die in the wilderness instead. In the same way, God may swear in His fiery wrath that the Hebrew readers will not be permitted to press on to spiritual maturity. As such, this will make it all but impossible to enter God's rest (4:11; 6:12). Just as the Exodus generation was confined in the desert with no possible way of going back to Egypt,[42] and just as it had no opportunity for spiritual growth in the Promised Land, the same can be said of the Hebrew readers if they continue in their own spiritual decline. This connects loss of opportunity for spiritual growth with loss of rest.

---

[42]   Even though the Exodus generation wanted to go back to Egypt (Num 14:2-4), this was virtually impossible. They had burned their bridges with Egypt. Egypt would not have taken them back, but probably would have pursued them with the sword just as the Amalekites did (Num 14:39-45).

Without spiritual maturity and growth, there can be no way of entering God's rest (4:1-11; 6:1-3). Moreover, just as the Exodus generation could not start over by going back to Egypt and was not allowed to enter the Promised Land, the Hebrew readers will also not be allowed to lay another foundation again (6:1), nor allowed to grow up spiritually (6:3), if they continue to follow the same slippery slope (6:4-6). This is the whole issue in Hebrews 6:1-8. The judgment in Hebrews 6 is not hell, but loss of opportunity for spiritual growth and maturity, which ultimately will lead to a loss of rest and eschatological reward (4:11; 12:25-29). If a Christian (6:4-5) has been sentenced to die in a spiritual wilderness, he simply will not have opportunity for spiritual growth, nor the opportunity to enter rest or to inherit his reward. Neither will God allow him to start over again, for in this particular case, it would be equivalent to re-crucifying Christ on the cross (6:6) – which is impossible. Therefore, death in a spiritual wilderness is the only remaining alternative.

The theme of Hebrews that Christ died once thus comes to the fore here in chapter six and it continues all the way through the following warning in chapter ten. This onceness is irreversible and unrepeatable. In light of the Hebrew readers' particular apostasy against the meaning of the cross, there can be no starting over again after having fallen away. Hebrews 10:26-27 clearly establishes this principle further, "For if we go on sinning willfully after receiving the knowledge of the truth, *there no longer remains a sacrifice for sins*, but a terrifying expectation of judgment and the fury of fire which consumes the adversaries." In Hebrews 10:10-14, 10:18 and 10:26, it is emphasized again and again that Christ died once for all, and so if the cross of Christ together with the high priestly results of His once for all death (6:19-10:18) does not motivate the Christian toward perseverance and sanctification, then judgment will be both certain and most severe (6:8; 10:27-31). God has already done everything possible to help prevent sin in the life of a Christian. Not only has Christ died for his sins, but He also now intercedes for him in heaven to prevent him from the daily practice of sin (4:14-16). As such, if all this grace is without result, then judgment is the only alternative, and this judgment will not only impact one's present spiritual life on the earth like the Exodus generation, but will also result in great negative consequences in the eschatological kingdom of God (12:25-29). The author of Hebrews even says in so many words that such a person may not be allowed to *see the Lord* (12:14).

If the Exodus generation, a redeemed people, refused to listen to God's Law and did not escape judgment (12:25), then how can the Hebrew readers expect anything different who are refusing to listen to the Son of God? Though there are two different covenants involved, the same God is in charge of both, "Our God is a consuming fire (12:29)." The Hebrew readers are therefore to beware of the bitter consequences of spiritual drifting (2:1-4). They may find themselves in a position just like the Exodus generation (4:1-11) in which there will be no way out of God's wrathful judgment (6:1-8; 10:26-31; 12:14-17). They may very well find themselves in a position in which they will have to endure and experience God's sentence of wrath for their sin. They will not be able to go back, and they will not be able to go forward, but will have to go through God's severe judgment instead, which is a loss of rest-inheritance or inheritance reward, but not loss of salvation.

Finally, the severity of the Hebrew warnings is all based upon the superior revelation of the Son of God which the Hebrew readers were rejecting (1:1-2:4). The Hebrew readers were somehow treating the New Testament as if it were a repeat of the old one. This, the author of Hebrews calls trampling underfoot the Son of God, regarding unclean the blood of the covenant, and insulting to the Spirit of grace. This is a great sin worthy of more severe judgment than anything under the Old Covenant (10:28-29). The judgments of the New Testament will not be softer than the judgments of the Old Covenant. The author of Hebrews indicates that they in fact will be worse. How were the Hebrew readers regarding New Testament revelation? What value were they placing on New Testament truth? What value were they giving to the cross? Would they go beyond the Old Covenant worship system and enjoy the New Testament worship system according to the Order of Melchizedek? This was the spiritual crucible in which they were about to fail miserably.

CHAPTER FOUR

The Danger of Careless Christianity – 2:1-4

Relating Hebrews 1 to the First Warning

In between the Old Testament doctrines of the glory (1:1-14) and the humiliation of the Messiah (2:5-18), the author writes these most solemn words to his brothers in Christ some 2000 years ago, the first warning in the book of Hebrews:

> For this reason we must pay much closer attention to what we have heard, so that we do not drift away from it. For if the word spoken through angels proved unalterable, and every transgression and disobedience received a just penalty, how will we escape if we neglect so great a salvation? After it was first spoken through the Lord, it was confirmed to us by those who heard, God also testifying with them, both by signs and wonders and various miracles and by gifts of the Holy Spirit according to His own will (2:1-4).

In chapter one the author of Hebrews writes about the glory of the exalted Son, the kind of Messiah that the Jewish people awaited so eagerly. However, in chapter two, he writes about the humiliation and suffering of the Son (2:5-18). It was this kind of Messiah, the suffering

Messiah, that the Jewish people struggled with. They failed to understand that it would not be until after His suffering and humiliation that the Messiah would achieve His ultimate glory. Paul summarizes this Jewish problem quite well in 1 Corinthians, "but we preach Christ crucified, to Jews a **stumbling block** ... (1:23)." It was this same stumbling block, the necessity of Messiah crucified and the cruciality of the cross, that was causing these particular Jewish believers in the book of Hebrews to stumble. However, here in chapter two, the author does not call it stumbling, but drifting. Unlike the Jewish population at large, they had already received Christ as their Savior. As such, they are being warned of spiritual drifting. They were being warned of drifting away from the Savior, of drifting away from the so great salvation which the New Testament revelation had conferred upon them.

The opening words of chapter two illustrate the author's habit of introducing his practical exhortations into the body of his sermon.[43] Both chapters one and two are loaded with Old Testament quotations concerning the Son and His theological relationship to Creation and to the angelic hosts. Both of these chapters are highly technical in nature, and they are filled with great theological meaning. However, right in the middle of this theological masterpiece, which consists of perhaps some of the most outstanding Christological statements found in anywhere in the New Testament, the Hebrew readers come across this warning, a serious warning indeed. This means at once that chapters one and two are not cold abstract theological doctrines about the Messiah. Though they are highly theological, and highly technical, they are not to be understood in a cold, abstract, philosophical way. These great theological doctrines are to have great impact on how the Hebrew readers are to live. Christology is the basis not only for this particular warning here in chapter two, but also for every subsequent warning that is found in the book of Hebrews. Here in Hebrews 1 and 2, Christology and severe warning go hand in hand. To be careless about Christology is to invite judgment and wrath. Christology can only be ignored at a Christian's peril.

The Old Covenant revelation was communicated merely by angels (2:2), but God's final eschatological revelation was communicated by His Son through the apostles (1:1-4; 2:3-4). Hebrews 2:1-4 makes it very

---

[43]   Vincent, _Word Studies in the New Testament_,(William B. Eerdmans Publishers: Grand Rapids, Michigan), Volume 4, p. 392.

clear that this New Testament revelation of the Son of God requires far more serious attention than the Old Covenant revelation of angelic intermediaries (2:2). To fail to listen to the Son is worse than to fail to listen to angels. With great interest, the author says the Old Covenent Law given at Mt. Sinai was mediated through angels. Though the book of Exodus mentions nothing of this, both the martyr Stephen and the apostle Paul understood that the Old Testament Law was given to ancient Israel through angelic mediators (Acts 7:53; Gal 3:19). While many become overly excited over messages from angels, here in Hebrew 2, it simply cannot compare to the message received from the Son. The agency of angels actually indicates a great limitation compared to the Son. The New Testament revelation of the Son, which was "first spoken through the Lord," and later "confirmed by those who heard," i.e., the apostles, requires far more serious attention. Moreover, this most superior revelation is here directly associated with "so great a salvation (2:3)." With greater privilege comes greater responsibility, and with greater responsibility comes greater peril.[44] Christianity is just as dangerous as it is gracious, and the reason why is precisely because of the superior nature of the Son of God, the central theme of the book of Hebrews (1:1-14; 3:1; 12:1-3).

This is why the author begins the warning with "because of this (2:1)." The natural question here, of course, is because of what? The answer is because of the entire contents of chapter one. Because the Hebrew readers have received a revelation superior to that of the Old Testament revelation (1:1-4), because they have received a revelation from One Who is the Heir of all things (1:2), because they have received a revelation from the One Who is both God and man at the same time (1:1-14), because they have received a revelation from the One Who created the universe (1:2), because they have received a revelation from One Who continues to uphold the universe by the power of His word (1:3), because they have received a revelation from One Who made purification for all sins (1:3), because they have received a revelation from the One Who is seated at the right hand of God (1:3), because they have a received a revelation from the One Who is superior to all the angels (1:5-14), because of all these great spiritual realities, they need to pay much more closer attention to the word which He gave to them (2:1-4). God has not spoken

44   Lane, p. 38.

to the Hebrew readers through mere prophets or angels, but through the glorified Son of God. There has therefore been progress both in revelation and covenant which the Hebrew readers have been ignoring. They are neglecting the progress of revelation which has culminated in Christ. They are thus over-inflating the Old Testament at the expense of the great glories of the New Testament.

This is the primary thrust of Hebrews 1 – that the progressive revelation of God has reached its climax in the Son. This magnificent theme stated in the opening paragraph (1:1-4) is the theme not only of the rest of the chapter, but also of the entire book. The final revelation of God by the Son is superior to the piecemeal and various revelations given to the Old Testament prophets, and this unique finality promises greater blessing for those who embrace it, but also greater discipline and judgment for those who fall away from it. This is essentially what the book of Hebrews is all about.

The great problem was the Hebrew readers were neglecting this final revelation given through the Son. They were somehow more impressed with the Old Testament of God than the New Testament revelation of the Son of God. The sacred author, therefore, warns them of the dire consequences of such an attitude. The final revelation of God through the Son has unique authority, with unique privileges, yet also unique responsibilities. As such, the author begins the book of Hebrews by explaining why the revelation of the Son is final and unique. It is precisely because of the Person of the Son of God. It is because of the nature of the Son. It is of because of the majesty of His Person. The Son, through whom God revealed Himself, is the Creator-Savior who is both God and Man. He is also superior to all the angels, and to all of the Old Testament prophets. This is why His Word is final and unique. To ignore what He has said is to literally play with fire.

The best illustration of the doctrine of progressive revelation is the Transfiguration. Hebrews 1:1-4 is like a doctrinal explanation of the Transfiguration.[45] What the Transfiguration demonstrated before the disciples is given a doctrinal explanation in Hebrews 1:1-4. In the Transfiguration, James, Peter and John were given a glimpse of Jesus' glory in contrast to Moses and Elijah. Moses is the Lawgiver and represents the Old Covenant Law. The great prophet Elijah represents the ministry

---

[45]   Dods, p. 247.

of the Old Testament prophets to the nation of Israel. Nonetheless, as good as these great Old Testament heroes were, they can in no way be compared to the Son. As such, rather suddenly, both Moses and Elijah disappear, leaving Jesus alone. God the Father aptly and solemnly speaks at this moment, "This is My beloved Son, with whom I am well pleased; listen to Him (Matt 17:5)." This is exactly what the Hebrew readers need to do. They need to listen to the Son, God's final word to them. God is more insistent that the Hebrew readers listen to His Son.

This is not to say there was something wrong with the Old Testament. The revelation of the Son is not more truer than the revelation given to the Old Testament prophets. The revelation given to the Old Testament prophets was just as pure and holy as is the New Testament. The difference is that the Old Testament revelation was not complete. This is the main thrust of 1:1-4, and the readers desperately need to understand this. They must pay **much more attention** to this final word of the Son which they have heard (2:1). As good as the Old Testament revelation was, it was incomplete. Throughout the Old Testament, God spoke to the fathers in a fragmentary way by the prophets, "He spoke in many separate revelations, each of which set forth only a portion of the truth. The truth as a whole never comes to light in the Old Testament. It appears fragmentarily, in successive acts over time."[46] In the Old Testament, God spoke by parables, by psalms, by the Old Covenent Law, by prophecies, by types, by miracles, by signs, etc.[47] However, upon the last of these days, God spoke by His Son, and this concluded the Old Testament prophetic office together with Old Testament time period. The Old Testament laid the foundation and groundwork for the coming Messiah. As such, it prepared the way for the New Testament revelation, but it was never intended to be treated as the final word. The problem here in the book of Hebrews is that the readers were treating the Old Testament revelation as if it were the final and eternal word. The author spends much time throughout the book refuting this assumption, even beginning his entire sermon with this particular issue in mind. Contrary to the thinking of the Hebrew readers, that which is last is best. The new is better than the old. This is precisely why the author of Hebrews begins his letter by contrasting the revelation given to the prophets, with the revelation

---

[46]   Vincent, p. 377.
[47]   Dods, p. 249.

given in the Son. The Hebrew readers need to understand the superior revelation of the New Testament in contrast to the Old Testament. This truth will rescue them from God's impending judgment.

However, while there is certainly a great contrast between the Old Testament prophet and the Son, the sacred writer is not advocating a total break between them. The main subject of both parties in Hebrews 1:1-2 is **God**. God is the source of both the Old Testament Prophet and the Son. As such, while God spoke to the Old Testament fathers by the prophets in various ways and at different times, in the last of these Old Testament days, God spoke through His Son. More to the point, if God the Father is the source of both revelations, then these revelations cannot be contradictory, but rather there has been a progress of revelation through the Son.

The difference therefore between the Old Testament prophet and the Son is not a contradictory one. Rather there is the same Author of both who does not change. However, the great problem in history is that man simply cannot take God in all at once. Biblical history is therefore God's schoolroom to teach the Jews and the world about the coming of Messiah, and so His revelation takes on a progressive character. The same Author of both revelations, the God who does not change, still has a time calendar. Over time therefore, throughout the history of the Old Testament, He revealed more and more of Himself to His people. Now, this great process has climaxed with the first coming of Messiah,"the Revelation of the Son is a continuation of the old so far as God is the author of both, but the Revelation of the Son is also completely new and separate in character so far as Christ is the mediator of it."[48]

With the coming of the Son, there is the final word, which has final authority. The New Testament revelation is just as final as the life and death and resurrection of Christ. There are no more Old Testament prophets to come. God has spoken once for all. Having fulfilled its God-destined purpose, the fragmentary nature of Old Testament revelation has been superseded because Christ has fulfilled its great aspirations,"the story of divine revelation is a story of progression up to Christ, but there is no progression beyond Him."[49] As such, the end result has been reached. More to the point, when one reaches the end result and begins to look

---

[48]   Westcott, Brooke F. _Hebrews_, p.7.

[49]   Bruce, p. 46.

back, he looks at the past differently, and unless one is a fool, he is not interested in going back to it. If one goes backwards, he loses the end result. He loses the goal which he has been working for all along. As such, the difference between the Old Testament prophet and the Son is a question of time and history, of prophecy and fulfillment, between that which is fragmentary versus that which is complete. It is therefore a question of eschatology, i.e., of Dispensations, not of two competing contradictory systems. What is being discussed is the progress of revelation on God's time calendar, and this progress of revelation has reached its peak or goal in the revelation of the Son. Eschatology, i.e., apocalyptic thinking, colors the author's outlook in the epistle of Hebrews. He looks at the Old Testament with an eschatological or apocalyptic perspective. He therefore calls the present age these last days (Heb 1:2), and the consummation of the ages (Heb 9:10, 26). The death of Christ has ushered in a new final period of salvation history characterized by a New Covenant and a new priesthood, the great theme of Hebrews. To go back to the old system is to forfeit the new system.

This is why the author of Hebrews begins his letter with doctrine of the climactic revelation of the Son. This is the answer to the crisis which the Hebrew readers are facing. Just as the Exodus generation was pining to go back to Egypt, so now these Jewish believers were pining to return to the good old days of the Old Covenant. The author therefore begins his letter by reminding them of God's progressive revelation of Himself which culminated in His Son, and once the Son has come finally and once for all, there is no turning back, unless they want to invite the fire of God's wrath into their lives.

The author, therefore, quickly gets to the point in chapter one. He begins his letter, without even mentioning his own name, by reminding them that the Son is God's most superior revealer. To go back to the old system is not only settling for less, but far worse – it is apostasy. The Hebrew readers, therefore, need to be occupied with the high priestly glories of Jesus Christ. They must stop pining for the good old days under the old system. As wonderful as the Old Testament and the Law of Moses was, as magnificent as angels are – they still cannot compare with the Son.

It is amazing that God's people can forget about the great glories of the Son of God. Giving due honor and homage to the Son is perhaps the greatest test in life to face as a Christian. As a Christian, one must accept the offense and starkness of the cross if he wants to press onto spiritual glories, something which the Hebrew readers were growing weary of. This test the author of Hebrews understood quite well. He therefore now gives his readers in Hebrews 2 his first warning (2:1-4). This immediately follows the great discussion on the glories of the Son in contrast to Old Testament prophets and angels (1:1-14). He warns them to give heed to the great glories of this New Testament revelation or suffer judgment (2:1-4).

Neglecting So Great a Salvation

In 2:1 in the Greek, the words '*to give heed*', or '*to pay attention*', is a present infinitive. This means that the Hebrew readers are *to pay attention* at all times to this New Testament revelation, not just some of the time. Moreover, this is strengthened by the phrase, '*we must*'. The Hebrew readers *must* at all times pay careful attention to what they have heard from the apostles, namely, New Testament truth, lest they drift away. In other words, apostolic doctrine will prevent them from drifting away. With interest, the author does not here say that they are drifting away. Grammatically, he uses the subjunctive mood, the mood of possibility, not of reality. They are in danger of drifting away if they do not pay much closer attention to this apostolic doctrine. If they do not watch out, they may be overtaken all at once and be caught without any kind of mooring to anchor them to the shore. The picture here is like a raft drifting downstream, and so if they are not careful to anchor themselves quickly to the dock, they will quickly lose their opportunity to secure themselves. To lapse from the truth is more often a result of inattention than of actual purpose.[50]

Structurally, Hebrews 2:1-4 consists of a direct statement in verse one, "*we must pay much closer attention*," followed by an explanatory condition in 2:2-4, "*how shall we escape if we neglect?*"[51] In other words, the Hebrew readers must pay much closer attention to apostolic doctrine. If they do not, they will reap a bitter judgment akin to the judgment of the Exodus generation (2:2-3). Moreover, if the Exodus generation was

---

[50]   Vincent, p. 393.

[51]   Lane, p. 35.

judged for their sin under the Old Covenant (2:2), then this will be no less true for the Hebrew readers under the new dispensation (2:3-4). If the Old Testament revelation meted out punishment for sin, then so will the New Testament revelation. If the Old Testament revelation mediated through angels proved valid and sure, and every transgression and disobedience received a just recompense, then how is it that the Hebrew readers think that they can escape if they neglect their own so great a salvation mediated through the Son of God and the apostles? Watch Out! Beware! The New Testament will judge disobedient believers just as the Old Covenant. The New Testament is not slack with regard to judging the saints for their sins. In short, the necessity of heedful care (2:1) is grounded on the certainty of retribution (2:2-3).[52]

Transgression (2:2) is a stepping over the line. It is the positive violation of a divine command. The *disobedience* described here (2:2) is a disobedience which results from the failure to listen up. *Recompense* (2:2) is a combination of both wages and punishment[53] or punishment as reward.[54] In the Greek, *having neglected*, is a conditional participle and so it is to be translated with the word *if*. This conditional participle indicates a condition which must be fulfilled before the action of the main verb can take place, and the main verb here is "how shall we escape?" This means that *if* they neglect their so great salvation, they will certainly not escape. Moreover, the salvation is *so great* precisely because of the greatness of the Son and His work. At the expense of their so great salvation, the Hebrew readers are hanging onto their outdated religious system.

Now, the Hebrews readers knew the Old Testament Law was certain in punishing transgressors, but they were not too sure about the New Dispensation.[55] Even today many Christians get careless about their own sins because they are under grace and not under the law. In the process respect for God is lost. It is perhaps very likely that the Hebrew readers were losing respect for New Testament truth. They liked the seriousness of the Old Covenent Law, but disdained the so-called easy-free life under New Testament grace, especially with regard to the antinomian behavior of the Gentile churches. And so here in Hebrews 2:1-4, the author of

---

52   Westcott, p. 37.
53   Kistemaker, p. 62.
54   Lane, p. 38.
55   Dods, p. 259.

Hebrews will now do away with this widespread opinion that the New Testament is lax. With regard to just retribution, the New Testament is just as trustworthy as the Old Testament. God is just as righteous in the New Testament as He is in the Old Testament. This has not changed. Jesus Christ loves righteousness and hates lawlessness (1:9). The source of the New Testament revelation is therefore unquestionably pure.[56]

New Testament truth has not been contaminated by sin any more than Old Covenant truth.[57] As such, the Hebrew readers were simply being careless with regard to holy purity of the New Testament. They were not taking it seriously. The old religious system was to them somehow more important and holy than the death and resurrection of the Messiah. The author of Hebrews therefore warns them of the dire consequences of spiritual carelessness. In Christianity, spiritual carelessness is very dangerous. In the New Testament, grace is not leniency. Grace is just as holy and pure as anything under the Old Covenant and does not condone the careless attitudes of God's people. Spiritual carelessness invites the wrath of God, even under the grace of the New Testament.

What the Hebrew readers do not spiritually appreciate is that the abolition of the Old Covenant is the freedom of man from subordination to the angels (2:1-18).[58] They have no idea as to how great their salvation really is (2:3-18). By quoting yet another Psalm to his readers (Ps 8:4-6), the author reminds them that the eschatological world to come will not be subjected to angels, but to man (2:5-9). Subordination to angels is inconsistent with man's ultimate destiny to be sovereign over all creation.[59] The quotation of Psalm 8 demonstrates that the salvation being emphasized in Hebrews 2 is that of man's universal dominion over the universe, i.e., God's rest, not justification:

> The temporary subordination of Christ to angels was followed by His permanent exaltation over them. He was only for a short time on the same plane as man under the administration of angels, but this temporary subordination to angels was followed by a permanent elevation over them.[60]

---

[56] Ibid, p. 260.
[57] Ibid.
[58] Vincent, p. 393-94.
[59] Ibid.
[60] Ibid., pp. 396-98.

While the old and present world has been entrusted to angels for administration (Dt 32:8 LXX; Dan 10:20; 12:1), this will not be true of the world to come. The Son of God and man, not angels, will rule the universe. It is therefore impossible to continue to be under the Old Covenent Law mediated by angels. Though for a little while the angels were higher than man (2:7), they are merely "ministering spirits, sent out to render service for the sake of those who will **inherit** salvation (1:14)." By remaining back in the old system under the authority of angels, the Hebrew readers may forfeit the right to rule with Christ in this great spiritual inheritance which is above all the angels. It is this aspect of their so great salvation which they are woefully neglecting. This great spiritual inheritance is later called God's rest (4:1-11), the major thrust of the next warning (3:7-4:13).

CHAPTER FIVE

SANCTIFICATION AND THE EXODUS DEBACLE

Sanctification: Salvation by Faith and Works

One of the great emphases of the book of Hebrews is that the salvation being prescribed by the author is conditioned upon faithful perseverance to the end, i.e., upon perseverant sanctification so as to enter God's rest, and this great theme carries throughout the epistle. This is precisely what the warning passages of Hebrews are all about. Time and time again, in passage after passage, there is a strong emphasis upon the conditional nature of salvation in the book of Hebrews (2:1-3; 3:6; 3:14; 6:7-8; 6:11-12; 10:23-24; 10:26-27; 10:35-39; 12:25). In order to be saved, i.e., enter God's rest, in the book of Hebrews, one must persevere in faith and obedience, and this is especially emphasized in Hebrews 3-4:

> ... but Christ was faithful as a Son over His house, whose house we are, *if* we hold fast our confidence and the boast of hope firm until the end (3:6) ... For we have become partakers of Christ, *if* we hold fast the beginning of our assurance firm until the end (3:14) ... therefore, let us fear if, while a promise remains of entering His rest, any one of you may seem to have come short of it (4:1) ... therefore, let us be diligent to enter that rest,

so that no one will fall, through following the same example of disobedience (4:11).

As such, the kind of salvation that is found in Hebrews *is* without question a conditional salvation. It is without question conditioned upon one's perseverance in faith and obedience. Like the Exodus generation, the Hebrew readers must persevere in faith and obedience or forfeit God's rest. God may certainly be faithful, which the author emphasizes over and over again in this epistle, but his readers may not be faithful.

The Hebrew readers therefore need to beware. They are not to follow the disaster of the Exodus generation. If the Hebrew readers are not faithful, if they continue to disbelieve God, then they will share the same fate as the Exodus generation who died in the wilderness. God saved them out of Egypt, but they failed to reach the salvation goal of the Promised Land. They passed the first salvation test, but they failed the second salvation test. Moreover, the problem was not with God, but with His people. The Exodus generation languished out in the wilderness. They were caught between their initial salvation out of Egypt and their salvation goal of rest in Canaan, and there they died by the edict of God.

The book of Hebrews does not teach the perseverance of the saints as is normally understood in theological circles. The book of Hebrews nowhere teaches that all real saints will eventually persevere to the end as this doctrine teaches. On the contrary, the book of Hebrews teaches that if one does not persevere in faith and obedience, then he will suffer the consequences of God's fiery judgment, and this fiery judgment is never said to be hell. Rather, it says in Hebrews that God will not allow such a person to enter His rest. Not entering rest is the judgment, not eternal hellfire. What the book of Hebrews does teach is that if one does not persevere in faith and obedience, then he will not inherit God's promised rest, certainly not in this life and perhaps not even in the eschatological future either. God will not take away his initial salvation, but He will not allow him to progress spiritually (6:1-3), and without spiritual progress one simply cannot reach the goal of rest (3:17-19; 4:11). To reach the goal of rest, one must progress spiritually, but God may not permit this (6:1-3), and this lack of spiritual progress will prevent him from finishing his work of endurance and faith here on the earth (4:11).

More to the point, if salvation is dependent upon faithful perseverance and obedience, then the kind of salvation being discussed here cannot be about being saved from the *penalty* of sin, but from the *practice* of sin. Theologically, there are three primary aspects of salvation: past, present and future. Past salvation is being delivered from the *penalty* of sin. In theology, this is generally called justification and is without works (Rom 4:1-8; Gal 2:16). Present salvation is being delivered from the daily *practice* of sin and is accompanied by works. This is called sanctification. Future salvation is being delivered from the *presence* of sin. This will occur at the future bodily resurrection of the saints and is called glorification.

With this in mind, a Bible interpreter must be able to identify which aspect of salvation an author of Scripture is emphasizing. As is always the case, an interpreter cannot ignore context, and contextually in the book of Hebrews, the author is primarily emphasizing the present aspects of salvation, i.e., sanctification, or the lack thereof, when he warns his readers. The author already recognizes that they have been saved once for all from the penalty of sin (3:1; 6:4-5; 10:10; 10:29; 12:22-24), but their being saved from the daily practice of sin is of course in doubt (3:6; 3:12-14; 4:1; 4:11; 4:16; 5:11-12; 6:1-3; 6:7-8; 6:9-12; 10:22; 10:26-39; 12:1-3; 12:11-15; 12:25; 13:1-22). Closely related, if they fail to live sanctified lives on the earth, they will not only experience God's wrath in this life (3:7-4:3; 6:7-8; 10:26-27), but also will lose out on the eschatological reward of God's rest in the future life (4:11; 6:12; 10:36). Though the Hebrew readers have been saved once for all and will therefore all receive glorified resurrection bodies, if they do not persevere in sanctification, they will miss out on their rest-inheritance, both in this life and in the life to come. If they want to receive the reward of God's rest, then they must persevere in faith and obedience.

In summary, justification, i.e., salvation from the penalty of sin, is unconditional, but sanctification and eschatological reward are highly conditional. The author of Hebrews is satisfied with their past salvation and so calls them all Christians, and this he can do precisely because a Christian is saved by grace without works (Rom 4:1-8; Eph 2:8-9). However, the author of Hebrews also knows that a Christian can only be sanctified by both faith and works (Heb 4:1-11; 11:1-40; Eph 2:10; Jam 2:14-26). Moreover, the author informs his readers that if they live a spiritual life of sanctification and perseverance, then God will reward them with His rest, both in this life and in the world to come (4:1-11; Col 3:23-25).

Only by understanding salvation in this way is it possible to appreciate how the author of Hebrews can call his readers saved in one breath, and then question their salvation in another. It is because the author is emphasizing different aspects of salvation in different contexts. His readers have already experienced past salvation, but they are having great trouble with their present salvation. Sanctification is very difficult. It is never an instantaneous act like past salvation. Past salvation requires but one act of faith in the cross for efficacy consistent with the historical fact that Christ died once. Sanctification on the other hand, is a process of spiritual growth requiring many acts of faith on a continuous ongoing basis. Sanctification always includes vigilant personal responsibility. In other words, the author is not trying to tell his readers how to get saved from the penalty of sin. Rather he is warning them to persevere in their faith. They are being warned to grow up spiritually so they can finish their course and receive the reward of God's rest. The author is talking about what happens after they get saved, not how to get saved in the first place. He wants them to persevere in faith and obedience now, so they will be able to inherit God's Promised Rest, both here and now (4:1-3), and in the eschatological world to come (4:11). However, if they act like the Exodus generation, this inheritance reward will be lost, perhaps for all of eternity (12:25-29).

This means that being saved from the penalty of sin does not automatically mean that a saint will automatically be a spiritual winner in the Christian way of life. This is the primary fallacy of the doctrine of the perseverance of the saints. It not only assumes that all Christians will be spiritual winners, which contradicts not only Scripture but reality as well, it also attempts the impossible. The perseverance of the saints tries to make something which is highly conditional by nature, i.e., sanctification, to be unconditional. Something which requires human responsibility, i.e., sanctification, is highly volatile and conditional by nature, and the risks involved here can only be eliminated at the expense of the free grace of God. In other words, conditions must be attached to the free grace Gospel message in order to ensure that no saint will abuse his spiritual freedom. In a sincere attempt to make sure that the free grace of God does not promote laxity in the Christian, strong adherents to the perseverance of the saints have taught that although all Christians may have spiritual ups and downs, in the end all real Christians will persevere until the final hour. This supposedly rescues the grace of God from being contaminated by libertarians who attempt to abuse their spiritual freedom under grace. This is actually very naïve. Regardless of the doctrines being taught, whether that be eternal security where a saint cannot lose his salvation, the perseverance of the saints where all real Christians will finally prevail, or the Arminian position that a Christian can lose his salvation, saints will still sin. In short, the doctrine of the perseverance of the saints can guarantee no better results than the Old Testament Law, or the threat of loss of salvation. If the Old Testament Law can be abused by people, even by Old Testament saints, then so can any other doctrine of Scripture, including the perseverance of the saints.

While the doctrine of eternal security is not free of difficulties, it can explain more passages of Scripture than the perseverance of the saints. It can teach that salvation is an absolute without disregarding the truly conditional nature of sanctification. Eternal security can also explain warning passages which threaten the Christian with judgment and loss of inheritance or reward. While not all of the problems have been resolved, it is still the best explanatory model without resorting to the Arminian position, which invariably leads to legalism. The doctrine of the perseverance of the saints cannot honestly explain the warning passages in Hebrews. The Arminian position is actually on much stronger ground because it has to assume so little.

The one who maintains the perseverance of the saints must in some way reject the judgmental consequences of the warning passages. It is inconceivable to him that a Christian can fall into God's fiery judgment. This is therefore a blind spot in his theological system. It would be so much cleaner theologically if all Christians would persevere in faith and obedience, but reality, even biblical reality, says otherwise. The Bible simply does not support the abstract theory that all saints will ultimately persevere until the final hour. The Bible demands perseverance, but nowhere guarantees it. There are actually many examples of believers who did not persevere in the Bible, the Exodus generation being the most infamous of all. Initial salvation may give one the platform for spiritual growth, but spiritual growth is never an automatic thing. Sanctification never just happens. It requires personal diligence on the part of the saint, and anytime human responsibility enters the equation, real failure is always a real possibility. The possibility of failure is real, and so the author of Hebrews writes a letter to warn them of failure. However, in the process of warning them, he does not doubt their past salvation, but he has does have many doubts and concerns about their personal sanctification. This is why he writes the book of Hebrews, precisely because his readers are not living saintly lives.

As such, following on the heels of the doctrine of the humiliation of the Son of God (2:5-18), the author warns his readers again about the danger of unbelief which can forfeit God's rest-inheritance (3:1-4:13). In chapter two, the express purpose of the high priesthood of Christ is to establish a Christian brotherhood of human dominion over the eschatological world to come (2:5-18).[61] This human dominion over the eschatological world to come is called entering God's rest in chapters three and four, and the author warns that this great privilege can be lost through unbelief and disobedience. Hence the thrust of wrath or rest becomes the primary theme.

A sinner becomes a saint without works. This is God's non-meritorious way of saving sinful people. A sinner gets exactly what he does *not* deserve, eternal life. However, a saint can only enter God's rest on the basis of faithful obedience and personal sanctification (3:1-4-11). In other words, he can only enter God's rest if he is worthy of it. Entering God's rest and inheriting promises is without question based on merit in the book of Hebrews (4:11; 6:9-15). Sinners cannot earn eternal life, but saints must earn the right to enter God's rest through spiritual perseverance. While sinners do not get what they deserve with regard to eternal life, saints do receive exactly what they deserve with regard to God's rest. A saint will either be punished in wrath for his disobedience, or will be rewarded with God's rest as a result of faithful obedience. The apostle Paul says it otherwise, "Whatever you do, do your work heartily, as for the Lord rather than for men, knowing that from the Lord you will receive the *reward of the inheritance*. It is the Lord Christ whom you serve. For *he who does wrong will receive the consequences of the wrong which he has done, AND THAT WITHOUT PARTIALITY* (Col 3:23-25)."

---

[61]   Dods, p. 267.

God's wrath or rest is therefore a certain consequence, depending only upon the spiritual behavior of the saint. The saint will receive one or the other based upon spiritual performance. This is why the author of Hebrews tells his readers, "The Lord will judge *His* people (10:30)."

While it may be true that God justifies a *sinner* by grace without works, it must never be forgotten that every *saint* will be judged by His works relative to his personal sanctification (Rom 14:10-12; 1 Cor 4:5; Jam 5:9; 1 Pet 1:17-18). It is one thing for a sinner to be justified by grace, but quite another for a saint to be considered worthy of the Kingdom of God (2 Thess 1:5; Rev 3:4-5). While it is certainly impossible for a *sinner* to be worthy of justification by his own works, it is nonetheless demanded of the *saint* that he be considered worthy of the kingdom of God through perseverant sanctification in this life. In short, a *sinner* is justified without works, but a *saint* is sanctified by works, and there is no confusion between these two great categories of people.

Historical Example of Irreparable Failure – the Exodus Generation

The Exodus generation is a typical key which unlocks the mystery of the Hebrew warning passages. Types are biblical histories which illustrate and even predict the future. They are thus very helpful in illustrating fundamental doctrines of Scripture. More importantly, types prevent theoretical speculation as they are solidly grounded upon the realities of history. Historical illustrations, especially biblical ones, thus help elucidate more concretely and clearly the principle which the author is trying to teach. This is especially true when almost two entire chapters are given over to the subject (3:1-4:11). The author dwells on the Exodus generation at great length precisely because his own readers are about to share the exact same fate. Furthermore, this strong emphasis is no detour, but is used as the primary warning illustration in Hebrews, and can only be ignored at the expense of sound biblical interpretation. In order to understand what the warnings in Hebrews are all about, it is first absolutely necessary to understand what happened historically to the Exodus generation. This historical understanding will prevent abstract theological theories, contrary to the context, from dictating the meaning of the book of Hebrews.

The primary warning in the book of Hebrews is not Hebrews 6, nor Hebrews 10, but Hebrews 3-4. As such, Hebrews 6 and 10 must be interpreted in light of Hebrews 3-4. To turn to Hebrews 6 and 10 first without understanding Hebrews 3-4 is to neglect context, and therefore meaning. Moreover, without context, one can make the enigmatic passages of Hebrews 6 and 10 say almost anything one wants them to say.

The Exodus generation teaches a critical theological principle which at first glance appears contradictory: one who has been redeemed freely by grace can lose his inheritance through disobedience. The Exodus generation, though saved out of Egypt, was forbidden by God to enter His rest inheritance in the promised land of Canaan. Thus the Exodus generation did not finish their course, but in fact died in the wilderness, halfway between their initial salvation and their salvation goal of rest-inheritance.

In 11:29, the author states that that Exodus generation crossed the Red Sea by faith. Their faith was of such value at this point that the author actually includes them among all of the Old Testament heroes of faith, the great theme of chapter 11 – *the Hall of Fame of Faith*. Thus the Exodus generation is considered by the author of Hebrews a generally saved generation.[62] Even the book of Exodus demonstrates this early in the book after Moses and Aaron delivered to them the initial message of their imminent salvation from Egypt, " So the people believed; and when they heard that the Lord was concerned about the sons of Israel and that He had seen their affliction, then they bowed low and worshiped (Ex 4:31)." Yet, in Hebrews 3-4, three times (3:7-11; 3:16-4:3; 4:11) the author also states the Exodus generation did not believe so as to enter God's rest. What this means is that their faith later faltered. Their faith was real when Moses and Aaron first announced salvation to them, and their faith was also real when God rescued them when they crossed the Red Sea, since the Egyptians drowned in their unbelief (11:29), but later on, their own unbelief prevented them from entering the promised land of rest (3:17-19). The Exodus generation thus presents a serious theological conundrum which has yet to be resolved even in the modern church.

The book of Hebrews presents that it is possible to be an unbelieving believer. Even Moses and Aaron suffered from this particular spiritual

---

62   This does not necessarily mean that every single person of the Exodus generation without exception was saved, but the general understanding that they were still remains.

ailment (Num 20:12). No matter how one looks at this, it cannot be denied that the Exodus generation believed so as to be saved out of Egypt, but later disbelieved so as not to enter God's inheritance rest. In other words, they did not persevere in their faith, and so were judged accordingly. Though a saved generation, they lost their right to enter God's rest because of unbelief.

At the same time, this does not mean the Exodus generation lost their salvation, nor that they never were saved in the first place, "When Israel was a youth I loved him, and out of Egypt I called My son (Hosea 11:1)." The psalmist says something very similar, "Our fathers in Egypt did not understand Your wonders; They did not remember Your abundant kindness, But rebelled by the sea, at the Red Sea. Nevertheless He *saved* them for the sake of His name, that He might make His power known (Ps 106:7-8)." This understanding is even reiterated in the New Testament. Paul says the entire Exodus generation was baptized into Moses, that they ate the same spiritual food and drink, and that Christ even followed them in the desert (1 Cor 10:1-4), "If this nation, at its peak of its national enthusiasm and spiritual power, is generally unredeemed, then Paul is telling us something very difficult to understand."[63] Indeed, the whole New Testament concept of redemption is entirely based upon the historical precedence of the Exodus generation, and countless passages in the Old Testament refer to the Exodus generation as being redeemed.

The problem in Hebrews is that both the Calvinist and the Arminian have generally assumed that entering rest is equivalent to obtaining salvation. As serious as loss of rest-inheritance is, it is very unlikely that inheriting rest means to obtain salvation. Both the Exodus generation example and the book of Hebrews actually distinguishes between being saved, and inheriting rest. If it is assumed that being saved and inheriting rest are the same thing, then both Moses and Aaron lost their salvation, along with a countless host of an entire generation of generally saved people. Joshua and Caleb were the only survivors of God's judgment. Only they inherited rest out of the entire Exodus generation.

It is assumed that Moses was certainly saved (Matt 17:3; Mark 9:4; Luke 9:30), but he too was forbidden to enter rest because of his own disobedience and unbelief (Num 20:8-13; Dt 32:48-52; Ps 106:32-33). Aaron is called the **saint** or **holy one of the Lord** (Ps 116:16), and yet he

---

63   Dunham, *Appendix*, p. 11.

too was denied inheritance rest (Num 20:12). The psalmist succinctly presents this particular issue quite well, "Moses and Aaron were among His priests. And Samuel was among those who called on His name. They called upon the Lord and He answered them. He spoke to them in the pillar of the cloud; They kept His testimonies and the statutes that He gave them. O Lord our God, You answered them; You were a forgiving God to them, and *yet an avenger of their evil deeds* (Ps 99:6-8)."

Thus the Exodus generation did not lose their salvation, nor did they commit the unpardonable sin.[64] In spite of their great unfaithfulness, God still forgave them (Num 14:20; Ps 78:38). However, even though God forgave them, this does not mean that they were released unpunished. God still judged them for their sin: no inheritance rest (Num 14:20-35; Ps 78:32-41). Though a forgiven people, they still reaped what they sowed, and were forced to live with the consequences of their sins. Forgiveness does not always mean that God's people will be spared the consequences of their evil actions.

The Exodus generation committed apostasy out in the desert (Num 14:1-10; Acts 7:39), and while God did forgive their sin, He still judged them. Though God saved them out of Egypt, he caused them to die in the wilderness through a long terrible period of 40 wasted years. They started out well, but God denied them their goal of the reaching and living in the promised land of Canaan. They were forced to live a meaningless life out in the desert, without a home, without rest, without any inheritance. Nonetheless, this does not mean that they were not saved, or that they lost their salvation, or that they were beyond the scope of God's forgiveness. In keeping with the Exodus illustration therefore, the judgment in Hebrews, while being very serious indeed, does not imply a loss of salvation. The Exodus illustration and Hebrews clearly indicates that being redeemed is one thing, but inheriting rest is quite another. Hebrews 10 clearly teaches that those who have been once for all saved (10:10-14) can fall into God's judgment (10:26-31). Hence the primary warning of the book of Hebrews, "Therefore let us be diligent to enter that rest, so that no one will fall, through following the same example of disobedience (4:11)."

---

[64]   Many interpreters have assumed in Hebrews 3:7-4:11 that failure to enter rest means failure to obtain salvation and that insulting the Spirit of grace in 10:29 is the unpardonable sin.

The Exodus generation is the most infamous generation of failure, nay even disaster, in the entire Old Testament. Countless passages throughout the Bible refer to it, and many passages describe its tragedy in full detail. Most notable in the Old Testament are Psalms 78 and 106, and in the New Testament are Acts 7:20-44, 1 Corinthians 10:1-11, Jude 1:5, not to mention Hebrews 3:1-4:13. Every one of these Scripture passages paint the Exodus generation in a negative, judgmental light. They are notorious for the fact that that though God saved them out of Egypt, He destroyed them out in the desert for their infidelity, unfaithfulness, disobedience and unbelief (Ps 78:12-33; 106:7-33; 1 Cor 10:1-11; Hebrews 3:1-4:13; Jude 1:5).

Only two men of this generation survived God's fiery judgment out in the desert: Caleb and Joshua (Num 14:30). Everyone else of that particular generation died in the desert. An entire generation failed. The Exodus generation is the most infamous generation of spiritual losers in all of the Bible, and this sad testimony is even more tragic precisely because they were a saved generation. This makes their failure even more heinous and inexcusable. The Exodus generation was almost a complete failure. It is the worst example of failure found anywhere in the Bible, and this horrible example is brought forward to warn the Hebrew readers of their own spiritual peril, not to mention the Church in Corinth for their own disobedient behavior (1 Cor 9:24-10:13).

Even Moses fell under God's judgment (Num 20:8-13; Ps 106:32-33) in spite of his faithfulness (Heb 3:5). Teachers or leaders are judged by a much more stricter standard (James 3:1). In his anger at Israel's rebellion, Moses failed at the waters of Meribah. He struck the rock twice instead of speaking to it (Num 20:8-13). Moses did not believe God so as to merely speak to the rock, but struck it instead, not once, but twice. This behavior the Lord judged, "Because you have not believed Me, to treat Me as holy in the sight of the sons of Israel, therefore you shall not bring this assembly into the land which I have given them (Num 20:12)."

In Deuteronomy 32, Moses died the sin unto death[65] by the command of the Lord. He was forbidden to enter the promised land, "Go up to this mountain of the Abarim, Mount Nebo, which is the land of Moab opposite Jericho, and look at the land of Canaan, which I am giving to

---

[65] The sin unto death does not imply loss of salvation, but is physical death meted out as a punishment against the sin of God's own people. 1 Corinthians 11:28-32 clearly distinguishes sin unto death from loss of salvation.

the sons of Israel for a possession. Then die on the mountain where you ascend, and be gathered to your people, as Aaron your brother died on Mount Hor and was gathered to His people, because you broke faith with Me in the midst of the sons of Israel at the waters of Meribah-kadesh, in the wilderness of Zin, because you did not treat Me as holy in the midst of the sons of Israel. For you shall see the land at a distance, but you shall not go there, into the land which I am giving the sons of Israel (33:51-52)." Moses however was allowed to at least see the promised land. He was certainly faithful for 40 years in his ministry to the Exodus generation. He taught Bible lessons for 40 years to a disobedient generation. Nonetheless, he was still denied to enter Canaan because of his own disobedience.

The Exodus generation saw more great miracles than any other generation in the history of the Old Testament, but they constantly rebelled and disbelieved God, and finally committed apostasy by deciding to return back to Egypt, "Our fathers were unwilling to be obedient to him[66] but repudiated him and *in their hearts* returned back to Egypt (Acts 7:39)." The Old Testament historical record of this apostasy is found in Numbers 13-14. After the 12 spies came back from scouting out the Promised Land, all of them except Joshua and Caleb complained that the people in the land were too strong to fight (13:27-33). The cities in the Promised Land were deemed too well fortified. The spies recognized their own lack of military ability and skills compared to the well-defended people of the land. Worse, they became preoccupied with this problem and somehow forgot about the sovereign power of God. They had just seen God destroy the greatest nation in the world at the time – Egypt – but they were scared of the much smaller kingdoms and tribes in the Promised Land. The Exodus generation simply did not understand God's ways of faith and promise (Heb 3:10), and so when they were on the frontier of the Promised Land, they trusted in their own experience rather than believe the promise of God to enter the Land of Rest. They trusted in their own pitiful works rather than in God's word which can work powerfully for them. They thus became afraid of the pagans rather than trust the all-powerful sovereign grace of God.

---

[66]   *Him* here is a reference to the Angel of the Lord who gave the Old Covenant revelation to Moses.

Two of the spies however, Joshua and Caleb, believed that God would deliver them from their hands as He did from Egypt. They did admit that the people in the Promised Land were very strong, but they understood that God promised them to enter His rest, and God's promise was more important than their own lack of experience. They encouraged the people of Israel to enter and take the Promised Land, "Do not rebel against the Lord, and do not fear the people of the land, for they will become our prey. Their protection has been removed from them, and the Lord is with us; do not fear them (Num 14:9)."

The other ten spies, however, could not make the same spiritual application, "We are not able to go up against the people, for they are too strong for us ... the land through which we have gone, in spying it out, is a land that devours its inhabitants, and all the people whom we saw in it are men of great size. There also we saw the Nephilim; and we became like grasshoppers in our own sight, and so we were in their sight (Num 13:31-33)." Here the fundamental contrast between belief and unbelief could not have been more pronounced. Two different groups of people looking at the same circumstances came up with two different conclusions. The very narrow minority of two believed in the gracious promises of God. The vast majority spurned them.

At the negative report, the people cried all night (Num 14:1). They then complained that they would have rather died in Egypt rather than have their wives and children become plunder at the hands of their enemies (Num 14:1-3). They decided they would have been better off in Egypt, and tried to appoint their own leader to return there (Num 14:4). It was here that they committed their irreparable apostasy. The scene was so bad that had not God Himself intervened, they would have killed Moses, Aaron, Joshua and Caleb. The people were about ready to stone them to death (Num 14:5-25).

It was at this juncture that God sentenced the Exodus generation to die in the desert through a long painful 40 years. This was the proverbial last straw that broke the camel's back. Moreover, death was not the worst part of the sentence. The worst part of the sentence was that they had to live in the desert – to live like a refugee – to live without a home – to live without rest – for 40 years. For every day the spies spied out the Promised Land, the people would have to live one year in the wilderness. As the 12 spies spent 40 days scouting out the promised land, this meant

40 years of punishment in the wilderness, "According to the number of days which you spied out the land, 40 days, for every day you shall bear your guilt for a year, even 40 years, and you shall know My opposition. I the Lord have spoken, surely I will do to all this evil congregation who are gathered together against Me. In this wilderness they shall be destroyed, and there they shall die (Num 14:34-35)." The Exodus generation literally walked in circles for an entire generation. There was no purpose to their life, and there was no hope of ever reaching their goal of home-rest, "So He brought their days to an end in futility and their years in sudden terror (Ps 78:33)." Their judgment was irreparable. They were not allowed to recover from their apostasy, nor press on toward spiritual maturity in the Promised Land. Their unbelief in God's promise prevented them from progressing spiritually into His Rest.

This judgment, however, nowhere implies loss of salvation. God may have been very angry with the Exodus generation, but He was only angry with them for 40 years (Heb 3:17), not for all of eternity. Indeed, immediately after God put a stop to their apostasy and show of rocks, Moses interceded for the children of Israel, "Pardon, I pray, the iniquity of this people according to the greatness of Your lovingkindness, just as You also have forgiven this people, from Egypt even until now (Num 14:19)." At Moses' intercession, the Lord responded by forgiving them, but He still punished them for their sin, "I have pardoned them according to your word; but indeed, as I live, all the earth will be filled with the glory of the Lord. Surely all the men who have seen My glory and My signs which I performed in Egypt and in the wilderness, yet have put Me to the test these ten times and have not listened to My voice, shall by no means see the land which I swore to their fathers, nor shall any of those who spurned Me see it (Num 14:20-23) ... your corpses will fall in this wilderness, even all your numbered men, according to your complete number from 20 years old and upward, who have grumbled against Me (Num 14:29)."

These verses alone show the infinite magnitude of the forgiving mercy of God. Forgiveness has no bounds, even the sin of apostasy. At the same time, this forgiveness did not condone their sin, nor did it overlook their sin. God still severely judged them. The forgiveness of God is a holy forgiveness. The Exodus generation is thus a story of a holy forgiving God who knows how to discipline His disobedient children without throwing them into hell:

> When He killed them, then they sought him; and returned and searched diligently for God. And they remembered that God was their rock, and the Most High God their redeemer. Nevertheless they deceived Him with their mouth, and lied to Him with their tongue. For their heart was not steadfast toward Him, nor were they faithful in His covenant. *But He, being compassionate, forgave their iniquity, and did not destroy them; and often He restrained His anger, and did not arouse ALL His wrath. Thus He remembered that they were but flesh, a wind that passes and does not return* (Ps 78:34-39).

Needless to say, though God's judgment against them was very severe and serious, these are not words which indicate that the Exodus generation lost their salvation, or that they were thrown into hell. Forgiveness, pardon and hell are not corollary concepts in the Bible. On the other hand, withholding hell from them does not mean that God condones sin. There was still wrath to pay, but it was not ***all His wrath*** (Ps 106:38).

After being saved out of Egypt, the Exodus generation had a choice: rest or wrath,[67] i.e., reward or punishment. Either they enter God's rest by faith or they will certainly experience the wrath of God. In other words, they will either enter God's rest or lose it through disobedience. The Exodus generation chose the latter, and reaped the bitter results of disobedience. The Exodus generation therefore lost the reward of God's inheritance, but this does not mean that they lost their salvation. On the contrary, "It has been well said that it took God only one night to get Israel out of Egypt but it took 40 years to get Egypt out of them. The former is an act of salvation, the latter a lifelong process of sanctification."[68] The Exodus generation is therefore a saved generation who endured God's holy discipline, not eternal hellfire.

To add further testimony, God did not allow the false prophet Balaam to curse Israel when they were in the desert (Num 22-24). Concerned about invasion, King Balak of Moab tried to hire the prophet Balaam to curse Israel for him. However, God specifically told Balaam that he

---

67   Wrath or Rest is the primary theme of Hebrews 4.
68   Geisler, Norman L. *A Popular Survey of the Old Testament*. (Baker Book House: Grand Rapids, MI, 1977), p. 65.

could not curse Israel precisely because they were blessed (Num 22:12). Balaam responded to Balak, "How can I curse whom God has not cursed (Num 23:8)?" Balaam further informs Balak:

> God is not a man that He should lie, nor a son of man that he should repent; Has He said and will He not do it? Or has He spoken and will He not make it good? Behold I have received a command to bless, when He has blessed then I cannot revoke it. He has not observed misfortune in Jacob; nor has He seen trouble in Israel; the Lord God is with him, and the shout of the king is among them. God brings them out of Egypt, He is for them like the horns of the wild ox. For there is no omen against Jacob, nor is there any divination against Israel (Num 23:19-23).

Thus Balaam could not curse Israel because of her divine blessing. God's punishment against Israel in the wilderness was a family affair, an affair which Balaam could in no way play a part.

The Gospel of Abraham (Gal 3:8-29; Rom 4:1-5), a gospel which has never changed in any dispensation, teaches that God's people are all saved by *faith without works*. This does not preclude the fact however that all of God's people will also be judged *by their works* (Rom 14:10-12; 1 Cor 3:10-15; Heb 10:30-31), not to maintain their salvation, but to inherit a great reward which in the book of Hebrews is called entering God's rest (4:1-11). If the Hebrew readers remain steadfast in their faith, they shall inherit a great eschatological reward, "Therefore do not throw away your confidence, which has a great reward. For you have need of endurance, so that when you have done the will of God, you may receive what was promised (Heb 10:35-36)." Salvation can only be received by the narrow way of faith without works. Inheritance, a post-salvation reward, can only be received on the basis of faithful perseverance, "And we desire that each one of you show the same *diligence* so as to realize the full assurance of hope until the end, so that you will not be sluggish, but imitators of those who through faith and patience *inherit the promises* (6:11-12)." The very fact that *promises* here is plural indicates further the author is not talking about salvation or justification, but eschatological rewards. The author of Hebrews still says it in another way, "therefore let us be *diligent* to enter that *rest*, so that no one will fall, through following the same example of disobedience (4:11)." The Hebrew readers, therefore, though saved once for all (10:10-14), are about to lose their spiritual inheritance rest if they continue in their disobedience (4:11; 6:1-8; 10:26-39), just like the Exodus generation.

CHAPTER SIX

WRATH OR REST – 3:1-4:13

The theme of Hebrews 3-4 is sharp and straightforward: wrath or rest, and the Exodus generation is the example. Much like the infamous Exodus generation, rather than enter God's rest, the Hebrew readers may invoke the wrath of God instead. Hebrews 3-4 clearly warns that the promise of entering God's rest will become a threat if they do not believe it. In fact, instead of bestowing blessing, God's promised word will become a lethal weapon of judgment (4:12-13). What was originally designed for promise and blessing can swiftly end up in wrath and judgment. As such, the author of Hebrews writes the second warning of the book to admonish the readers to enter God's rest, and to warn against forfeiting it.

There is a promise of entering God's rest (4:1), but an unbelieving heart not only forfeits the promise, but invites the fiery judgment of God as well. If the Hebrew readers do not pay close attention to the apostolic message and persevere in it, they will not escape this judgment. Enter rest or experience judgment – this is the issue at hand. There is no neutral ground. Entering God's rest is conditioned upon faithful obedience to the promises of God. There is a one to one relationship between the necessity of sanctification and entering God's so great Sabbath rest.

Cut Off From the House of God – 3:1-6

In Hebrews 3:1-6, the author tells his readers that both Moses and Jesus were faithful in God's house. He then warns them about how the Exodus generation was disobedient (3:7-19). This naturally brings up the question about the faithfulness of his own readers (4:1-11), the great issue in the book of Hebrews. Just because Moses and Jesus were faithful in God's house does not mean that the Hebrew readers will be. The Exodus generation failed and so can they. Outstanding leadership does not necessarily mean that the team will be outstanding. The Exodus generation had one of the greatest leaders of all time, if not *the* greatest leader in all of the Old Testament in Moses. However, they still failed in the wilderness. In the New Testament era, the Hebrew readers have Jesus as their leader. He is God manifest in the flesh who is superior to all the angels (1:1-14). He is their faithful high priest (2:17-18) who is able to come to their aid in moments of sin and temptation (4:14-16). Even though He is also superior even to Moses, this perfect leadership and accessibility does not mean that the Hebrew readers cannot fail. They still have the personal responsibility to believe and obey God (3:7-19; 4:1-3; 4:11). They still have the need to hold fast their confidence and persevere until the end (3:6, 14; 4:16). It is not how they started that counts, but how they finish.

This being the case, chapter three opens with a strong tension between the unconditional and the conditional nature of salvation. In 3:1, the author unconditionally calls them all holy brethren. They are considered to be saints in the full sense of the word since a holy brother is precisely what a saint is. Yet both 3:6 and 3:14 are highly conditional. The Hebrew readers may be holy brothers, but they are **God's house** and **have become partakers with Christ** only if they persevere in faith and holiness. In the Greek, both 3:6 and 3:14 are third class conditional sentences, i.e., probable future condition. As such, there is hope that his reader will meet the conditions of being God's house and being a partaker with Christ. Nonetheless, there is still uncertainty. The spiritual experience of being God's house and being partakers with Christ is conditioned by the subjunctive mood in the Greek. Unlike the Greek indicative mood, the subjunctive mood is not the mood of reality but of possibility, and so the author emphasizes, "*if* we hold fast." 3:1 therefore refers to their heavenly position as saints, but 3:6 and 3:14 refer to their heavenly experience of that position, or lack thereof.

The author is clearly distinguishing here between being a **holy brother** and being **God's house** and a **partaker with Christ**. Being a **holy brother** is one thing. Being **God's house** and a **partaker with Christ** is another. The first is an unconditional reality. The latter is conditioned upon faith and obedience. The first is automatic. The latter is not. This may seem contradictory, but there is no mistake here. The tension between the indicative mood of reality in 3:1 and subjunctive mood of possibility in 3:6 and 3:14 cannot be ignored. The Hebrew readers are saints who have been saved from hell, but they need to persevere in faith and holiness if they want to experience **God's house** and be a **partaker with Christ** so as to enter God's rest (4:1-11).

The key to understanding this difficult tension is by determining what the author means by **house** (3:6). Many assume that this is a reference to one's salvation, that being saved and being God's house is one in the same thing. However, the context clearly indicates that the author is talking about something experiential, and not positional as in 3:1. He is talking about one's personal experience of the house of God, not whether or not they are genuine saints. He is talking about their personal worship experience with regard to the New Testament house of God.

House here is first a reference to earthly tabernacle in 3:2, and then to heavenly tabernacle in 3:5-6. Moses was faithful in the earthly house or tabernacle as a **servant** (3:2), but Jesus was faithful as a **Son** in the heavenly house or heavenly tabernacle. The issue again is not initial salvation, but worship service. The author is not saying that both Moses and Jesus were saved, but that they were faithful in their respective houses of worship. The contrast of houses given here in chapter three is therefore a contrast between two worship systems, between the Old Covenant worship system and the New Testament worship system, and question is over spiritual faithfulness, not whether or not someone is saved. This emphasis is later confirmed in chapter ten:

> Therefore, brethren, since we have confidence to enter the holy place by the blood of Jesus, by a new and living way which He inaugurated through the veil, that is, His flesh, and since we have a great high priest over the **house of God**, let us draw near with a

sincere heart in full assurance of faith, having our hearts sprinkled clean from an evil conscience and our bodies washed with pure water. *Let us hold fast the confession* of our hope without wavering, for He who promised is faithful; and let us consider how to stimulate one another to love and good deeds, *not forsaking our own assembling together*, as is the habit of some ... (10:19-25).

This passage is directly parallel to 3:6, only further expanded. The author again mentions the house of God. The house, as in 3:6, is the heavenly tabernacle (10:19-21). The necessity of faithful perseverance is again brought up (10:23-25) as in 3:6. This passage is also clearly stressing Christian worship *experience*. He is talking about the conditions necessary for faithful Christian worship under the New Testament heavenly tabernacle system. The author is actually encouraging his readers to experience the New Testament heavenly tabernacle in their souls. Through faithful perseverance, they can experience this heavenly tabernacle since Jesus is their resurrected and faithful high priest. Moreover and with great interest, the author also says that some have quit coming to church. Therefore, such ones are not the house of God (3:6), though they are saved once for all (10:10-14, 26, 29).

In 3:1-6 and 10:21, the *house of God* is the heavenly tabernacle of which the earthly tabernacle was a type. In so many words, the author actually states that the Old Testament tabernacle was a type, model or copy of heaven, "... just as Moses was warned by God when he was about to erect the tabernacle; for, 'See,' He says,' that you make all things according to the pattern which was shown you on the mountain (8:5)." The Old Testament tabernacle was therefore not the real worship system. It was only a model or copy of the real one in heaven. As far as models go, it was a great tool to teach the Jewish people about the realities of heaven, but the Old Testament tabernacle was never heaven on earth. This emphasis is explained even further and in great detail in 9:1-14. The word *house* is not mentioned there, but the theme is identical with 3:1-6. In 9:1-14, the contrast is not between Moses the servant and Christ the Son (3:1-6), but between the high priestly functions of the Old and New Testaments. Whereas the Old Testament high priests performed their priestly duties in the earthly tabernacle, Christ performed his priestly duty in the heavenly tabernacle:

But when Christ appeared as high priest of the good things to come, He entered through the greater and more perfect tabernacle, not made with hands that is to say, not of this creation; and not through the blood of goats and calves, but through His own blood, He entered the holy place once for all, having obtained eternal redemption ... (9:11-12)

The contrast, therefore, between houses in 3:1-6 is parallel to the contrast between the old earthly tabernacle and the new heavenly tabernacle in 9:1-14. It is nothing other than the same contrast that is later developed between the Aaronic priesthood and the Order of Melchizedek. This helps elucidate exactly the problem set before the Hebrew readers. How can they possibly be considered the New Testament house of God if they are trying to go back to the old one? As such, the author warns them, "... whose house we are, if we hold fast our confidence and the boast of our hope firm until the end (3:6)."

This *house* (3:6) is not an indication or even a spiritual test to examine whether or not the Hebrew readers have saving faith. It is however, a spiritual test with regard to their present spiritual experience. The author of Hebrews never questions the reality of their initial salvation, but he is deeply concerned about their present spiritual conduct. He already knows they are saved as he calls them holy brethren in 3:1. What he is questioning is their spiritual experience of the heavenly tabernacle, of being Christ's house. More to the point, the author knows that it is this great spiritual experience, of experiencing Christ's house in the heavenly tabernacle, that will rescue his readers from their spiritual sloth. The problem is that his readers want to go back to the old system. His readers are pining for the house of Moses. They have failed to grasp that the house of Moses can be nothing more than an earthly model, and as long as they fail to see this, they simply cannot experience the New Testament heavenly tabernacle according to the Order of Melchizedek in their souls. They are missing out on the priestly resurrection life which the heavenly tabernacle is offering them. As long as they are maintaining their present spiritual course, they are not God's house.

Even the Exodus generation did not properly worship God in the Old Testament tabernacle. Though they were saved out of Egypt, they were not God's house in the desert. Rather than worship the true God, they became idolatrous instead. They worshiped foreign gods in spite of the presence of the tabernacle. Even the very existence of the Old Testament tabernacle itself did not prevent them from worshiping falsely:

> Our fathers were unwilling to be obedient to him, but repudiated him and in their hearts turned back to Egypt, saying to Aaron,' Make for us gods who will go before us, for this Moses who led us out of the land of Egypt, we do not know what happened.' At that time they made a calf and brought a sacrifice to the idol, and were rejoicing in the works of their hands. But God turned away and delivered them up to serve the host of heaven; as it is written in the book of the prophets,' It was not to Me that you offered victims and sacrifices 40 years in the wilderness, was it, O house of Israel? You also took along the **tabernacle** of Moloch and the star of the god Rompha, the images which you have made to worship ... (Acts 7:39-43).

Though the Exodus generation had the right worship tabernacle, they still committed apostasy in their hearts against God. The Exodus generation therefore was not the house of God even though they had the right building. On the contrary they were the house of Moloch. Thus the author of Hebrews warns his readers about the same example of apostasy and disobedience (3:7-4:11). His readers may be holy brothers, but their present spiritual conduct is forfeiting their experience of God's house, just as the Exodus generation did.

King Uzziah can also be used as a further example to illustrate how one can be saved, but still not be considered the house of God. 2 Chronicles 26 records that King Uzziah was a faithful believing King for most of his life (2 Chron 26:1-15), but at the height of his success, he became arrogant (2 Chron 26:16). With blatant disregard for the **house** of God, he presumed upon the priesthood. The priests warned him of the consequences. However, Uzziah became enraged at them (2 Chron 26:17-18). As such, God cursed him with leprosy, "King Uzziah was a leper to the day of his death; and he lived in a separate house, being a leper, for he was **cut off from the house of the Lord** ... (2 Chron 26:21)." For most of his life, King Uzziah was one of the most faithful kings Israel ever had, so faithful that it was a notable day of great sorrow for Isaiah the prophet when he finally died (Isa 6:1). However, in spite of his earlier faithfulness, he later committed apostasy, and so lost the right to be God's house. He was cut off from the house of the Lord for his disobedience. Here again, the house of God is related to sanctification, and not to initial salvation. The Hebrew readers, though saved once for all, may also be cut off from the house of God if they continue in their spiritual decline.

In the New Testament, the apostle Peter also relates the house of God to sanctification. 1 Peter 2:5 reads the recipients of the letter are "*being built up as a spiritual house* for a holy priesthood, to offer up spiritual sacrifices acceptable to God through Jesus Christ (1 Peter 2:5)." Being built up as a spiritual house is without doubt a question relating to the spiritual life and sanctification, not to initial salvation and justification. Peter even talks about offering up spiritual sacrifices to God. This again is a question of spiritual service, not of how to become saved. Peter also uses here the imagery of the Old Testament tabernacle to teach his readers about serving the Lord spiritually in the New Testament priestly house of God. He recognizes his readers cannot offer up Old Testament sacrifices, but they can most certainly still offer up *spiritual sacrifices acceptable to God through Jesus Christ* (1 Peter 2:5). Through the priesthood of Christ, his readers can offer up spiritual sacrifices in the heavenly tabernacle by living godly lives. As they obey the Lord in this way, they will be *built up as a spiritual house for a holy priesthood*. Peter also calls his readers a royal priesthood consistent with the great meaning of the Order of Melchizedek found later in the book of Hebrews.

Not too far removed from this same emphasis, the apostle Paul correlates building upon the foundation of the temple of God with receiving or losing a reward, dependent upon spiritual faithfulness (1 Cor 3:9-17). Paul uses the temple terminology a bit differently, emphasizing both its positional and experiential aspects, rather than just the experiential aspect that is seen in Hebrews. Paul reminds the disobedient saints of Corinth that they are in fact God's building (1 Cor 3:9). By position, they are the temple of God (1 Cor 3:16). However, the problem is that they are destroying this temple through disobedient behavior (1 Cor 3:17). Like Hebrews, the temple imagery refers without question to the New Testament heavenly tabernacle of which the Old Testament temple was a type. And like Hebrews, the Corinthians believers are actual saints (1 Cor 1:1), but they are still in the process of destroying God's temple though persistent disobedient behavior, again just like the Hebrew readers. As such Paul warns them, "If any man destroys the temple of God, God will destroy him … (1 Cor 3:17)." Like Hebrews, punishment is certain for those who are disobedient. The only real difference between Corinthians and Hebrews is that the Corinthians are committing Gentile sins, while the Hebrews are committing Jewish sins. The same punishment however is being warned of.

The Corinthian believers must be wise and careful how they build in God's *building* (1 Cor 3:9-10). This again is a question of sanctification and spiritual service, and not initial justification. Sloppy Christian service, i.e., wood, hay and stubble, will not be acceptable in the house of God. It will all be burned up at the judgment seat of Christ for the *church* (1 Cor 3:11-15):

> Each man's work will become evident; for the day will show it because it is to be revealed with fire, and the fire itself will test the quality of each man's work. If any man's work which he has built on it remains, he will receive a reward. If any man's work is burned up, he will suffer loss; *but he himself shall be saved*, yet so as through fire (1 Cor 3:13-15).

Just as Hebrews distinguishes between being saved and entering God's rest (3:1; 4:11), so here Paul clearly distinguishes salvation from receiving a reward for faithful obedience. Paul warns the Corinthian believers that they may enter heaven, but they will do so without eternal reward. The book of Hebrews teaches the same principle with regard to the Exodus generation. They were originally saved by faith, but lost the *reward of the inheritance* through disobedience. Like the Hebrew readers, the Corinthian believers were failing with regard to their personal sanctification, and this was having negative consequences with regard to the house of God. By their spiritual conduct, they were denying what they really were, the temple of the Holy Spirit, and if this process continues, God will destroy them (1 Cor 3:17), but this destruction nowhere suggests loss of salvation (1 Cor 3:15). At the same time, this does not mean that the Corinthian believers will get away with sin. Destruction and fire are words which speak of great pain and divine punishment.

Loss of reward is not something trifling, but something which involves pain, destruction, and fire.

Forfeiture of Spiritual Partnership with Christ – 3:14

Hebrews 3:14 is actually an expansion of 3:6, "For we have become partakers of Christ, *if we hold fast the beginning of our assurance firm until the end.*" 3:14 further clarifies what the author means by being God's house in 3:6. To spiritually experience the heavenly house of God and to become partakers with Christ are two sides of the same coin. A Christian can spiritually experience the heavenly tabernacle only insofar as he partakes of the priesthood of Jesus Christ. This is further substantiated by the clause, "… let us hold fast (3:14)." Every other exhortation to hold fast found in the book of Hebrews occurs in contexts of the heavenly priesthood and tabernacle (3:6; 4:14-16; 10:19-23). 3:14 is to be interpreted along the same lines. To partake of Christ is to partake of His priesthood and the heavenly tabernacle. To partake of Christ is to spiritually experience the heavenly house of God.

Both 3:6 and 3:14 are actually abbreviated exhortations of 4:14-16 and 10:19-23. Common to all four passages is the exhortation to hold fast. 4:14-16 exhorts the Hebrew readers to hold fast their confession since they have a great high priest who has passed through the heavens. The Hebrew readers have a great high priest in Jesus who not only can sympathize with their weaknesses since He too was tempted in every way as they (4:15), but more importantly, can provide them with the solution to their temptations. Jesus does not merely sympathize with His people like a glorified psychologist, but also provides spiritual answers to combat sin in their lives. Jesus provides them with a spiritual platform, i.e., the throne of grace in the heavenly tabernacle, which will enable them to "receive mercy and find grace to help in time of need (4:16)." 4:14-16 clearly defines what it means to partake of Christ. It means to partake of His heavenly priesthood so that one can use resurrection life and power to overcome sin and temptation. Resurrection life and power is conferred through the heavenly priesthood of Christ, but this life-giving power is available only insofar as the Hebrew readers hold fast. This is the new and living way according to the Order of Melchizedek wherein the saints can enter with boldness into the heavenly holy of holies because of the blood of Christ (10:19-20). The Hebrew readers have a great high priest over the *house of God* (10:21). As such, they are to draw near and hold fast their confession of hope (10:22-23). The sacred writer even warns them of not forsaking their own assembling together, "as is the habit of some, but encouraging one another; and all the more" as they see the day of judgment drawing near (10:25). To be the house of God and to partake of Christ is therefore to exercise the spiritual priesthood of Christ in their own lives by faith. By faith in the priesthood of Christ, the Hebrew readers can experience resurrection life and power. As they put into practice the heavenly priesthood of Christ, they will find spiritual victory, which is also the avenue into God's rest (3:6-11; 3:14-19).

Exercising the priesthood of Christ (4:14-16), being a partaker with Christ (3:14), and being the house of God (3:6) is the way into God's spiritual rest. It is no coincidence that the warnings of not entering rest follow immediately after both of the conditional statements of being the house of God (3:6-11) and being partakers with Christ (3:14-19), not to mention the fact that it also immediately precedes the exhortation to put into the practice the priesthood of Christ (4:14-16). There is therefore a strong parallel between being God's house, being a partaker with Christ, entering God's rest, and putting into practice the priesthood of Christ. The Hebrew readers are the house of God *if* (3:6), and then there is the warning to enter rest (3:7-11). The Hebrew readers have already become partakers with Christ *if* (3:14), and then the warning to enter rest (3:15-19). Entering God's rest is predicated upon faithful perseverance in the house of God, i.e., by putting into practice the great high priesthood of Jesus Christ into their lives and thus being a heavenly partaker with Him. By faith, the Hebrew readers are to maintain themselves in the house of God, and are to continue to be partakers with Christ so that they can experience God's spiritual rest, both in this life (4:1-3), and in the eschatological world to come (4:11).

The word *partaker* here means partner or co-worker. The same word is used in the Gospels to describe Peter and Andrew as partners in the fishing trade. So again, the author here is not telling the Hebrew readers how to get saved. He is concerned about their duty and devotion in spiritual service inside the heavenly holy of holies. He wants them to personally experience being a partner with Christ in this life, to actually work with Christ as a partner in spiritual service together as Peter and

Andrew worked together in the fishing business. Being a co-worker or partaker with Christ is conditioned upon faithful obedience. If a Christian wants to be a partaker with Christ, certain spiritual conditions must be met. Being a partaker with Christ does not come automatically. Faithful perseverance in the spiritual life is required. Closely related to this is Roman 8:17 where Paul teaches that if one wants to be a co-heir with Christ, he must suffer with Him in faithful obedience.

So again, the author of Hebrews stresses that his readers must hold fast their assurance firm until the end (3:14). In this lifetime, throughout this lifetime, they are to hold fast until end, and if they do this, they have already become partakers with Christ. Now this, of course, is a bit confusing and seems contradictory, for it says they have already become partakers, but only if they hold fast until the end. How can this be? How can one already be a partaker of Christ if he has not yet held out until the end? It seems here that the author is teaching his readers the biblical principle of already/not yet. They have already become partakers with Christ, but not yet. As long as they hold onto their assurance, they have already become partakers or partners with Christ. However, what they did yesterday is no guarantee of what they will do tomorrow. The author uses the already/not yet principle here to assert the highly conditional nature of sanctification. The experience of resurrection life is no automatic experience. This is certainly the problem facing the Hebrew readers. They were more impressed with the earthly experience of the Old Testament tabernacle than they were with the resurrection life of the New Testament tabernacle. They were on the verge of drifting and falling away, and so the author warns them that they are partners with Christ so long as they hold fast their assurance. If they fall away, they will certainly lose the spiritual experience of being a partner with Christ. This will be their judgment. They will not be considered a partaker with Christ. This however, does not mean loss of salvation. The immediate context of chapter three is clearly present salvation or present experiential privilege in the house of God. They must faithfully persevere. They may be holy brothers (3:1), but this does not automatically mean that they are Christ's partners or co-workers. Through personal sin, disobedience and unbelief, one can always forfeit such a privileged status, the great emphasis of 3:7-19.

Forfeiture of Divine Rest – 3:7-4:13

Beginning in 3:7, the author of Hebrews warns about what will be forfeited if the Hebrew believers continue their disobedience. The rich reward of God's rest, both in this life and in the life to come (3:11; 3:15-4:3; 4:11), will be squandered if the Hebrew readers harden their hearts in unbelief and sin:

> Therefore, just as the Holy Spirit says, Today if you hear His voice, Do not harden your hearts as when they provoked Me, as in the day of trial in the wilderness, where your fathers tried Me by testing Me, and saw My works for 40 years. Therefore I was angry with this generation, and said, they always go astray in their heart, and they did not know my ways, as I swore in My wrath, ***they shall not enter My rest*** (3:7-11).

At this point, the author of Hebrews has not told his audience what God's rest is. That is coming up in chapter four. The author does, however, identify *how* rest can be forfeited. Hardness of heart (3:8), provoking God (3:8), testing God (3:9), continually going astray (3:10), ignorance of God's ways (3:10), apostasy (3:12), an unbelieving heart (3:12), falling away (3:12), the deceitfulness of sin (3:13), disobedience (3:18), and unbelief (3:19) are all mentioned as the reasons why the Exodus generation did not enter God's rest, and all of these statements of Scripture are integrally related.

The first one mentioned in this long list is **hardness of heart**. This is contrasted by listening daily to the voice of God, "Today if you hear His voice, do not harden your hearts ... (3:8, 15)." In this particular context, to listen means living obedience to the word of God as in James 1:22-25, not merely using one's ear to physically hear something. When parents discipline their children, they often ask, "Why didn't you listen to me?" In other words, "Why did you disobey me?" Here in Hebrews, the reason why is because of hardness of heart,[69] a stubborn refusal to acknowledge the truth. Rather than allow the Word of God to penetrate the heart in

---

[69]   In the Bible, the heart is often a virtual synonym for the mind, and is not to be seen in opposition to the mind which is so characteristic of the modern liberalism where feelings take priority over the intellect. Many passages in both the Old and New Testaments depict that the mind is the heart, and vice-versa.

order to make it pliable, the heart hardens itself against spiritual instruction and correction. When the heart hardens itself against the Word of God, it magnifies and reinforces its own evil ways. The antithesis to hardness of heart is listening/obeying the voice of the Spirit (Heb 3:7), which in this context is the written Word of God (Heb 3:7-11; Ps 95:7-11), penned by King David. The voice of the Spirit is not some fuzzy impressionistic intuition, but is clearly stated here to be the written Scriptures. Biblical spirituality is determined by the Scriptures, and is something which must be practiced daily.

David uses the word **today** (Heb 3:7, 15) to emphasize the fact that biblical spirituality is not a one shot experience of deliverance, but is a daily process. The battle against hardness of heart is therefore both daily and taxing. It is also a very deceitful battle (Heb 3:13), a deceit which only the clarity of the written Scriptures, applied by the Holy Spirit, can arrest. If the Word of God is not taken seriously, hardness of heart automatically sets in. This simple teaching of Scripture is very simple and straightforward, but is often very hard to accept. Hardness of heart often gets in the way of accepting the Scriptures as **the** method of spiritual progress and sanctification. An entire generation, the Exodus generation, hardened itself against the Word of God and so forfeited their spiritual progress and divine inheritance. The Hebrew readers are themselves walking down the same self-destructive path which God will certainly judge if this problem is not spiritually corrected. As the author of Hebrews so often warns, they need to listen up, "For this reason we **must** pay much closer attention to what we have heard, so that we do not drift away from it (Heb 2:1)."

Closely related to hardness of heart and disobedience is unbelief (Heb 3:15-19). Hebrews 3-4 teaches that one obeys God by believing Him (Heb 3:12; 18-19; 4:1-3). This is stated most clearly by the author of Hebrews later on in the book, "and without faith it is **impossible** to please Him ... (Heb 11:6)." Faith in God's Word is what pleases Him. God rewards those who believe and rely on His Word (Heb 3:17-4:3; 11:6). Such people progress spiritually and are greatly blessed of God. To disbelieve God is actually the greatest sin. To not trust His Word is to treat God disrespectfully. To disbelieve God is to depend on self or even upon a group of people not in step with the Scriptures. While many people seem to understand that self-dependence is a distorted view of life, they do not realize so is group dependence.

Many assume that the individual is evil, and the community is somehow good. However, every community is made up of individuals, and if the individuals are evil, then so the community will be evil too. Communities are not somehow magically good any more than an individual is naturally good. In fact, the Bible often contrasts the faith of individual people verses the corrupt communities at large, "Do not follow a multitude to do evil (Ex 23:2)." This is precisely what happened with the Exodus generation. The Exodus community was thoroughly corrupt with only a few exceptions. Rather than believe in God's promise to enter the land of rest, the Exodus community cried and died in the desert.

The way of faith is actually a very narrow and dogmatic way of spiritual progress. It is generally not even very popular among God's own people. God does not work through the popular ways of men. God works **exclusively** through His own promises, and the only way to avail oneself of these promises is to believe them. Faith and promise is God's way of spiritual progress and sanctification. Faith prevents evil human works from polluting the glory of God. Had the Exodus generation believed God's promise to enter the rest of Canaan, all of the glory would have gone to God since He was the One who made the promise. It would have been God's promise that caused Israel to take the land, not their own human ability.

On the other hand, faith does not mean that no works are being done. Faith would have moved the Exodus generation out of the desert into the promised rest of Canaan. In such a scenario, God would have worked through them, fulfilling His promise to them as they believed Him. In this way, it would have been their trust in God's all-powerful grace that would have been the cause for their spiritual works and success, not naked humanism. Moreover, the ultimate merit is in the object of faith, i.e., God's promise, not in the act of faith itself, much less in the evil works of the Exodus generation.

Humanly speaking, the Exodus generation was ill-prepared to make war against the warriors of Canaan, but had they trusted in God's gracious promises to deliver them, then they would have conquered the Promised Land, even though they were physically outmatched. The Exodus generation knew they were outmatched, but this should have been beside the point. If God delivered them out of Egypt, then certainly He can destroy the much smaller kingdoms in the Promised Land. However, they forgot about God's glorious promises, not to mention the whole historical event of the Exodus, "They were rendered weak by their unbelief and hardness of heart."[70] Their horizontal viewpoint forfeited their spiritual progress and God's promised rest.

The Exodus community simply did not depend upon God promises. They were in fact ignorant of how God worked (Heb 3:10). They were ignorant of the fact that God blesses people through faith in His powerful Word. Faith in God's Word is what produces spiritual progress, something which an entire generation and community, forfeited, "So we see that they were not able to enter because of unbelief (Heb 3:19)." Even though the Exodus generation saw God miraculously save them out of the great judgments upon Egypt, they did not trust In His Almighty power to conquer the Promised Land. Depending upon themselves, looking at their own inability, recognizing only their own weaknesses, they complained against God's clear direction. Every time God tested them with a difficult situation, they quickly complained about what He was doing. Rather than believe in God's provisions and care, they tested and provoked Him instead (Heb 3:9). By their unbelief they forfeited the spiritual experience of God's promise, and so He punished them for 40 years in the wilderness with no possibility of spiritual recovery. The Exodus generation fell into apostasy, and the same fate awaits the Hebrew readers if they do not wake up spiritually, "Take care, brethren, that there not be in any one of you an evil, unbelieving heart that falls away from the living God, but encourage one another day after day, as long as it is still called Today, so that none of you will be hardened by the deceitfulness of sin (Heb 3:12-13)."

The sin of departing from the living God in 3:12 is the Greek word to **apostasize**. The Exodus generation repudiated their salvation from Egypt. They wanted to return (Num 14:1-10). Having been worn out by the deprivations of the desert, they yearned for the garlics of Egypt. They also committed idolatry not long after they received the Old Covenent Law and tabernacle worship system (Ex 32:1-10). They even worshiped false gods (Acts 7:39-43). They repudiated God's person, His salvation, and His direction. In other words, they apostasized from the

---

70   Dods, p. 278.

living God. As such, this particular sin, as heinous as the description is, **was** committed by God's own people in the past, and can be committed even today.

Technically speaking, apostasy is something which only God's people can commit anyway. An apostate person is someone who has known the truth, and yet later repudiates it. Moreover, this is precisely what the author of Hebrews is warning his readers about. If they do not pay much more closer attention to the Word of God (2:1), which is the truth they have previously known (10:26) and experienced (6:4-5), then they will commit apostasy, and share the same fate as the Exodus generation, i.e., no rest (3:7-4:11).

The author of Hebrews typologically uses the failure of the Exodus generation to enter the Canaan rest to warn his readers of the greater danger and greater peril of forfeiting God's Genesis rest (4:1-11). The **Rest** spoken of with regard to the Exodus generation was the inheritance of Canaan. This was the promised land given to Abraham, Isaac and Jacob. This was the inheritance which the Exodus generation lost because of their apostasy. The rest which the Hebrew readers are about to lose however, is not the promised land of Canaan, but something far greater. The principle of forfeiting rest through disobedience remains the same for both the Exodus generation and the Hebrew readers, but the inheritance rest which the Hebrew readers are about to lose is actually far more consequential. New Testament saints have greater privileges than Old Testament saints, but with greater privileges comes greater responsibilities and greater perils. The rest which the Hebrew readers are about to forfeit is not a piece of real estate, but God's own personal rest which He himself ushered in after He created the universe (4:1-10), "The rest which God promises to His people is a share in that rest which He himself enjoys."[71] This Genesis rest which God is now enjoying is being offered to the Hebrew readers (Heb 4:4; 4:9-10), but it can be lost through spiritual unfaithfulness (4:11). The book of Hebrews makes clear that God's rest can be entered only upon the one condition of perseverance in faith. Just as the entrance into the Canaan rest was conditioned upon the faith-obedience of the Exodus generation, so the Genesis rest can only be entered upon the one condition of faith-obedience, "Therefore let us fear, while a promise remains of entering His rest, any one of you may seem to

---

[71]   Bruce, p. 106.

have come short of it. For indeed we have had the good news preached to us, just as they also; but the word they heard did not profit them, because it was not united *by faith* in those who heard (4:1-2)."

Quoting the Genesis creation account, the author of Hebrews defines for his readers what God's rest is, and what it is they are about to forfeit, "For He said somewhere concerning the seventh day: and God rested on the seventh day from all His works (4:4)." Here the author carefully distinguishes between God's rest from His works of Creation.[72] This being so, God's rest cannot be a cessation of *all* activity, for God continues to work in holding the universe together and exercising His sovereignty in history (John 5:47; Heb 1:3). However, God has stopped creating. In this sense He is now resting and continues to rest, "The word actually means *cease* more than *rest* as understood today. It is not a word that refers to remedying exhaustion after a tiring week of work. Rather it describes the enjoyment of accomplishment, the celebration of completion."[73]

God is now enjoying what He has created. As such, God's rest consists primarily of His satisfaction with what He has done[74], "God saw all that He had made, and behold, it was *very good* (Gen 1:31)." The Sabbath rest itself was a sign between God and Israel, "For in six days the Lord made the heaven and the earth, but on the seventh day He ceased from labor and was *refreshed* (Ex 31:17)." So God's rest consists of divine satisfaction and refreshment, and along with this, comes rulership and dominion. Since God created the universe, and was very pleased with what He had made, He now enjoys the created universe which He has made, and one of the primary ways in which He enjoys it is through His dominion of it. In this sense God continues to work even though He is resting.

So rest from Creation brings on the divine responsibility to govern. Resting and ruling therefore are closely related:

> Thus says the Lord, Heaven is My *throne* and the earth is My footstool. Where then is a house you can build for Me? And where is a place that I may *rest*? For My hand made all these things, thus all these things came into being, declares the Lord (Isa 66:1-2).

---

72   Lane, p. 99.
73   Ross, Allen P. *Creation and Blessing*, (Baker Book House: Grand Rapids, MI, 1987), p. 113.
74   Dunham, *The Hebrew Warning Passages*.

Rest from creation ushers in a different kind of work, i.e., governing the universe. It is this rest which God is offering to the Hebrew readers, and it is this rest which can be forfeited through spiritual disobedience.

At this juncture, the eschatological world to come mentioned back in Hebrews 2, wherein redeemed humanity will rule the new universe with the Messiah, becomes closely allied to God's rest in chapters three and four. The eschatological world to come in Hebrews 2 is God's rest-inheritance in chapter four, prefigured by the land of Canaan. If this is the case, then what the Hebrew readers are about to forfeit is their right to rule or to exercise their right of inheritance in the eschatological world to come. As is true in any inheritance, there is a distinction between living on an inheritance and possessing the rights of ownership of an inheritance. In the ancient world, the king ruled the inheritance and passed it down to his son, the heir, but there were still many subjects who lived on the inheritance who did not have the right to rule it. They were servants, but not rulers. In the same way then, the Hebrew readers may be saved, and thus they shall be glorified and live in heaven, but they shall be denied the right to rule God's most majestic eternal inheritance. In this way, they will not inherit rest. They will not inherit the kingdom of God.

The most difficult problem relating to God's rest in chapter four is that there is a strong tension between present rest and future rest, between experiential rest and eschatological rest. Both aspects of rest are said to be available to the Hebrew readers (Heb 4:1-3; 4:11). Thus, the emphasis upon the already/not yet first noted back in 3:6 and 3:14, becomes much stronger in 4:1-11. Rest is something which can be experienced *today* (Heb 4:3-7), but is also something which will be experienced later on in the eschatological world to come (Heb 4:11).

The author makes this principle very clear by making a rather startling statement, "For if Joshua had given them rest, He would not have spoken of another day after that (Heb 4:8)." With great irony, the sacred writer is here teaching that Joshua's generation did not enter God's rest, even though they took the Promised Land by faith. They obeyed God whereas the Exodus generation did not, but this does not mean that they completely fulfilled the meaning of God's rest. Moreover, God's rest was not appropriated under David either (Heb 4:5-7). The promised rest was therefore not believed by the Exodus generation, but neither was it exhausted under Joshua or David.[75]   The settlement of Canaan under Joshua and the existence of the kingdom under David's day did not fulfill the divine promise of rest, but rather pointed to another day yet future[76], "So there remains a Sabbath rest for the people of God (Heb 4:9)."

The experience of rest in Canaan was only a type or symbol of the complete rest that God intended for His people. The settlement of Canaan did not in any way finish God's so great salvation history program. On the contrary, it only prefigured what God would one day provide eschatologically, "You will bring them and plant them in the mountain of Your inheritance, the place, O Lord, which You have made for Your dwelling, the sanctuary, O Lord, which Your hands have established. *The Lord shall reign forever and forever* (Ex 15:17-18)." The generations of Joshua and David did experience God's rest in their own lifetime, but they did not experience its ultimate fulfillment. Joshua's generation did not exhaust or fulfill God's rest, and David's generation was warned against losing it (Ps 95:7-11), but both of these generations did get a taste of God's rest in the present life, a taste which was denied the Exodus generation because of their unbelief.

With this in mind, the author of Hebrews tells his readers that they can both have rest *today* (4:1-7), and also in the eschatological future (4:8-11), *if* they do not harden their hearts in unbelief and apostasy. The author warns his readers about coming short of God's Rest (4:1), and then tells them that those who have believed (the promise of entering rest) are right now in the process of entering rest (4:3). However, they must still strive throughout this lifetime to enter into God's eschatological rest (4:11). They are already, but then again, not yet. The days of the already/not yet are days of trial and testing, but since those being tested *already* have, they have the potential to survive the fiery tests of the *not yet*. Thus the Hebrew readers must continue to strive to receive and use the blessings which they already have. Otherwise they will end up like the Exodus generation, depending on self rather than on God's promises. If his readers want rest both in this life, and in the eschatological life to come, they must faithfully obey by holding fast their confession of faith.

---

75   Dods, pp. 279-80.
76   Lane, p. 101.

God has already done many things for His people. The death, resurrection and ascension of Christ have been completed historically once for all (Heb 1:3-4). However there are still many things which are **not yet** in people's personal experience, and this **not yet** is a great test of the soul, nay even a present crisis of faith. The things which are **not yet** can only be approached by faith, and so faith here in this context is primarily an eschatologically orientated faith, a present grasp upon future reality, "faith brings into the present the reality of that which is future, unseen, or heavenly."[77] Hebrews 11:1 makes this clearer still, "Now faith is the assurance of things hoped for, the conviction of things not seen." Thus, if the Hebrew readers maintain themselves by faith in the heavenly priesthood of Christ during this **not yet** time period on the earth, then they will receive great blessing and eschatological reward, both in this life and in the life to come. Conversely, if they do not survive this **not yet** crisis period, God will certainly judge them, both on the earth and at the future judgment (Heb 4:11; 12:25-29).

The author therefore warns his readers, "Let us fear ... (Heb 4:1)." In the Greek this is an emphatic exhortation. The Greek also suggests that beforehand his readers were not fearful. Even chapter two suggests this in that they were careless and not fearful of the responsibilities under the New Testament. To the sacred writer, they are coming short of entering God's rest (Heb 4:1), "Our author therefore urges his readers again to press on and attain that goal precisely because it will not be reached automatically. They will do well to fear the possibility of missing it."[78] The Hebrew readers' position, just like the Exodus generation, is one of trial, "To have been brought to Christ is only the beginning. It is by no means the end:"[79]

> God's original promise of rest remains unchanged and still holds good. Such being the case, he who doubts the promise itself runs a risk ... Since this promise remains – let us fear to distrust it.[80]

Now fear here does not mean to be scared, but it means to have a healthy respect and awe for the promises of God. While conferring great

---

[77]   Ibid, pp. 98-99.
[78]   Bruce, p. 105.
[79]   Westcott, p. 92.
[80]   Vincent, p. 421.

blessings, God's promises are also very fearful if His people come short of obtaining them. A promise of entering rest remains, but it has not yet been fulfilled by the Hebrew readers. Let them, therefore, fear lest they come short of it, "But to this one I will look, to him who is humble and contrite of spirit, and who trembles at My word (Isa 66:2)."

Hearing the word without obedience is disrespectful. Moreover, it runs the risk of God's judgment (Heb 4:2-3). Just as the hearing of the good news of entering rest did not benefit the Exodus generation, so the same could also happen to the Hebrew readers themselves, "Hearing the good news does not mean that you will automatically reach the goal for which you set out."[81] The Hebrew readers may have started out well, but they need to press on and finish what they started, something which the Exodus generation did not do.

Now, the **good news** here in the Greek literally means **we who have been evangelized**. Upon seeing this here, many immediately think of the gospel, the salvation message that Christ died for their sins. However, this is not at all what is being said here. The **gospel** in this context is actually a reference to the good news of entering God's rest. As is always the case, context determines meaning, and the context is clearly God's rest, which here can only mean post-salvation experience. This is also supported by the historical context of the Exodus generation as well. What they failed to believe was not with regard to their initial salvation out of Egypt, but for their spiritual advancement into God's rest. They did not believe the good news or gospel of entering God's rest, and so forfeited its benefits.

In 4:3, the Greek emphasizes that those who have believed God's promise about entering rest are now in the **process** of entering that rest. In the Greek, **entering rest** is in the present tense, and so it must therefore be a present possibility now, although it cannot be a complete rest as the later verses indicate (4:7-11). Moreover, **entering rest** is a gnomic present. This means that the statement itself is a truism, a given truth that is generally true. If one has believed God's promise of entering rest, then he is entering rest right now. The following phrase, "As I swore in My wrath, they shall not enter My rest (Heb 4:3b)," supports this even further. Unbelief forfeits the promise of entering rest. This means conversely that those who do believe God's promised rest will enter rest, and that they will begin to do so immediately because of the

81   Bruce, p. 105.

present tense. This rest can be experienced in this lifetime (4:1-3), but then again, not yet (4:8-11).

The conquest of Canaan under Joshua is actually very illustrative here to help alleviate some of the confusion which the concept of the already/not yet places on the interpreter. Unlike the Exodus generation, Joshua's generation did believe the promise to enter God's rest. As such, they entered into the land of their rest-inheritance. However, when one reads the book of Joshua, it took a while to conquer the Promised Land. Unlike the Exodus out of Egypt, entering God's Rest in Canaan did not happen all at once, but took place little by little, step by step. Moreover, this is why the author later exhorts his readers to continue to be diligent to enter God's rest (4:11). He understands that like the conquest of Canaan it will not happen overnight but requires faithful patience and vigilance:

> Behold, I am going to send an angel before you to guard you along the way and to bring you into the place (the Promised Land) which I have prepared ... I will send My terror ahead of you, and throw into confusion all the people among whom you come, and I will make all your enemies turn their backs to you. I will send hornets ahead of you so that they will drive out the Hivites, the Canaanites, and Hittites before you. *I will not drive them out in a single year* that the land may not become desolate and the beasts of the field become too numerous for you. *I will drive them out little by little, until you become fruitful and take possession of the land* (Ex 23:20; 27-30).

The Hebrew readers must learn to continue to persevere in their faith so as to take more and more of their rest inheritance like Joshua's generation did. Thus, believing God's promise of rest is not a one-shot experience like initial salvation, but rather requires faithful perseverance over an extended period of time, and in the case of the Hebrew readers, they must hold out until the end.

Unlike initial salvation, participation in God's rest requires an element of merit on the part of the believer. Salvation is a non-meritorious gift, but entering rest is a meritorious reward for faithful obedience. Entering rest is therefore something which is earned by the believer in obedience to the will of God.

On the other hand, however, entering rest is a gracious opportunity which God grants in addition to salvation. God graciously provides the spiritual platform and the spiritual resources so that the child of God can enter His rest. Nevertheless, the child of God still has a great responsibility to use these spiritual resources as God directs. There is therefore a strong interplay between the faithfulness of God and the faithfulness of God's people in the process of entering rest. The only ones who will be able to enter rest will be those who use God's grace, not for salvation, but to get beyond the basics and grow up into spiritual maturity. Only those who consistently depend on the supernatural power of God, which in the book of Hebrews is the Melchizedekian Priesthood of Christ, will enter rest. God's rest must therefore be merited, but it can be merited only by depending upon the grace of God. God will therefore greatly reward those who use consistently His grace to advance spiritually.

In being consistent with the meaning of God's promised rest, in the conquest of Canaan, Joshua's generation certainly fought many battles, but they fought in the strength of the Lord, and they took cities for which they did not work:

> Then it shall come about when the Lord your God brings you into the land which He swore to your fathers, Abraham, Isaac and Jacob, to give you, great and splendid cities which you did not build, and houses full of all good things which you did not fill, and hewn cisterns which you did not dig, vineyards and olive trees which you did not plant, and you eat and are satisfied (Deut 6:10-11).

In this sense, the land of Canaan truly was a land of rest. The Israelites moved into cities, houses and farms which were already built. What's more, even though they had to fight off the inhabitants of the land, God was the one who did the real fighting. Under Joshua, Israel trusted in God's powerful and gracious promises, and so God worked on their behalf:

You shall consume all the peoples whom the Lord your God will deliver to you; your eye shall not pity them, nor shall you serve their gods, for that would be a snare to you. If you should say in your heart,' These nations are greater than I; how can I dispossess them?' You shall not be afraid of them; you shall well remember what the Lord your God did to Pharaoh and to all Egypt: the great trials which your eyes saw and the signs and the wonders and the mighty hand and the outstretched arm by which the Lord your God brought you out. So shall the Lord your God do to all the peoples of whom you are afraid. Moreover, the Lord your God will send the hornet against them, until those who are left and hide themselves from you perish. You shall not dread them, for the Lord your God is in your midst, a great and awesome God. The Lord your God will clear away these nations before you little by little; you will not put an end to them quickly, for the wild beasts would grow too numerous for you. But the Lord your God will deliver them before you, and will throw them into great confusion until they are destroyed. He will deliver their kings into your hand so that you will make their name perish from under heaven; no man shall be able to stand before you until you have destroyed them (Deut 7:16-24).

Thus even the conquest of Canaan was a result of God's grace. God fought for Israel against her enemies as long as they trusted in Him. The key was that Israel was to rest in God's promises, and as long as they did, God brought them into His rest more and more until they conquered the whole land. Yes, Israel did eventually conquer the land. Yes, they did work and they did struggle. They did therefore merit God's rest. However, the cause of the success was not that they were such good fighters, but that that they rested in God's powerful promises.

The conquest of Canaan therefore illustrates how rest can be both already and not yet at the same time. It also illustrates how the Israelites rested in God's gracious promises to conquer the land. They were personally responsible to take the land of rest, but they had to do this by trusting in God's promises. God swore to Abraham, Isaac and Jacob that the Promised Land would be given to their descendants. If the Israelites personally believed this promise, then they would experience the Promised Land of rest. If they did not, then they would personally experience God's judgment instead like the Exodus generation.

The Israelites were personally responsible to believe and trust in God, and armed with His promises, they were to conquer the land of Canaan in spite of all the opposition they might encounter. Though militarily outmatched, the promises of God were stronger than any pagan army. As such, it would have been the promises of God that caused Israel to take the land, not their own human abilities. So long as they rested in the promise originally given to Abraham, Isaac and Jacob, then they could take the Promised Land away from their enemies. Thus the act of conquest too was a question of God's rest. God's rest was theirs, if they rested in God's promises by faith. The burden of conquering the land was placed upon God's shoulders, lessening greatly the burden upon the Israelites. Again, this is the whole point of rest.

This teaches the spiritual principle that the Christian must learn to rest in God's gracious promises if he wants to enjoy God's rest-inheritance. But resting in God's promises does not mean that the saint does nothing. On the contrary he must fight spiritual battles in order to obtain this rest. While this may seem contradictory, it really is not. Even today it is often said, "I am trying to get some rest."[82] There is therefore effort involved in the attempt to enter rest. Nonetheless, this effort is to be done according to the gracious supernatural power of God. By faith, the Christian, the Hebrew readers, can rest in God's gracious promises. As they do so, little by little and step by step, they can enter God's rest. Moreover, God will lead them into His rest just as Joshua's generation conquered the land.

This same tension between working and resting is also seen when Jesus speaks about rest in the Gospels, "Come to Me, all who are weary and heavy-laden, and I will give you **rest**. Take my yoke upon you and learn from Me, for I am gentle and humble in heart, and you will find **rest** for your souls. For My yoke is easy and My burden is light (Matt 11:28-30)." This spiritual rest can be experienced in the soul right now so long as the Christian rests upon Jesus. This does not mean that the Christian will not do anything at all. Just as the Israelites still had to conquer the Promised Land, Jesus will still give him a yoke. Moreover, the Christian must still learn, and he still must carry a burden, but the

---

[82]   Dunham, *The Danger of Distrust*.

yoke is said to be easy and the burden is said to be light. The Christian can carry such a burden because the almighty God of the universe is sustaining him. This is the rest which the Christian can have right now, but this rest is a daily spiritual battle which can be lost under the pressures of spiritual warfare. Like any soldier, the Christian must still persevere and continue the course in this faith-rest operation.

In summary, Hebrews 4:1-3 teaches the Hebrew readers can enter rest right now, but then 4:11 clearly indicates that they must continue to strive to enter God's rest. While 4:3 stresses the present reality of rest, 4:10-11 stresses eschatological rest. Only those who have been faithful to the end, only those who have completed their work on the earth in this lifetime, will be able to enter God's eschatological consummation-rest (4:10-11). Just as God rested after the completion of His work after Creation, so the Hebrew readers need to finish their work of faithful perseverance in order to enter rest, "For the one who has entered His rest has himself also rested from his works, as God did from His (4:10)."

Just like in everyday life, only after someone finishes something can he truly enjoy and rest in his labor later. It is the same in the spiritual life. God finished his work of creation and rested (Heb 4:4). Jesus Christ finished His work of salvation on the cross and sat down and rested (Heb 1:3-4). Now the question is – what about the Hebrew readers? What about the Christian? The Christian is to be diligent to enter God's rest by faith, piece by piece, little by little, step by step, if he wants to enjoy it later on. The author here is teaching that what a Christian will enjoy in heaven will be determined by how much of God's promises or of God's rest, he has utilized in this lifetime. However, if a Christian is not diligent, then God will judge rather than bless (4:12-13), "Let us strive earnestly for the peril is great."[83] If the Hebrew readers are faithfully resting in God today until the end, then they shall be richly rewarded both in this life and especially in the eschatological future (Heb 4:1-11; 6:9-12; 10:35-36). However, if they act like the Exodus generation, they will not only lose out on their future reward, but will also be punished severely for their failure in this life (3:7-11; 3:14-4:3; 4:11-13). Thus the theme of wrath or rest encapsulates well the theme of these crucial chapters.

---

[83]   Westcott, p. 99.

Spiritual Warfare and Inheritance in the Book of Ephesians

In Ephesians, the apostle Paul speaks about putting on the full armor of God so that his own readers may be able to stand firm against
the schemes of the devil (Eph 6:11). He commands them to be **strong
in the Lord**, and in the strength of **His might** (Eph 6:10). He reminds
them that the battle they face is spiritual, "For our struggle is not against
flesh and blood, but against the rulers, against the powers, against the
world forces of this darkness, against the spiritual forces of wickedness
in the heavenly places (Eph 6:12)." The Christian does not have to face
Canaanites. He faces a far greater foe in fallen angels. These are forces
which a Christian cannot defeat armed with the flesh, "Therefore, take
up the full armor of God, so that you will be able to resist in the evil day,
and having done everything, to stand firm (Eph 6:13)." Direct contact
with these forces is ruinous as they are simply too strong and powerful
to defeat. However, the best defense against these spiritual forces of
darkness is living a godly life in truth and righteousness (Eph 6:14),
presenting the gospel to a lost world (Eph 6:15), walking by faith (Eph
6:16), trusting in eternal security (Eph 6:17), using the Word of God (Eph
6:17), and praying regularly and consistently in the power of the Spirit
for all the saints (Eph 6:18). Recalling the conquest of Canaan, Paul
describes all these necessary spiritual activities with military figures of
speech. However, the spiritual battle is no figure of speech, but is very
real, and extremely serious.

Closely connected, the first chapter of Ephesians declares to the
saints all of the spiritual assets available to the Christian, "Blessed be
the God and Father of our Lord Jesus Christ, who has blessed us with
every spiritual blessing in the heavenly places in Christ (Eph 1:3)." It is
these great spiritual assets, unlimited in potential, which the saints are
to use in the their spiritual battle against wicked forces (Eph 6:10-18).
Furthermore, these spiritual assets are later called an inheritance (Eph
1:18). Recognizing that the utilization of this divine inheritance is nothing to be taken for granted since it is closely tied to sanctification, Paul
prays for the Ephesian saints:

> … that the God of our Lord Jesus Christ, the Father of glory, may
> give to you spirit of wisdom and of revelation in the knowledge

of Him. I pray that the eyes of your heart may be enlightened, so that you will know what is the hope of His calling, **what are riches of the glory of His inheritance in the saints,** and what is the **surpassing greatness of His power toward us who believe.** These are in accordance with working of **His might,** which He brought about in Christ, when He raised Him from the dead and **seated Him at His right hand in the heavenly places,** far above all rule and authority and dominion, and every name that is named, not only in this age, but also in the one to come. **And He put all things under subjection under His feet,** and gave Him as head over all things to the church, which is His body, the fullness of Him who fills all in all (Eph 1:17-23).

Paul prays the Ephesians may learn to use this great spiritual inheritance so they might live sanctified godly lives. He then adds that faith in this inheritance is what grants spiritual power (Eph 1:18-19). The power of God's might works through His inheritance (Eph 1:18), wherein a saint has been blessed with every spiritual blessing possible (Eph 1:3), *if* he rests in these most glorious and gracious provisions by faith (Eph 1:19). Faith-rest is therefore also taught in Ephesians 1, and not just in Hebrews 3-4.

Also parallel to Hebrews in Ephesians 1 is the emphasis upon the ascension of Christ. It is through the avenue of the ascended Christ that the Christian can begin to experience this divine royal inheritance. In Hebrews, this is called the king-priest Order of Melchizedek wherein the royal priesthood of Christ confers resurrection power to overcome sin and temptation. Ephesians also mentions the heavenly places in Christ (Eph 1:3), which would be the heavenly tabernacle in Hebrews. Thus Paul's prayer in chapter one for the Ephesian saints that they come to spiritually experience their rich spiritual inheritance, can easily be understood as prayer to enter God's rest-inheritance. Moreover, like Hebrews, Paul warns the Ephesian saints about the real possibility of losing this inheritance through disobedience (Eph 5:1-7),"For this you know with certainty, that no immoral or impure person or covetous man, who is an idolater, has an *inheritance* in the kingdom of God (Eph 5:5)." This is precisely why Paul prays for them in chapter one, and then later commands them to be diligent in spiritual warfare in chapter six.

Like the Hebrew readers, the Ephesians saints too must be diligent to enter God's rest or face the same consequences of disinheritance.

However, this disinheritance of the kingdom of God does not mean loss of salvation, or even loss of all of the heavenly inheritance. The Holy Spirit is a guaranteed pledge of the saints' inheritance which will not be taken away, "In Him, you also, after listening to the message of the truth, the Gospel of your salvation – having also believed, you were sealed in Him with the Holy Spirit of promise, who is given as a pledge of our inheritance with a view to the redemption of God's own possession, to the praise of His glory (Eph 1:13-14)." This aspect of the inheritance cannot be lost since it has been sealed by the Holy Spirit. As such, they must not, "grieve the Holy Spirit of God, by whom you were sealed for the day of redemption (Eph 4:30)."

Thus the Ephesian saints have an aspect of their inheritance which is sealed for all of eternity based upon the activity of the Holy Spirit of *promise*, even if they grieve the Holy Spirit (Eph 1:13-14; 4:30). However, if they continue to grieve the Holy Spirit so that their lives are characterized by sin, they will have no inheritance in the Kingdom of Christ and God because this aspect of the inheritance is based on faith and obedience (Eph 4:31-5:7). To inherit the kingdom of God one must be an imitator of God (Eph 5:1-5). The same issues therefore of rest-inheritance, eternal security, disinheritance, faith and perseverance are also at the heart of the book of Ephesians. Entering rest is not just something which peculiarly appears in Hebrews, but can be found in Ephesians as well.

Other New Testament Parallel Passages

It is no coincidence that almost every time a church or believer is being warned about losing something, it is almost always related to either inheritance, rest, reward or prize (1 Cor 3:10-15, 6:9-10, 9:24-27; Gal 5:19-21; Eph 5:3-5; Heb 3-4; 2 John 8), which a Christian can only receive by continued perseverance and sanctification. All of these expressions are virtually synonymous, as Colossians 3:24 makes so clear, "Whatever you do, do your work heartily as for the Lord rather than for men, knowing that from the Lord you will receive the *reward of the inheritance* (3:23-24)." Reward and inheritance are thus identical synonyms, and they are distinct from initial justification and salvation (Rom 4:4-5; 1 Cor 3:10-15). In Romans 4:4-5, Paul says that justification is not a ***reward***,[84] which can only be received by works. This is consistent with 1 Corinthians 3:14-15 which warns that a Christian worker can lose his reward at the judgment seat of Christ and yet still be saved. This means that initial salvation must not be confused with receiving a reward. Rewards are received on the basis of faith and obedience (Col 3:23-24), whereas justification is received on the basis of faith without works (Rom 4:1-8; Gal 2:16).

There is therefore no contradiction in the New Testament which teaches that a Christian cannot lose his salvation (John 6:35-40; 10:27-29; Rom 8:28-39; Heb 10:10-14), but that he can lose his reward or inheritance through disobedience. While this would appear to be contradictory to many, it is still a doctrine which the Bible teaches not in a few places. This tension between receiving salvation by faith without works, yet gaining or losing inheritance or reward on the basis of faith plus works, is actually maintained throughout the New Testament. In fact, the warning against losing inheritance is a consistent warning throughout the New Testament, and the book of Hebrews contains the most systematic explanation of this theological conundrum. Those who have been once for all sanctified and perfected forever (3:1; 10:10-14) are also in great danger of losing God's rest inheritance (4:1-11) just like the Exodus generation (3:7-19).

In Colossians 3, right after Paul speaks about the importance of working heartily unto the Lord so as to receive the reward of the inheritance, he immediately warns them, "For he who does wrong will receive the consequences of the wrong which he has done, and that without partiality (3:25)." The warning passage of Colossians 3:23-25 is also parallel to the warnings in 1 Corinthians 6:9-10, Galatians 5:19-21, and Ephesians 5:3-5. In Colossians 3:23-25, Paul speaks of the judgment of God with regard to the ***reward of the inheritance***. In the other three passages, he essentially gives the same warning, but rather speaks of ***inheriting the kingdom of God*** instead. Paul may use a bit different terminology, but all the warnings are essentially the same here.

---

[84]   Paul uses the Greek word misqoj, i.e., wages or reward, in Rom 4:4 – *to the one working, the **reward** is not being reckoned according to a gift, but according to a debt.*

In Colossians 3:23-25, Paul warns that God will judge impartially those who do wrong, strongly implying the loss of the inheritance reward. Specifically in this context, the warning is given to slaves that they must do their work heartily as unto the Lord, rather than to men. They must be obedient to their masters, not only when he is watching, but at all times throughout each work day. To fail to do so on a consistent basis is a serious sin, and will reap bitter consequences at the judgment seat of Christ. How a Christian slave worked in the Roman Empire was no trifling matter to the apostle Paul. A genuine spiritual work ethic was critical to present a strong Christian testimony to the Roman world.

The same warning of disinheritance is also brought up in 1 Corinthians 6:9-10, Galatians 5:19-21, and Ephesians 5:5-6. In those warning passages, Paul threatens disinheritance to those Christians whose lives are characterized by continual sin. If Christians persist in willful sin, Paul categorically says that such persons will not inherit the kingdom of God (1 Cor 6:9-10; Gal 5:19-21). In Ephesians 5:3-6 states with certainty that such people will have no inheritance in the Kingdom of Christ and God. While many have assumed that these warnings apply to unbelievers rather than to believers, there is little reason to doubt that that they are also being applied to real Christians just like the book of Hebrews. In every one of these passages, the context is very clear. Paul is charging the saints not to be involved in various sins. He then warns them of disinheritance. How all of the sudden these warnings are then taken as applying to unbelievers is most difficult to understand when he has been talking all along about the sins of the saints. Indeed, in Galatians 5:21, Paul points out rather tersely to the Galatians, "Of which I forewarn you, just as I have forewarned you, that those who practice such things will not inherit the kingdom of God." How this warning can apply to unbelievers is none too clear when Paul explicitly directs this against the Galatian saints. Moreover, it is too obvious for words that no unbeliever can inherit the kingdom of God. How can this possibly be a warning of any kind for a Christian? It would be a very strange warning indeed, if not superfluous, if Paul was warning each one of these churches, "Don't you know that all unbelievers are not going to heaven?"[85] While it may be too obvious for words that no unbeliever can inherit the kingdom of God, it is not so obvious that a believer can

---

[85]   Dillow, p. 71.

lose his kingdom inheritance. But here in these passages Paul actually warns believers of losing their inheritance (1 Cor 6:9-10; Gal 5:19-21; Eph 5:3-5; Col 3:23-25), though he never questions their salvation (1 Cor 6:11; Gal 3:2; Eph 1:13-14, 4:30; Col 1:13-14, 2:9-15). Thus we are left with the exact same problems between warning and eternal security that we see in Hebrews. Paul agrees with the sacred author of Hebrews that inheriting the kingdom of God is just as distinct from initial justification as entering rest is.

These parallels become even more striking if we compare Colossians 3:23-25 with Hebrews 4:11. These verses are remarkably identical as illustrated below with Hebrews 4:11 being placed in parenthesis:

> Whatever you do, do your work heartily as for the Lord rather than for men (*Let us therefore be diligent*) knowing that from the Lord you will receive the reward of the inheritance (*to enter that rest*). For he who does wrong will receive the consequences of the wrong which he has done, and that without partiality (*lest anyone of you should fall through following the same example of disobedience*).

By comparing these verses, receiving the reward of the inheritance is identical with entering rest. While Colossians 3:23-25 primarily relates receiving the reward of the inheritance connected to slaves doing their job under the authority of their masters, this still cannot be divorced from Christian ethics. The warning of disinheritance is a general principle taught throughout Scripture directed against any kind of continual sin. Both Colossians 3:23-25, and Hebrews 4:11 clearly teach that diligent perseverance is necessary to either receive the reward of the inheritance or to enter rest.

Furthermore, since the concept of rest is based on the promised-land illustration, rest means inheritance. Entering rest in the Old Testament means to share in the temporal blessings of the promised-land, but in order for Israel to inherit the promised-land, faithful perseverance was required. If this was true in the Old Testament, this is no less true in the New Testament which is specifically spoke of in 1 Corinthians, Galatians, and Ephesians (1 Cor 6:9-10; Gal 5:19-21; Eph 5:3-5). These warning passages demand sanctification as a prerequisite before one can inherit the kingdom of God. Inheriting the kingdom of God does not mean to become justified or be ultimately saved. Such a conflation of sanctification would contradict salvation by free grace. These three warning passages make it very explicit that if a Christian's life is characterized by continual sin, he will not inherit the kingdom of God. Just as the Exodus generation did not inherit the kingdom of God on earth, neither will the Christian inherit the eschatological kingdom of God if he continues to sin willfully. He will forfeit his God-given right to participate with Christ as a ruling heir over the full eternal blessings that the kingdom of God offers. This however does not imply that he will lose his original salvation inheritance which is provided for apart from works (Rom 4:13-16; Eph 1:13-14).

At this point, Romans 8:17 is helpful to make this principle more clear. The problem with this verse is that the English translation is a poor one, virtually obliterating a distinction in the original Greek which Paul was trying to make. In the English translation it reads as if both being an heir of God and being a fellow heir of Christ mean exactly the same thing. This would also mean that being an heir of God and being a fellow heir of Christ are conditioned upon suffering with Christ as the English text reads as follows, "And if children, heirs also, heirs of God and fellow heirs of Christ, *if indeed* we suffer with Him so that we also may be glorified with Him (Rom 8:17)." In the original Greek however, Paul makes a most interesting distinction, "And if children, also heirs. Heirs of God *on the one hand*, but fellow heirs of Christ *on the other hand*, if indeed we suffer in order that also we may be glorified[86] (with Him)."

Why this distinction was glossed over in the English translation is of course of some debate, but the Greek is actually clear on this. If we have the Holy Spirit then not only are we saved, but we are also children of God (Rom 8:15-16). This also means that if we are children of God, we are heirs of God also (Rom 8:17). In a limited sense therefore, all children of God are heirs and will have an inheritance in heaven with the only condition being that they are saved, that they have been adopted into the family of God, that they possess the Holy Spirit (8:15-17a). However, Paul does more than suggest in the remaining part of the verse that being a fellow heir of Christ is a different issue, requiring obedience and

---

[86] Glorified here cannot mean ultimate glorification in the general sense of a receiving a resurrection body, but sharing with the glories of the exalted Christ in a very special way.

sanctification. He purposefully adds that if one wants to be a glorified fellow heir with Christ, he must suffer with Him in sanctification and spiritual perseverance. This is a special designation, a tremendous addition really, to being just an heir of God. Those who suffer with Jesus will be rewarded just as Jesus was rewarded.

Revelation 2:26 says it another way, "He who overcomes, and he who keeps my deeds until the end, to him I will give authority over the nations, and he shall rule them with a rod of iron, as the vessels of the potter are broken to pieces, *as I also have received authority from My Father* (Rev 2:26-27)." Here Jesus Christ promises that those Christians who persevere until the end will rule with Him in the coming Millennium. Revelation 3:21 adds further, "He who overcomes, I will grant to him to sit down with Me on My throne, *as I also overcame* and sat down with My Father on his throne (Rev 3:21)." Those Christians who overcome will be blessed with a glorified position with Christ Himself. Just as Jesus had to faithfully endure to receive this exalted position, so must the Christian. Sitting with Christ on his throne is also certainly consistent with entering God's rest, and can also just as easily be understood as inheriting the kingdom of God. Indeed, inheriting a kingdom makes sense only if the heirs are considered to be kings themselves, and this special royal designation will only be given to those who by faith and perseverance inherit the promises.

This being the case, since salvation and inheritance are closely connected, just as there is past, present, and future salvation, so there is also a past, present and future inheritance as well. Past inheritance, based exclusively on the promise of God, is received by faith alone apart from works. However, the present experience of that inheritance requires faith and works, based on the believer faithfully using the promises of God in his life. The future inheritance is a mixture of both. All Christians are heirs of God apart from works, and therefore will all have a limited future inheritance in heaven. Nonetheless, only those who have faithfully put into practice their present inheritance on the earth will receive an eschatological inheritance in heaven. In this way, they will become co-heirs of Christ, enter rest, receive the reward of the inheritance, and inherit the kingdom of God in the same way that Christ did, i.e., through suffering obedience.

Thus the promised inheritance of God has both unconditional and conditional clauses attached to it. Past salvation inheritance is unconditional. It is without works. God will keep His side of the contract regardless of the merit of the recipient, even to His hurt. Indeed, this is exactly what promises are. This also means that every Christian will have a limited heavenly inheritance with God in the eschatological future, even if they have not lived lives which God has demanded of them. Present and future inheritance however has conditional clauses attached to it, and these clauses demand faithful obedience on the part of the recipient. This aspect of the inheritance is meritorious. Hence it is called a reward, yet it is also consistent with the grace of God in the sense that this opportunity was still given by God's gracious provision. Those who persevere in the grace of God will be rewarded accordingly to their works.

2 Timothy 2:11-13 provides a good summary of this great theological conundrum, "It is a trustworthy statement: For if we died with Him, we will also live with Him (past salvation inheritance). If we endure, we will also reign with Him (future salvation inheritance of being a co-heir with Christ). If we deny Him, He will also deny us (the future salvation inheritance of being a co-heir with Christ will be denied). If we are faithless, He remains faithful, for He cannot deny Himself (past salvation inheritance is eternally secure regardless of the activity of the saint for the simple reason that God promised it)." Only seen in this light can salvation inheritance be seen in its full orbed entirety which the Scriptures present in more than a few places.

Regardless of how one looks at all of these verses, they are all teaching one thing: perseverance and sanctification are required for any Christian to enter rest, to receive the reward of the inheritance, to inherit the kingdom of God, or to be a fellow glorified heir with Christ. Inheriting the kingdom of God is far more than simply entering heaven on the merits of the crosswork of Christ. To inherit the kingdom of God means to be a co-reigning heir with Christ sharing in God's great eschatological Sabbath rest. Since it is based on sanctification and obedience, it cannot be confused with ultimate basis for salvation, but must be seen as something in addition to initial salvation.

Whether or not inheriting the kingdom of God or entering rest means to rule in the Millennium, or to rule the universe from the New Jerusalem in heaven, is perhaps a moot point. The fact of the matter is that the Scriptures supports both of these spiritual possibilities conditioned upon faithful obedience. Hebrews 2:5 speaks of ruling the eschatological world to come. Hebrews 12:24 speaks of Mt. Zion and the city of the living God, the heavenly Jerusalem. Revelation 2-3 pronounces great spiritual inheritance rewards in both the Millennium and the heavenly New Jerusalem for those who faithfully persevere until the end, "Now in a large house there are not only gold and silver vessels, but also vessels of wood and of earthenware, and some to honor, and some to dishonor. Therefore if anyone cleanses himself from these things, he will be a vessel for honor, sanctified, useful to the Master, prepared for every good work (2 Tim 2:20-21)."

The Sword of the Lord – 4:12-13

In Numbers 14, the good news of entering rest became a lethal weapon to the Exodus generation because they did not believe the promise, the theme of Hebrews 4:12-13. In the same way the Exodus generation was cut down by the sword after committing apostasy in the desert, the same may happen to the Hebrew readers if they do not wake up spiritually, "for the word of God is living and active and sharper than any two-edged sword, and piercing as far the division of the soul and spirit, of joints and marrow, and is able to judge the thoughts and intentions of the heart. And there is no creature hidden from His sight, but all things are open and laid bare to the eyes of Him with whom we have to do (Heb 4:12-13)." God may cut the Hebrew readers down in judgment with a spiritual sword, which is the Word of God.

Numbers 14 is the place where the Exodus generation committed apostasy in the desert when they tried to appoint their own leader to bring them back to Egypt, attempting to stone Moses, Aaron, Joshua and Caleb to death in the process. Here the Lord personally intervened to stop the mob verdict from being executed against them, and pronounced His judgment: 40 years in the desert until they all die. With great interest is, after Moses related this sentence against the congregation of Israel, they all cried (Num 14:39). They then presumed this show of tears would perhaps move God to rescind His judgment. Thus, they decided to try and enter the Promised Land after all. However, it was too late.

Even though they cried, and even though they may have changed their minds about the evil they had wished upon their leaders, God was not going to change His mind about His sentence that they would indeed die in the desert. God made an oath. He swore in His wrath that the Exodus generation would not enter His rest. Therefore, there was no opportunity for a repentance (Heb 12:16-17) that would get them into the Promised Land to inherit rest. They may have cried and felt deep regret. They even tried to change their destiny, but their tears would not move the settled disposition of God against them.

In their arrogance, while Exodus generation knew God was a forgiving God, and had forgiven them many times, they decided that they would try again to enter the Promised Land of rest, "Here we are; we have indeed sinned, but we will go up to the place which the Lord has promised (Num 14:40)." They freely acknowledged their sin to God, and presumed this would be enough to atone for the consequences of their action. They had actually done this many times before. However this time it was too late. They had gone too far. Even though they acknowledged their sin, God still did not repent. Though God did forgive them, this time the Exodus generation will have to permanently live with their previous evil decision-making. God emphatically declared that they will indeed die in the wilderness through a long period of 40 wasted years.

Thus Moses warned them again, "Do not go up, or you will be struck down before your enemies, for the Lord is not among you. For the Amalekites and the Canannites will be there in front of you, and you will fall by the *sword*, inasmuch as you have turned back from following the Lord (Num 14:42)." As usual, the congregation of Israel did not listen to Moses and went up anyway. They even went up without the ark of the covenant and without the instructions of Moses. This being so, they were quickly defeated by their enemies (Num 14:45).

The original promise, therefore, to enter rest, instead became a lethal weapon. They did not believe in the good news of entering rest, and so God sentenced them to die in the wilderness. When they heard that, they did not want that either, so they decided to go into the land by their own initiative, presuming that God would fight for them in spite of their sin. Thus, they were immediately struck down by the sword. It was too late.

The Hebrew readers, therefore, need to beware the same fate. There may indeed come a time when God may not permit spiritual progress (Heb 3:11; 4:3; 6:1-3), but mete out judgment instead (Heb 4:12-13; 6:7-8), the theme of the next warning of Hebrews. There may come a time when even confession of sin cannot make up for the consequences of one's actions. If the Hebrew readers continue to disbelieve the promise, then that promise will turn into a lethal weapon, a lethal sword which will, "judge the thoughts and intentions of the heart (Heb 4:12)." The Hebrew readers will not only have to pay the consequences of God's punitive judgment, but it will also prevent them from spiritual growth as well, not to mention eschatological reward.

The Hebrew readers need to watch out. There is no escaping the all-encompassing surveillance of God's judgment (Heb 4:12-13). The Word of God has an incisive and penetrating quality. It is also, "living and active and sharper than any two-edged sword (Heb 4:12)." This expression here is poetical, "It signifies that the Word penetrates to the inmost recesses of our spiritual being just like a sword cuts through the joints and marrow of the body."[87] More to the point, "a double-edge sword is a more formidable weapon than a single-edged. It offers less resistance and therefore cuts deeper and quicker."[88]

Hebrews 4:13 adds further, "There is no creature hidden from His sight, but all things are open and laid bare." This speaks of complete exposure, if not complete defenseless before the presence of the Word of God.[89] In addition, in the Greek, the force of verse 13 is to assert that the exposure to the Scripture entails the exposure to God Himself. The English has great difficulty in translating the last phrase of 4:13. In the Greek it literally reads, "and all is naked and laid bare to His eyes, toward whom to us *the Word* (4:13b)." Total intimacy and transparency with God is not only uncomfortable and judgmental, but occurs through personal experience with the Word of God. The fact that the author of Hebrews nowhere makes any sharp distinction between the written Scriptures and the Personal Word emphasizes this principle further. How can one have intimacy with an invisible God? Without the Word of God, without the written Scriptures, it is not possible. What's more, intimacy with God

---

[87]   Vincent, p. 428.
[88]   Dods, pp. 281-82.
[89]   Lane, p. 103.

involves intense divine scrutiny. The surveillance of God is exhaustive. Nothing escapes the scrutiny of God.[90]

---

[90]   Ibid.

CHAPTER SEVEN

THE DANGER OF PERSISTENT SPIRITUAL DULLNESS – 5:11-6:8

Their Spiritual Sloth is Inexcusable – 5:11-14

In Hebrews 5-6, the writer of Hebrews interrupts his comparison of the Aaronic priesthood with the priesthood of Christ (4:14-5:10) in order to warn his readers to be better students of the Word (5:11-14).[91] He therefore continues his comparison with the Exodus generation. Just as they did not listen to the Old Testament Law, so the Hebrew readers too were neglecting the New Testament. In fact, this neglect was beginning to become a chronic problem, and so the sacred author must address the issue. He wants to share the glories of Christianity with them through the Word, but instead, he must stop and begin to warn them yet once again. As such, he begins the warning at the end of chapter five by telling them how their spiritual growth has been stunted by their persistent spiritual lethargy:

> And having been made perfect, He became to all those who obey Him the source of eternal salvation, being designated by God as a high priest according to the Order of Melchizedek. Concerning him we have much to say, and it is hard to explain, since you have become dull of hearing. For though by this time you ought to

---

91   Kistemaker, p. 147.

be teachers, you have need again for someone to teach you the elementary principles of the oracles of God, and you have come to need milk and not solid food. For everyone who partakes only of milk is not accustomed to the word of righteousness, for he is an infant. But solid food is for the mature, who because of practice have their senses trained to discern good and evil (Heb 5:9-14).

The writer desperately wants to speak to them about the Order of Melchizedek, "concerning him we have much to say (Heb 5:11)." Indeed, in his comparison between Aaron and Jesus in chapter five, he had already begun this discussion. However, as he thinks about the spiritual condition of his readers, he stops the forward progress of his argument, and goes back to the fact that they have not shown the spiritual poise and maturity necessary to appreciate what the Order of Melchizedek is all about.

The problem here is not that the Order of Melchizedek is difficult to explain, but precisely because his readers were spiritually dull. The author of Hebrews is afraid that they are not ready for it. This is to a large extent what the book of Hebrews is all about. The writer wants his readers to get a hold of the great spiritual truths of the Order of Melchizedek, but he is afraid that his readers are not spiritually able to accept these great truths. Worse, since they have been Christians for so long now, there is no excuse for their spiritual dullness, "For though by this time you ought to be teachers, you have need again for someone to teach the elementary principles of the oracles of God, and you have come to need milk and not solid food (Heb 5:12)." Moreover, the fact that they are so spiritually dull at this point in their spiritual life is to their shame (Heb 5:11). As such, instead of re-teaching them the basics of the truth, which his readers need, he warns them instead (Heb 6:1-8). Great spiritual inspiration is not enough to motivate these people. The Order of Melchizedek may be great inspiration, but the author must still warn them severely to awake them from their spiritual slumber.

The author had planned to continue his teaching on the Order of Melchizedek but his material is too advanced for his readers. "His theology is too deep for them precisely because his students are too lazy. The subject matter is difficult to explain, not because of the lack of the writer's skills, but because of the readers' inability to comprehend."

[92] What's more, the perfect tense in the Greek **have become** indicates that the recipients had already fallen into this state of spiritual dullness (Heb 5:11), "and since they have fallen into this state, the author then is forced to divert his attention away from the topic of the priesthood."[93] The author of Hebrews therefore warns them very severely yet again (5:11-6:8), but with great interest, he then follows up with a great encouragement (6:9-20).

In short, the author does not want his readers to fall into despair. How does one severely warn people without throwing them into despair? The writer of Hebrews shows how this is done, and so here in Hebrews 5-6, he leaves his readers with a wonderful example of what he means by a **word of exhortation** (Heb 13:22). To motivate his readers, the author warns, sometimes very severely. However, all of his warnings are administered with a tone of grace, tenderness, and encouragement (Heb 6:1-20).

Something has gone drastically wrong at the most basic level in the discipleship process. By all normal spiritual standards the readers should have graduated by now. In fact, they should all be teachers by now. They have had ample time to grow spiritually, but because of lack of interest, because of spiritual sloth, because of spiritual dullness, they are still but babes in the faith. Even worse, they need to be taught the basics all over again, "**Elementary principles** here signifies the basic lines or principles of elementary doctrines."[94] To their spiritual shame, this process needs to be repeated. It is therefore an inexcusable situation.

The picture being presented here by the writer is that of a 20 year-old still drinking baby milk. More to the point, the problem is not because of a lack of good training. Hebrews 6:7 clearly indicates that they have been well provided for. God has been watering them with good teaching for a long time now, but the results have been thorns and thistles rather than fruit (Heb 6:7-8). Worse, this process has been dangerously protracted. As a result, 5:13 indicates the Hebrew readers are untrained or unskilled in the **word of righteousness**. They have not been exercised by the truth (5:14). They have had relatively little practice in the word of truth. Someone who drinks only milk cannot exercise or train very much. Even in a baby's stomach, milk does not last very long.

---

[92]   Ibid, p. 148.
[93]   Ibid.
[94]   Ibid, p. 151.

In order to train, one needs solid food (Heb 5:14). Without solid food, it is simply impossible to train or exercise properly. Here the author draws from common sense in everyday life to try and make a similar application to his readers. They are like athletes who are drinking only milk, and milk is simply not enough to sustain an athlete in training. As such, drinking only spiritual milk, they are left untrained, not really knowing the difference between good and evil. This lack of spiritual discernment has placed them under the sway of evil, and they are way beyond the time of patiently waiting for them to grow up. Now, much more drastic measures must be taken to get them to wake up, the main point of 6:1-8.

The Judgment of Hebrews 6:1-3 – God May Not Permit Spiritual Maturity

While not a few interpreters get bogged down in the difficulties of Hebrews 6:4-6, they tend to overlook the overall context and quickly lose their way. What is so often neglected is that the author of Hebrews has already informed his readers what the warning is all about before the infamous verses of 6:4-6, "therefore, leaving the elementary teaching about the Christ, *let us press onto maturity ... if God permits* (Heb 6:1-3)." In other words, the writer of Hebrews is not warning them about losing their salvation here in chapter six, but is warning them about lost opportunity for spiritual growth, consistent with the Exodus generation disaster. God may not permit the Hebrew readers to press onto maturity. Closely connected, this will also forbid them God's rest. This is the real force of the warning in Hebrews 6 which so often is ignored in favor of more cryptic interpretations derived from 6:4-6. Like the Exodus generation, God will not give the Hebrew readers opportunity for spiritual growth if they fall away (6:3-6), but will judge them instead with irreparable consequences (6:7-8).

5:11-14 clearly states the problem with the Hebrew readers is not that they are somehow unsaved, but rather that they have not grown up spiritually in spite of ample time and opportunity to do so. As such, the warning in Hebrews 6:1-8 must respond to the direct problem of the persistent spiritual sloth which the readers have been experiencing. This means that no matter how 6:4-6 is understood, it cannot be divorced from the immediate context that the judgment in mind here is not loss of salvation, but lost opportunity for spiritual growth. The author so states this in so many words. 5:11-14 states the spiritual problem. 6:1-3 warns that God may not permit the Hebrew readers to press onto maturity, and then 6:4-6 explains why not.[95] 6:7-8 then gives an illustration to clarify the situation further. This is the judgment at hand here in Hebrews 6, i.e., God may not permit the Hebrew readers to press onto maturity into God's rest parallel to the Exodus debacle.

Although recognizing his readers need to be taught again the elementary teachings of the faith (5:11-14), the author refuses to consider doing this. They have already been through basic training once, and there has been more than enough time to grow up as real genuine disciples of the Lord. The writer of Hebrews, therefore, is not going to give them the opportunity to re-learn the basics – even though they may really need this. Their time is up. It is now time to press on toward spiritual maturity and growth:

> Therefore leaving the elementary teaching about the Christ, let us press onto maturity, not laying again a foundation of repentance from dead works and of faith toward God, of instruction about washings and laying on of hands, and the resurrection of the dead and eternal judgment. And this we will do, *if God permits* (6:1-3).

Let us press onto maturity is the main verb of the sentence in 6:1-2. Therefore the clause, "this we will do, if God permits (6:3)," corresponds to the phrase, "Let us press onto maturity." Closely related, to leave the elementary teachings about the Christ (6:1) means to not lay down again another spiritual foundation (6:2). *If God permits* is a third class condition in the Greek, which is the probable future condition. It is therefore likely that God will allow them to mature spiritually. Nonetheless, there is still some doubt on this possibility. In the Greek, the author does say *if indeed* or *only if* God permits, and then 6:4-6 warns the readers why this possibility may still be in doubt. In other words, if the readers fall into the trap of 6:4-6, then God will not permit them to press onto maturity

---

[95]   The explanatory *gar* in the Greek is often overlooked here. The author of Hebrews says at the beginning of 6:4 *for*, referring back to the previous clause in 6:3, "And this we shall do if God permits." 6:4-6 must therefore explain 6:1-3.

(6:3). Perhaps some already have fallen into this trap? Hebrews 10:25 notes some have quit coming to church.

The warning begins in 6:1 with a ***therefore***, "therefore ... let us press onto maturity." Now the natural question is why therefore? The reason why is because of 5:11-14, i.e., because they are spiritually immature, because they have had plenty of time to grow up, because God has watered them well – they need to press onto spiritual maturity leaving behind the basics of the faith. This is why the author will immediately begin his in-depth discussion on the Order of Melchizedek (6:9-7:28), precisely because this royal priesthood is what will spur them on toward spiritual advancement. This means at once that the Order of Melchizedek is the perfect cure for the readers' spiritual dullness. The Order of Melchizedek is the antidote to their spiritual crisis. "Their particular condition of immaturity is such that only an appreciation of what is involved in Christ's priesthood will cure it. Their minds need to be stretched and the Order of Melchizedek can stretch their minds as nothing else can." [96] In other words, since they have remained immature too long, ***therefore*** he will teach them about the Order of Melchizedek to push them out of their immaturity, and this whole emphasis begins in 6:9 immediately following the warning (6:1-8).

The great problem here is that the Hebrew readers lack the spiritual understanding that Christianity is greater than Judaism. Christianity does not have all of the elaborate holy rituals which were such an important part of Judaism. Where is priestly holiness in Christianity? It cannot be seen with the physical eye. What happened to the magnificence of the Old Testament priesthood? The author of Hebrews will therefore demonstrate from this point forward that Christianity is indeed very holy, and that Christianity is indeed very magnificent. The author will then tell his readers that the great holiness and majesty of Christianity consists in the fact that Christ is now in the real heavenly holy of holies in heaven, far above the earthly tabernacle. More to the point, this heavenly tabernacle is based on the eternal Order of Melchizedek, not according to temporal order of Aaron. This means that the Order of Melchizedek is far superior to the order of Aaron since it is both indestructible and eternal, the great theme of chapter seven. The author tells his readers that though he is warning them very severely (6:1-8)

---

[96]   Bruce, p. 138.

because of their inexcusable persistent lethargy (5:11-14), he is actually, "convinced of better things" for them, and the "things that accompany salvation, though we are speaking in this way (Heb 6:9)." Moreover, the things which accompany salvation *is* the Order of Melchizedek, "This hope we have as an anchor of the soul, a hope both sure and steadfast and one which enters within the veil, where Jesus has entered as a forerunner for us, having become a high priest forever according to the Order of Melchizedek (6:19-20)."

The Order of Melchizedek is what the writer of Hebrews is pushing his audience to. He wants them to spiritually experience the Order of Melchizedek in their souls, the greatest human experience available to man, far greater than anything the earthly tabernacle could ever provide. However, in order to have this rich spiritual experience, his readers must press onto maturity. His readers must leave behind the elementary teachings of Christianity and follow their pioneer to heaven through faith, and spiritually experience the Order of Melchizedek right now. If they do this, then they will experience the house of God (Heb 3:6), be partakers with Christ (Heb 3:14), and enter into God's rest (Heb 4:1-11). The way into God's spiritual rest is through the Order of Melchizedek (Heb 4:11-16). In other words, by being God's house, by being partakers with Christ, by using the Melchizedekian Priesthood in their lives, they will be able to press onto maturity into God's spiritual rest. If they do not do this, they will fall irreparably into God's judgment. Their time is almost up.

Now the writer of Hebrews gives a peculiar list of the elementary teachings of the faith in 6:1-2. He lists *repentance from dead works, faith toward God, instructions about baptisms, the laying on of hands, the resurrection of the dead* and *the eternal judgment.* These are the foundational doctrines which were originally taught to the Hebrew readers when they first became Christians. It is also quite evident that this rather peculiar list is geared for Hebrew converts, and not for pagan ones. A list of basics like this would be almost incomprehensible if they were originally given to pagan converts at the point of salvation.

The references to repentance from dead works, baptisms, and the laying on of hands are issues that deal with Jewish priesthood. The Old Testament worshiper approached God through the priesthood, which consisted of dead works, i.e., animal sacrifices,[97] baptisms and the laying on of hands. They are also dead works by definition since they are dead sacrificial works which can neither perfect the worshiper nor take away sin (Heb 10:1-4).

Baptisms cannot be Christian baptism since it is plural. Hebrews 9:9-10 speaks of various **baptisms** which were only symbols imposed by the Levitical priesthood until the time of the reformation when under the authority of the New Testament and/or Covenant. The laying on of hands most probably refers to the act whereby the Old Testament worshipers would lay their hands on the heads of the sacrificial animals, confessing their sins in the process before the animal was killed, thus transferring the guilt of the worshiper onto the offering.

With regard to Christian conversion and its relationship to such priestly operations, the Hebrew readers needed to repent. They would have had to change their minds about the dead works under the Old Testament system and accept the cross of Christ for the forgiveness of their sins. While the animal sacrifices and the various baptisms could not forgive anyone, even under the Old Covenant, this was not a widely accepted understanding of scriptural teaching. In fact, many a Jew throughout the history of the Old Testament missed the typological significance of ritual sacrifices. Ritual sacrifices in the Old Covenant could only depict in picture form what Christ would do later in reality on the cross (Heb 9:1-14). While this teaching may be obvious from a Christian standpoint, it was not to the Jews of the day.

Repentance away from Judaism would have been very difficult to accept. Nonetheless, a repentance from slavishly and legalistically depending upon these rituals was imperative, and so the Jews had to learn these basic elemental truths of Christianity in order to become saved. It is also true that a strong distinction between ritual and reality was simply not as clear in the Old Testament, a clarity which only Christ and New Testament teaching could bring about. As such, when these Hebrew readers became Christians, it was no simple changeover, but one which involved a great spiritual transition away from the old to the new.

Lastly, the writer also briefly mentions basic principles like faith toward God, the resurrection and the eternal judgment. These basic principles are general enough for both the Hebrew and the pagan convert.

---

[97] Animal sacrifices are called **dead works** in Hebrews 9:11-14.

Regardless, however, while the references here in 6:1-2 may be a bit cryptic because they are so brief, the main point is still clear. The Hebrew readers need to get beyond the baby stuff. It is time to leave these basic principles of conversion. What's more, even though the readers seem to have forgotten the significance of these basics, the author refuses to teach them all over again. He therefore charges them to press onto the spiritual heights of the Order of Melchizedek, not repeating again the basics of the faith.

It is Impossible to Start Over Again – 6:4-6

Three times in Hebrews 5:11-6:8 the author uses the word *again*, "... *again* you have need to be taught the elementary truths of the Word of God (Heb 5:12) ... not *again* laying a foundation of repentance ... (Heb 6:1) ... it is impossible ... *again* to renew to repentance (Heb 6:4-6)." *Again* in 6:1 refers to a second beginning. It refers back to the elementary truths of the Word of God (5:12), to the foundational principles of the faith (6:1). Moreover, this second beginning the author refuses to teach them. Then in 6:6, if the Hebrew readers fall away into apostasy, a second beginning is impossible anyway, and the reason why is because they have already become Christians *once* for all (6:4). Therefore *again* here is to be contrasted with *once* in 6:4. The Hebrew readers are having a difficult time accepting the final once for all nature of Christianity. They had grown so accustomed to repetitive religion under the Old Covenant, they had very little appreciation for the once for all significance of the cross. They were actually favoring the repetitions of Judaism over against the finality of Christianity. By their spiritual behavior, they were in effect, perhaps without realizing it, treating the cross as if it were merely another repetitive animal sacrifice.[98] In this way, they were neglecting their so great salvation.

Following on the heels of the warning in 6:3 that God may not permit the Hebrew readers to press onto maturity, the word *impossible* is emphatically placed at the beginning of the sentence in 6:4 in the original Greek. The author is further warning his readers. He now talks about something which is absolutely impossible. Literally in the Greek, 6:4-6 reads as follows:

---

[98]   The Catholic mass is not to much different than this.

It is **impossible** for those who have been **once** enlightened, having tasted both the heavenly gift and have become partakers of the Holy Spirit, and having tasted both the good word of God and the powers of the coming age, and having fallen away, **again** to renew into repentance, **re-crucifying** to themselves the Son of God and exposing Him to public shame (Heb 6:4-6).

The author makes very clear that it is impossible for those who have **once** become Christians (6:4-5), who later fall away (6:6), to renew them **again** to repentance. Then, the reason why it impossible is because it re-crucifies to themselves the Son of God, exposing Him to public shame. The Hebrew readers desperately need to understand that Christ died once, and this means once for all, meaning that they must accept the spiritual realities of the New Testament priesthood rather than stay back under the Old Covenant system. More to the point, since Christ died only once, one can become saved only once. This salvation process cannot be repeated any more than the Son of God can be crucified all over again. As such, if the Hebrew readers fall away into apostasy back into the old system, it is impossible to repent again to get back on track, precisely because this will be equivalent to re-crucifying Christ to themselves again, both a historical and spiritual impossibility. By apostasizing backwards into the repetitive nature of Old Testament religion, the Hebrew readers were setting themselves up for a judgment which will have irreparable consequences.

Just as Hebrews 2:1-4 warned the readers about drifting too far away from the dock, so Hebrews 6:1-8 warns them that this spiritual drifting will take them so far downriver into the Old Testament religion that they will not be able to recover their way. What they gained initially by striving upstream will have been permanently lost. It is one thing to stop rowing upstream when one is far ahead of his initial starting point. It is quite another to drift downstream altogether past his initial starting point, especially if it cannot be navigated upstream because of foaming whitewater.

By His death on the cross, Christ has brought the Hebrew readers to a new starting point beyond the foaming whitewater of the Old Testament Law. Because of the cross, the Hebrew readers were placed in a new superior position beyond the whitewater in which they could navigate upstream, provided they believe in His gracious promises. However, the Hebrew readers are now at the point of drifting down past this initial starting point. They are about to lose their moorings and be swept downstream by a spiritual river of foaming whitewater. Furthermore, once they get caught in the whitewater, not only will they not be able to row upstream, but neither will they be able to start all over again. There comes a point in time when someone gets so far a field that he does not have time to recover his way.

Another good illustration would be that of a runner who tries to start his race all over again after having been disqualified, an illustration which Paul entertains seriously in the warning passage of 1 Corinthians 9-10 (1 Cor 9:26-27). Once the runner is disqualified, he cannot start over again, even if he repents or cries or changes his mind or whatever. His disqualification is permanent.

Now the word *for* is near the beginning of the sentence in 6:4. It is an explanatory *for* in the original Greek, and goes back to 6:3, "if God permits." In other words, the writer is explaining why God may not permit the Hebrew readers to press onto maturity. 6:3 states the primary judgment that God may not permit spiritual growth, and then 6:4-6 explains why not. The explanatory *for* is so often overlooked by many interpreters. However, its presence here requires that 6:4-6 must in some way explain 6:3. There is no way around this. 6:4-6 must explain why God may not permit the Hebrew readers to get back on track, i.e, to press on toward spiritual maturity.

Like **impossible**, the word **once** is also emphatic, being placed near the beginning of the sentence in 6:4. As such, it conditions the following four participial phrases in the Greek. This means the Hebrew readers have been **once enlightened**, they have **once tasted of the heavenly gift**, they have **once been made partakers of the Holy Spirit**, and they have **once tasted the good word of God and the powers of the age to come**. The author is giving here a rather impressive list of what happened originally to the Hebrew readers. He is talking about their initial, yet very rich, salvation experience.

Once enlightened speaks of the fact that God originally gave them divine illumination to receive the Gospel message. Having tasted the heavenly gift speaks of the fact that they have experienced the gracious riches of heaven. They had also become partakers of the Holy Spirit. This indicates that the readers initially understood they were also participants in the privileges of the New Covenant. The spiritual experience of the Holy Spirit is basic to what the New Covenant is all about in contrast to the Old Covenant (8:8-10). They also had experienced the good word of God in their lives.

Furthermore, the author refers to the fact that they have experienced the powers of the age to come, which are the coming eschatological millennial powers of the kingdom of God promised in the Old Testament, foreshadowed by apostolic miracles (2:3-4). This, of course, is closely allied to the promise of spiritual powers of the Holy Spirit and the New Covenant. The "powers of the age to come" thus reveal the fact that the Hebrew readers received these great spiritual privileges ahead of time, before the kingdom of God actually becomes visibly manifest on the earth during the Millennium. As such, there can be no doubt that these Hebrew readers are genuine believers.

These participial phrases here are undeniably expressive of a tremendous one-time salvation event. One of the great themes of Hebrews is that Christ died once (Heb 7:26-28; 9:11-12; 9:24-27; 10:10-14; 10:18; 10:26). Here in 6:4-5, the author categorically states that like the death of Christ, so the initial conversion experience is also a once for all unrepeatable event. The one time conversion experience of 6:4-5 corresponds directly to the fact that Christ died once for all. When the writer emphasizes this *once* in 6:4, he is talking about something which is once for all, something which is parallel to the death of Christ, something which cannot happen *again*. Christian salvation is an irreversible, unrepeatable one-time event.

Now this brings up the question that if salvation is a one-time once for all event, does this mean that a Christian will automatically persevere in his faith until the final hour? The writer of Hebrews answers this question with an emphatic "*no*" as the participle *fallen away* in 6:6 demonstrates. The author makes this remarkably clear by using only one article to control all of the participial phrases. In the Greek, the same article agrees with all of the following participles. This means that the same ones who were once enlightened are also the same ones who have fallen away. In other words, the same ones who were once saved later have fallen away into apostasy. However, while these participles are all grammatically connected to demonstrate that the author is talking about the same group of people, the last participle, *fallen away*, is distinguished from the others by meaning and the experience of time. While the first four participles are positive in declaration that the Hebrew readers are indeed real genuine Christians, the last participle, *fallen away*, is negative in describing their apostasy away from their initial salvation. It is also something which could have only happened at a later time, in distinction from the other participles, describing their initial conversion which was simultaneously experienced when they accepted Christ as their Savior. This means at once that Hebrews 6:4-6 denies the doctrine of the perseverance of the saints as is commonly taught within Calvinistic circles. These verses teach that it is possible for a Christian to fall away who will have no chance of spiritual recovery. This is the force of Hebrews 6:1-6. Just as the Exodus generation wanted to go back to Egypt, and just as they worshipped other gods in the wilderness, so these Hebrew readers want to go back to corrupt Judaism at the expense of holding fast their Christian confession. They are not persevering in their faith, and so the author of Hebrews warns them of the consequences of this.

Fallen away[99] in the Greek is in the past tense. This seems to indicate that the Hebrew readers have already fallen away. Grammatically this is the natural interpretation, but the immediate context actually goes against this interpretation. The fact the Hebrew readers have not yet committed apostasy, though they are very close to it, goes back to the explanatory *for* in 6:4. This explanatory *for* is dependent upon the subjunctive mood of 6:3 as to why God may not permit the Hebrew readers to spiritually mature. In the Greek, *if God permits*, is in the subjunctive mood. This is the mood of possibility and not of reality, and this potentiality carries over into 6:4-6. 6:3 therefore states that God may not permit the Hebrew readers to grow up spiritually, and then 6:4-6 explains under which circumstances God will not allow this to happen. Even the English picks up on the subjunctive character of 6:4-6, beginning with the clause, "for in the case ...." 6:4-6 is stating the case in which God will not allow a Christian to press onto maturity. If a Christian falls away into apostasy, he will lose the opportunity to get back on track, which, by definition,

---

[99]   It is important to note that Greek participles do not have mood, but are dependent upon the main verb of the sentence as to whether or not the writer is talking about something which has actually happened, or may happen. In 6:4-6 there is no main verb, only the predicate *it is impossible*. *It is impossible* is describing a potential case dependent upon the subjunctive mood in 6:3, *if God permits*, and is not necessarily indicative of the Hebrew readers, at least not yet anyway.

will also prevent him from growing up spiritually – and this loss will be an irreparable one. The author has not really stated that his readers have fallen away yet, but in the case that they do fall away, his readers need to know it is impossible to renew them again into repentance.[100]

Even the broad context of Hebrews teaches that the Hebrew readers have not yet committed apostasy, though they are awfully close to it. 2:3 states that the Hebrew readers will not escape *if* they neglect their so great salvation. They must pay carefully attention to the Word of God, *lest* they drift away (Heb 2:1). The Hebrew readers are both Christ's house and partakers with Him, *if* they hold fast (Heb 3:6; 3:14). They are also to be diligent so as not to fall away like the Exodus generation (4:11). Furthermore, *if* they go on sinning willfully after receiving a knowledge of the truth, there no longer remains a sacrifice for sins, but a certain terrifying expectation of judgment (10:26). The author of Hebrews then warns his readers at the end of the book, "See to it that you do not refuse Him who is speaking (12:25)." These verses clearly indicate that apostasy or the falling away has not yet happened, but the writer warns them of this because they are so close to it. Moreover, if the Hebrew readers have already committed apostasy, then there would be no point in warning them. To warn someone after the fact is a waste of time, and nullifies the whole point of what a warning actually is.

It has been difficult for many to decide whether or not *renew again into repentance* (6:6) refers to salvation-repentance or a repentance to recover fellowship with God. The enigmatic nature of 6:4-6 makes the decision even more difficult to make. Either way, however, the results will be the same. There can be no recovery for the one who commits apostasy. While this may sound excessively harsh, the sacred writer of Hebrews is saying nothing significantly different than what he said of Esau in 12:16-17. Esau found no opportunity for repentance either. Though this big hairy man even cried when he realized he lost his blessing, Isaac still did not change his mind, i.e., he did not repent to give it back to him. Likewise, the Exodus generation found no opportunity for repentance either. Once they committed apostasy, even after they

---

[100]   The other alternative here is that Hebrews 10:25 says that some of the Hebrew readers have quit coming to church. Hence the sacred author may be using their example of already haven fallen away to warn his readers of what could also happen to them. In any case, whether or not the apostasy has been committed is perhaps beside the point. The same principle of no recovery still applies.

cried, they could not enter the promised-land so as to recover what they had lost. God had sworn in an oath that they will not enter rest, and that was it. Even so-called repentant tears could not gain back what they foolishly had forfeited. God may have forgiven them, but he did not grant them an opportunity for repentance to enter rest. There is thus a strong connection between the permissible will of God and the impossibility of repentance here (6:3-6). It is God who graciously grants repentance, not the other way around, and the time may come when it will be too late, just as when Paul commanded Timothy in the Ephesian church to refute the false doctrines of his hearers "with gentleness correcting those who are in opposition, if perhaps God may grant them repentance leading to the knowledge of the truth and they may come to their senses and escape the snare of the devil ... (2 Tim 2:25-26)."

Seen in this light, the author of Hebrews can categorically state that it is impossible to repent again after having fallen away, which does not necessitate loss of salvation. Neither is it a repentance to recover fellowship with God, nor even a repentance related to receiving the forgiveness of a particular sin. God may indeed forgive the Hebrew readers of their persistent spiritual lethargy as He did with the Exodus generation, but this does not mean He will change His mind so as to allow them to enter His rest. The repentance being emphasized here is a repentance which presumes that a simple change of mind, and closely connected to this, a change in a course of action, can bring back again what was already foolishly forfeited through persistent apostate thinking. It is a repentance which thoughtlessly assumes that it can make another decision after a decisive decision has already been made. In other words, the Hebrew readers may confess their sin before God like the Exodus generation did (Num 14:40), and God may forgive them (Num 14:20), but God will still discipline and withhold the spiritual blessings which they otherwise would have received had they not acted in the way they did (Num 14:21-23, 44-45). What is being discussed here is a repentance which cannot change the consequences of a previous pivotal decision.

Though Esau and the Exodus generation are good examples to help the readers understand what kind of falling away cannot be repented of, the sacred author updates these Old Testament illustrations to fit the New Testament situation at hand. What is presented in Hebrews 6 is the New Testament doctrine and application of this particular Old

Testament truth. As such, the author therefore establishes a one to one relationship between *repent again* and *re-crucifying*. The Greek preposition *ana* is placed on the verb *to crucify* which changes it to mean, "*re-crucify.*" The Greek preposition *ana* very often means *again* when it used as a compound. With interest, *ana* has also been tacked onto the infinitive *to make new* so as to mean *renew*. The connection therefore between *again to renew into repentance* and *re-crucifying* cannot be overlooked. This further creates a strong contrast between the *once* in 6:4, and the *again* in 6:6. Here in the context of Hebrews 6:4-6, a second repentance, after having once become a Christian and then later having fallen away, is impossible.

However, the real onus here is upon *having fallen away*, a decisive decision to move away from fundamental Christian truths into the shadows of Judaism, and not upon the second repentance. In other words, it is the falling away which brings about the situation in which a second repentance or renewal is impossible. If the Hebrew readers fall away from the faith by going back into Old Covenant teaching, then they cannot repent or change their mind, or change their course of action to recover what they have forfeited. Under such a scenario, not only will God not permit them to grow up, but they would not be able to grow up spiritually anyway. One simply cannot use the Old Covenant priesthood to advance himself spiritually into the heavenly realities of the Order of Melchizedek. To relapse back into another form of Judaism is to go back before the cross which automatically forfeits the priesthood of Christ and its heavenly tabernacle. With regard to the Hebrew readers, it is also to favor the Old Testament priesthood over the New Testament priesthood. As such, if they fall away back into the Old Covenant religion, then they must repent about the cross and the New Testament priesthood yet again in order to get back on track. In other words, if they want to grow up spiritually after having fallen away, then they must start over again if they want to recover. This would involve a second repentance which the author says is impossible.

This second repentance is a therefore a *repentance from apostasy* so as to recover what they have already lost. In the context of Hebrews, it is an apostasy which denies the final once for all significance of the cross, and this means nothing other than losing out on the experience of the heavenly realities of the Melchizedekian Priesthood, which is also the way into God's inheritance rest. By relapsing back into the Old Covenant priesthood, they will permanently lose out on their New Testament priesthood for good. A second repentance to regain the experience of the Melchizedekian Priesthood after committing apostasy back into the old Levitical system is out of the question. They have simply drifted too far downstream to recover what was lost, and no amount of crying or even a repentant change of mind or heart can bring it back.

Moreover, the author of Hebrews leaves no doubt this repentance is impossible because it resembles all too closely an initial conversion repentance, which is both unrepeatable and irreversible. Once a Christian repudiates the great spiritual meaning of the cross, i.e., regards common the blood of the covenant (Heb 10:29), there is no such thing as another repentance which can remedy the situation. The writer of Hebrews puts it yet another way, "There no longer remains a sacrifice for sins, but a terrifying expectation of judgment and the fury of fire which will consume the adversaries (10:26)." If one could repent again after this particular apostasy, it would be equivalent to re-crucifying the Savior a second time, exposing Him yet again to the public shame which He experienced while on the cross. The Melchizedekian Priesthood is a final priesthood based on the one time death of Christ, which cannot be re-bartered for again once given up. The fact of the matter is that God Himself will not repent with regard to the Melchizedekian Priesthood (7:21). Thus the inverse is also true. The Hebrew readers cannot repent if they go back to the Levitical priesthood, precisely because God has sworn with an oath in which He will not repent, "Thou are a priest forever according to the Order of Melchizedek (7:21)." This means that that there can be no going back to the Old Covenant Levitical system. To go back to such a system is to go contrary to the supernatural oath of God. It also goes contrary to the whole import of what the cross really means.

Now the author knows that objectively the great humiliation of the cross cannot be repeated, but it still can be attempted subjectively through apostate carnal thinking. The author therefore says here, "re-crucifying *to themselves* the Son of God (Heb 6:6)." If the Hebrew readers commit apostasy against the meaning of the cross, and then later try to repent, they would be *subjectively* crucifying the Son of God to themselves once again. It is not that objectively speaking Christ could be crucified again, but that their apostate practices show their evil rejection of the meaning of the cross. As such, God will swiftly judge them for this.

This is why God will not allow the Hebrew readers to press onto maturity, much less recover what they lost. In such a scenario, their attempt to return again to the cross brings about a blasphemous situation which can only bring about judgment, and never spiritual recovery. If they commit this apostasy against the meaning of the cross, there will be no way out of God's judgment. Even if the Hebrew readers admit their sin, God will certainly forgive them, but this does not mean that He will let them go without punishment. If the Hebrew readers do relapse back into the old system, then they will be stopped dead in their tracks without any hope for spiritual recovery. They may perhaps even confess their sin, but they will not be able to repent in the sense of recovering the spiritual assets which they have forfeited. Their loss will be just as irretrievable as what happened to the Exodus generation and what happened to Esau. God will not grant another repentance to those who go back to the old system precisely because it is a sacrilege against the cross. In this way, divine discipline actually intervenes to prevent such a course of action. In this way, it is perhaps better to speak of the perseverance of God, rather than the perseverance of the saints. Here in Hebrews 6, God intervenes to put a stop to a total apostate situation. By refusing another opportunity for a second repentance, God places a limit on the scope of the apostasy. In this way, by the saving judgment of God, they would not be condemned with the world (1 Cor 11:30-32). This is the force of, "if God permits (6:3)."

An Illustration of Further Clarification: Bad Crops are Burned – 6:7-8

In Hebrews 6:7-8, the writer uses an ancient agricultural practice to help clarify his point further:

> For ground that drinks the rain which often falls on it and brings forth vegetation useful to those for whose sake it is also tilled, receives a blessing from God; but if it yields thorns and thistles, it is worthless and close to being cursed, and it ends up being burned (Heb 6:7-8).

That the writer uses another explanatory *for* at the beginning of the sentence means the agricultural illustration given must in some way explain the warning of 6:1-8. Recognizing the difficulty of the doctrines taught in 6:1-8, the writer wants to illustrate what he means by comparing the situation at hand with an agricultural field. Just as a farmer will burn up a field that consistently brings forth thorns and thistles rather than useful vegetation, so this will also happen to the Hebrew readers if they do not wake up spiritually from their sloth. The writer here likens their spiritual sanctification to thorns and thistles, rather than genuine fruit, and the impending consequences of this will be an inevitable fire.

The writer refers his Hebrew readers to the soil. Just as the ground drinks the rain which often falls upon it, so God has watered them very well. God has done everything possible here to expect the best results. Their spiritual sloth is not God's doing. God has watered them, and he has given them ample time to mature properly (5:11-14). Just as a farmer expects useful vegetation from a well cared for garden, so God expects the spiritual fruit from the Hebrew readers. The problem is the spiritual life of the Hebrew readers may wind up being characterized by thorns and thistles rather than genuine spiritual fruit. **Worthless** is the more frank term in describing their spiritual condition. This brings up the natural question: what will a farmer do in such a scenario? Well, the Hebrew readers know that he will set fire to the worthless thorns and thistles, "it ends up being burned (Heb 6:8)." Moreover, the drastic effects of the fire are permanent. Once a worthless garden is burned, a farmer cannot expect any more fruit from it. The time for planting is over. The crop has been lost.

Now this burning does not refer to a loss of salvation, but to the burning of worthless fruits. Just as Paul states that all wood, hay and stubble, i.e., worthless works, shall be burned up at the judgment seat of Christ when God judges the saints (1 Cor 3:10-17), so likewise here in Hebrews. The illustrations are different of course, but the meaning is the same. God will not accept worthless fruit, but will burn it up instead. The fact that the author also says, "***close*** to being cursed," further suggests that he is not talking about loss of eternal salvation. It may perhaps be close, but it is still not eternal hellfire. Even Paul in 1 Corinthians 3:10-17 boldly asserts that God's fiery judgment against the saints does not imply loss of salvation. The fire will burn up everything that is worthless, but not the Christian himself, though the Christian will still experience the pain of the fire. Likewise in Hebrews, the readers themselves are compared to the ground, which cannot be burned. When interpreters see fire they all too often think of hell. However, God often warns His own people, both in the Old and New Testaments not in a few places, about the fires of judgment which do not imply loss of salvation.

CHAPTER EIGHT

THE GREAT SIGNIFICANCE OF THE ORDER OF MELCHIZEDEK – 7:1-10:25

The Order of Melchizedek Demands a New Covenant – 7:1-8:13

Through the priesthood of Christ (2:17-18), through His identification with man (2:9-14), through His death on the cross (2:9), the transcendent, sinless, Son of God is now in a position to elevate man from his current slavery into sonship (2:14-18). The enslaving fear of death (2:15) contradicts the whole idea of sonship and universal dominion as mentioned in Hebrews 2:5-8.[101] Contrary to the original divine will, man is actually held under the dominion of death and Satan (2:15), but through the exalted priesthood of the Son of God who is above all the angels, including Satan himself, man can be delivered from this slavery.

In Hebrews 2 we have one of the first discussions of the high priesthood of Christ (2:17-18). This is what the author of Hebrews really wants to emphasize. He wants to teach the Hebrew readers about their so great high priest in the heavenly places. Later in the book of Hebrews, the high priesthood of Christ will be called the Order of Melchizedek, the royal eternal priesthood positioned at the right hand of God in the heavenly tabernacle (7:1-9:28). As such, this theme, first mentioned

---

[101] Dods, p. 268.

briefly in 2:17-18, will later become the main argument of the book (4:14-10:25).

Hebrews 5-10 is actually an extended theological discourse on the meaning of the first communion service at the Last Supper. There Jesus told His disciples, "This cup which is poured out for you is the **New Covenant** in My **blood** (Luke 22:20)." This is exactly the precise theme of Hebrews 7-10, where the author brings together both Psalm 110 and Jeremiah 31 from the Old Testament. It is no coincidence that immediately after the discourse on the Order of Melchizedek in chapter seven the author quickly begins to explain to the Hebrew readers in chapter eight that the apocalyptic days of the New Covenant now have a spiritual application to them inside the church, albeit ahead of schedule. Moreover in chapters nine and ten, the reason why the eschatological days of the New Covenant and/or Testament have been inaugurated is because Christ has made a once for all eschatological sacrifice (9:11-10:18). There is thus a strong relationship between priesthood and covenant, the latter being based on the former (7:11), and if the priesthood is changed, then of necessity there must also be a change of covenants as well (7:11-12; 9:15-22).

As such, when Jesus told his disciples that the cup was the New Covenant in His blood, this means that the cup pictured His priesthood so that it is possible to say, "This cup which is poured out for you is the New Covenant in my **priesthood** (blood)." The relationship between priesthood and covenant is one of the great themes in the book of Hebrews, so much so that chapters seven and eight indicate that the inauguration of the New Covenant is based on the Order of Melchizedek. This explains why there has been a change of covenants from the old to the new. The Order of Melchizedek has replaced the order of Aaron and Levi. This being so, there must also be a change from the Old Covenant to the new. It is this vital truth which the Hebrew readers need to desperately understand. If Jesus Christ is their new heavenly high priest in the heavenly holy of holies, then they can no longer be under the authority of the Old Covenant whose priesthood was on the earth.

From 4:14-10:18, the author of Hebrews teaches about the New Testament Order of Melchizedek in contrast to the Old Covenant Aaronic order, with Hebrews 10 being the climax of the epistle in regard to both theological explanation and warning. Here in this chapter, the theological explanation of the Order of Melchizedek comes to an end in 10:18. Then in 10:19, the book of Hebrews shifts into a new direction as to how to put this Melchizedekian Priesthood into daily practice, and this shift of emphasis carries all the way through to the end of the book. Here the author speaks about putting the Melchizedekian Priesthood of the New Testament into practice by faith, and this whole process begins in 10:19 as the author calls his readers to worship God in a new and living way inside the heavenly holy of holies (10:19-25). Moreover, this is a great spiritual privilege which can only be conferred through the priestly Order of Melchizedek. The Old Covenant Aaronic order never could provide such a majestic position in heaven. In fact, the Old Testament high priest could only enter the earthly holy of holies once a year (Heb 9:7). However, a saint under the authority of New Testament grace, under the authority of the Order of Melchizedek, can personally experience the heavenly holy of holies at all times, provided that he continues to persevere in faith. He can personally experience this heavenly house of God as he perseveres every day in these great spiritual privileges (3:6; 4:14-16; 10:19-23).

However, this spiritual priesthood can only be practiced by faith. This is why the author emphasizes the principle of faith both at the end of chapter 10 and then especially throughout chapter 11. This being so, they are to occupy themselves with their great high priest in heaven, the person of Christ Himself, in the midst of adversity and divine discipline (12:1-13). Following this, a final warning is given at the end of chapter 12 before finally concluding the letter with a series of general ethical injunctions listed in chapter 13. Thus, there is a strong emphasis upon practical spiritual living from 10:19-13:19, not that the other chapters were not practical, but that the theological arguments and severe warnings are to lead them to live a godly life. In other words, the Order of Melchizedek is presented in a such a glorious and majestic way, if not in holy reverence, that this is to be a great inspiration for the Hebrew readers to live godly lives. It could also be put in yet another way: if the Order of Melchizedek does not inspire the Hebrew readers to godly living, then they will be judged. This means the Order of Melchizedek is not a theological theory which is only to be discussed among doctors of theology, but is to be put into practice just as the Levitical priesthood was put into practice.

The Order of Melchizedek is an order of worship which must be put into practice just like the Levitical priesthood. This is what Hebrews 7:1-10:18 is all about. The major difference between the priesthoods is not only the Order of Melchizedek is far superior, but it is also real, even though it is carried out on an invisible spiritual plane. The Levitical priesthood was a mere model of the heavenly one (Heb 8:5; 9:9-10). The Order of Melchizedek on the other hand is real, although it is an invisible order in contrast to the visible fleshly Old Testament tabernacle (9:1-28). It is therefore a priesthood which cannot be seen, touched, felt or sensed. This places great stress on the worshiper. One can worship God only by faith (Heb 11:6), and in the case of the Hebrew readers, this means that one cannot worship God through the conveniences of Old Testament religious rituals. The Order of Melchizedek is so awesome it cannot be reduced to fleshly religion, and this places a great temptation before the Christian worshiper: is Christian worship real?

How does one worship an invisible God? This is precisely the question the author of Hebrews answers throughout the book, and here in 7:1-10:18, he lays the theological foundation to help understand it from a New Testament point of view. Since the Messiah has already come and gone, and since His priestly role on the cross is an unrepeatable act which fulfilled the great meaning of the tabernacle sacrifices, God has thus removed all of Judaistic religious traditions and rituals which the worshiper could see with his eyes, listen with his ears, and smell with his nose. The sacred writer, therefore, is trying to convince his Jewish-Christian readers that everything they grew up with were only shadows (Heb 8:5-10:18) of the heavenly reality relative to New Testament worship. This is a very tall order indeed. How does one worship God in the heavenly holy of holies right now even though he is still physically on the earth? This is answered by Hebrews 7-10, and the writer of Hebrews makes it very clear that one worships God not by the religious form which he practices, but by the spiritual principles he believes and implements into his life. The whole thrust of Hebrews is that Christ died once for all, the major theme of Hebrews 10. Such an incredible sacrificial act has inaugurated a glorious new eschatological order of history, covenant, and worship, which can only be ignored at the worshiper's peril.

Immediately following the severe warning of 6:1-8, the author begins to encourage his readers once again (Heb 6:9-20) before embarking on the discussion of the Order of Melchizedek (7:1-28). He is actually convinced of better things than judgment for them (Heb 6:9). He is convinced they will spiritually mature, that God will allow this yet to take place in their spiritual walk with the Lord. Though they are close to it, they have yet to commit apostasy.

Moreover, they have been saved once for all (Heb 6:4-5), and God is not unjust so as to forget their previous good works (Heb 6:10). In the past they have ministered to God's name, and some of them continue to minister to God (Heb 6:10). As such, even though God may not permit them to grow up (Heb 6:1-3), God is still not unjust to forget their previous good works (Heb 6:10). At the same time, what they did yesterday needs to be maintained throughout the rest of their lives, "And we desire that each one of you show the same diligence so as to realize the full assurance of hope until the end, so that you will not be sluggish, but imitators of those who through faith and patience inherit the promises (Heb 6:11-12)." They still are required to persevere in their faith to receive their inheritance, and the Order of Melchizedek can give the spiritual power necessary to enable them to continue to endure.

So finally, after having severely warned the Hebrew readers about their great peril, that they will not escape if they neglect their so great salvation (Heb 2:1-3), that God may not allow them to enter His rest (Heb 3:7-4:11), that God may not permit them to grow up (Heb 6:1-3), the author really begins to explain to them what he has wanted to teach them all along, i.e., the Order of Melchizedek. The author may severely warn his readers, but he is still convinced of better things for them, not only because they have already been once for all saved and that God will not forget their previous good works, but more than that, because Jesus Christ is their heavenly High Priest according to the Order of Melchizedek. The Hebrew readers have available to them an indestructible, eternal priesthood which confers resurrection powers to its recipients. This is the now the subject of discussion for the next three chapters, the great theme of the entire book.

Thus, even though the Hebrews readers may not be spiritually ready for the Order of Melchizedek (Heb 5:11-14), the author is going to teach them about it anyway (Heb 7:1-28). He refuses to teach them the basics all over again (Heb 6:1). They have already been Christians much too long to re-teach them the basics (Heb 5:12). The Hebrew readers therefore have no choice but to press on to maturity or face God's fiery judgment (Heb 6:1-8). There is thus a strong ultimatum here: grow up or suffer judgment. As such, regardless of their spiritual condition, the author pushes on ahead to begin discussing the lofty matters of the Order of Melchizedek in chapters 7-10. More to the point, if the Hebrew readers do not get a hold of this truth, then judgment is certain (Heb 10:26-31). *Today* is their day to stop hardening their hearts and start believing the divine promises which accompany salvation, divine promises which they need to hold onto, divine promises which will richly reward them with great blessing,   "Therefore, brethren, since we have confidence to enter the holy place by the blood of Jesus, by a new and living way which He inaugurated through the veil, that is, His flesh, and since we have a great high priest over the house of God, let us draw near ...(Heb 10:19-22a)."

Hebrews 10:19-23 is the goal that the author wants his readers to reach, i.e., to personally experience the heavenly Order of Melchizedek in their souls. He desperately wants them to experience the priesthood of Christ as this will satisfy their longing for a genuine priesthood like no other. This will also enable them to endure to the end, and give them great motivation to serve the living God. Hebrews 10:19-23 is the spiritual goal the author has been heading towards all along. It is this spiritual transcendence in the heavenly house of God that he wants his readers to know about. However, before he gets there, he first must teach them the doctrinal principles behind all of this, and this is all laid out in Hebrews 7-9. Before he talks about this new spiritual worship experience (Heb 10:19-23), he first must teach them the hows and whys of all this (Heb 7:1-10:18). This he begins to do in Hebrews 7 by describing the significance of the person of Melchizedek as found in both Genesis 14 and Psalm 110.

Hebrews 7 is divided up into three major parts. The first part is 7:1-3. Here the author establishes the historical person of Melchizedek is a messianic type. The second part begins in 7:4 and goes up until 7:10. These verses establish the historical person of Melchizedek is actually superior to both Abraham and Levi. Then, the final section begins in 7:11 and goes through the end of the chapter. This section establishes the superiority of the Melchizedekian Priesthood compared to the Levitical priesthood, and the whole thrust here is that the eschatological days of Psalm 110 have begun. David prophesied in Psalm 110 that there would be a messianic King-Priest who will be given a royal eternal priesthood according to the order or Melchizedek far above all earthly rule and authority. The author of Hebrews now proclaims that these days have now started, and this means not only an abrogation of the Levitical priesthood, but also of the entire Old Covenant as well (Heb 7:11-8:13). It is no coincidence that the discussion of the New Covenant immediately follows the discussion on the Order of Melchizedek. Just as the giving of the Old Covenant was established upon the Levitical priesthood, so the giving of the New Covenant is established upon the Melchizedekian Priesthood. The inauguration of the Melchizedekian Priesthood is why the Hebrew readers are now under the New Covenant as opposed to the old. This is also why the New Covenant is far superior to the Old Covenant, precisely because it is based on a superior priesthood. So here in these verses, the writer of Hebrews asserts that what the Levitical priesthood could never produce, namely perfection (Heb 7:11-19), the Order of Melchizedek has done (Heb 7:21-28). Moreover, the implications of all this is nothing less than eschatological, and the natural question is why would the Hebrew readers want to hang onto the old system?

This was the spiritual test for the Hebrew readers. It is also a perennial problem even in the modern church. Generally speaking, Christian people would rather hang onto cultural religious traditions full of dead works than experience the spiritual privileges of the New Testament grace. Like the author of Hebrews, it becomes very difficult to teach straight Bible. When the Bible starts to contradict people's religious cultural traditions, the majority tends to side with religious culture rather than with the Bible. The average Christian seems to be more generally impressed with his own religious traditions than he is with the Order of Melchizedek, and the reason for this is very simple – unbelief. The modern Christian faces the same problems the Hebrew readers faced. The Order of Melchizedek is too spectacular to believe. It is simply too good and too heavenly to be really true. As such, religious culture often trumps genuine Christianity. The end result is the glory of God is clouded out by human religious traditions.

In the book of Hebrews, the awesome glory of Christianity was being overshadowed and squelched by the shadows of Judaism. The sacred writer thus writes to tell his readers the Old Testament worship system was only an earthly model of the coming eschatological reality – the Order of Melchizedek – and that this priesthood is what they really need. Moreover, if they truly understand and believe in the glorious Order of Melchizedek, they will not want to go back to the old system. In Christianity, giving up the Old Covenant and priesthood is not a loss, but in fact a great improvement in both spirituality and holiness. Once they taste of the superiority of Christianity, they will not settle for anything less. This is why the author begins his discussion on the Order of Melchizedek.

How does the author of Hebrews establish the Old Covenant has been outdated? How does he convince a group of Jewish people who prided themselves in the Old Covenant that times have changed? This is precisely the problem set before the writer of Hebrews, and he tackles this problem first of all by going back to a primitive historical event in Abraham's life recorded in Genesis 14.[102] This was when the great king-priest Melchizedek met Abraham. This meeting between Abraham and Melchizedek even occurred before God entered into covenant with Abraham (Gen 15:1-21). So here in Hebrews 7:1-10 the sacred writer will remind his readers about the historical personage of Melchizedek, the king-priest who blessed Abraham. Then he will explain to them the great spiritual significance of Abraham's historical encounter with Melchizedek. This rather obscure Old Testament historical encounter will later on become the basis for the abrogation of both the Levitical priesthood and the entire Old Covenant as well. The author here uses the Old Testament Scriptures themselves to show his readers the Old Covenant has been superseded. He will thus show them this spiritual principle is something which the Old Testament itself actually teaches. To put it another way, to teach the Old Covenant is outmoded is not an attack on the Old Testament. It is, in fact, completely consistent with

---

[102] It is no coincidence that before Abraham entered into covenant with God in Genesis 15, he was first visited by the king-priest Melchizedek in Genesis 14. As such, even with the Abrahamic Covenant, priesthood precedes covenant.

what the Old Testament teaches about itself.[103] Such is the great spiritual significance of Abraham's encounter with Melchizedek.

Bible history precedes Bible doctrine. Bible history is the basis for Bible doctrine. As such, the author will draw from the history of the Old Testament and will then explain the great spiritual significance of that historical event. In 7:1-3, there are inserted 5 historical facts taken from Genesis 14. In 7:4-10, the author then provides the theological or spiritual interpretation of those facts, which, in turn, have great eschatological consequences the Hebrew readers need to understand (7:11-28). The historical encounter between Abraham and Melchizedek in Genesis 14 thus points to the future eschatological reality of the royal priesthood of the Messiah the readers need to appropriate into their lives daily. This is what Hebrews 7-10 are essentially all about.

With great interest, the office of king-priest was forbidden under the Old Covenant. In fact, the great spiritual leader of Judah, King Uzziah, was stricken with leprosy because he presumed upon the priesthood (2 Chron 26:1-21). Though a positive believer for most of his life, he did not persevere in the spiritual life prescribed for him by God. He presumptuously invaded the office of the priest, which God forbade. This brings up the problem of Melchizedek. Melchizedek was both a king and a priest at the same time. Thus the historical person of Melchizedek contradicts what was forbidden by the Mosaic Law. How can this be?

The author of Hebrews gets out of this dilemma by stating that Melchizedek was a messianic type. In 7:3, Melchizedek was made **like** the Son of God. Even though the kings were not were not allowed to usurp the office of priest, the Son of God can. The amalgamation of king-priest is something designed only for Messiah and for no one else. This was Messiah's prerogative (Dan 7:1-13). Moreover, Melchizedek was both **before** the Old Covenent Law which forbade this union, and he is an historical type of the future Messiah **after** the Old Covenent Law.

The literal historical event of the king priest Melchizedek mirrors the future eschatological event of the Messiah. This is what is meant by a type. The historical person of Melchizedek is a type. This means that his office is exaggerated or treated like a hyperbole. However, this exaggeration or hyperbole will later be fulfilled by the antitype, by the

---

[103]   It is also true that the Old Testament is far more than just the Old Covenant, something which many seem to forget.

Messiah Himself. Thus it can be said that Melchizedek is, "without father, without mother, without genealogy, having neither beginning of days nor end of life, but made *like* the Son of God, he remains a priest perpetually (Heb 7:3)."

Now this verse is a purposeful exaggeration. Melchizedek is not the Messiah, and he must still have a genealogy, father and mother and so forth. Even Jesus had a mother. However, his genealogy is never traced or discussed with regard to his priesthood. The author of Hebrews therefore seizes upon this silence to teach that the Melchizedekian order has no succession. The whole Melchizedekian order is occupied by Himself. This one man constitutes the entire order. He succeeds no one in office and no one succeeds him, "he is thus a type of a messianic priest precisely because he discharges forever all priestly functions in his own single person – no predecessors nor successors."[104] Such is the legacy of Melchizedek. "Since Melchizedek did not belong to any successional priestly order, but was himself the entire order, the author of Hebrews says this is just like the Son of God."[105] Since Melchizedek is a type of Christ, the author can exaggerate the historical event about Melchizedek because Christ will fulfill all of the exaggerated things said about him. Moreover, this is not without precedent since David's messianic psalms do exactly the same thing. The person of David was exaggerated, not for mere hyperbole, but so that he might picture what the Messiah will later do in eschatological reality.

Now the main point of the author's argument is that this Melchizedek indeed was a great man, "Observe how great this man was to whom Abraham, the Patriarch, gave a tenth of the choicest spoils (Heb 7:4)." The author reminds his readers that Abraham gave the king-priest Melchizedek a tenth of the choicest spoils of war. More than that, Abraham was under no such law to pay a tithe to Melchizedek as "the payment of tithes to him was a tribute to his personal greatness."[106] Furthermore, Melchizedek blessed Abraham, not the other way around (Gen 14:19-20; Heb 7:7). This means at once that Melchizedek was indeed greater than Abraham, "Without any dispute the lesser is blessed by the greater (Heb 7:7)." These two historical realities therefore establish that Melchizedek

---

[104]   Dods, pp. 306-08.
[105]   Ibid., p. 306.
[106]   Ibid, p. 309.

is superior not only to Abraham but also to the Levitical priesthood, and the reason why is very simply stated, "and, so to speak, through Abraham even Levi, who received tithes *paid* tithes, for he was still in the loins of his father when Melchizedek met him (Heb 7:9-10)." If Abraham paid a tithe to Melchizedek, then Levi did as well since all Levites are descendants of Abraham. Through the patriarch Abraham, the Levitical priests also paid a tithe to Melchizedek, and this is more than interesting precisely because under the Law, Levi does not pay tithes, but rather receives them instead. The author of Hebrews sharply points out that well before the Old Covenent Law, Levi already paid a tithe to Melchizedek, "The act of Levi's father Abraham determined his relationship to Melchizedek."[107]   What's more, Levites are mere mortal men (Heb 7:8), but the Order of Melchizedek is eternal since no genealogy is mentioned with reference to his priesthood (Heb 7:1-3).

Melchizedek is therefore without question superior to the entire Jewish Old Covenant system, and this has tremendous eschatological consequences. The superiority of Melchizedek will now be used to show that the Old Covenant has been superseded precisely because the Messiah is a high priest according to a new heavenly order above Aaron, a theme which carries over into the rest of the chapter. In 7:11-14, the author asserts the Levitical priesthood was only provisional, whereas the Melchizedekian is permanent.[108] Then, in 7:15-19, the Levitical priesthood was hereditary, whereas the Melchizedekian Priesthood is eternal.[109] In 7:20-22, the Levitical priesthood came without an oath, whereas the Melchizedekian Priesthood came with an oath, i.e, that of Psalm 110:4.[110] In 7:23-25, the Levitical priesthood was both plural and successional, whereas the Melchizedekian Priesthood is both singular and enduring.[111] Then finally in 7:26-28, the author categorically states the Order of Melchizedek is an eternally perfect high priestly order without any rivals or competitors. It stands alone because of its eternal perfection.

Now what all of this means is that Old Covenent Law and priesthood has been superseded by a superior covenant and priesthood. In other words, the efficacy of the Old Covenent Law is entirely dependent

---

[107]   Westcott, p. 177.
[108]   Dods, p. 306.
[109]   Ibid.
[110]   Ibid.
[111]   Ibid.

upon the efficacy of the Levitical priesthood.[112] This being the case, if the Levitical priesthood is inefficient, then so is the entire Mosaic legislation. The inability of the Levitical priesthood to achieve the goal of perfection under the Mosaic Law implied its own abrogation.[113] The imperfection of both the Levitical priesthood and the Mosaic Law is proved by the fact that another priestly order was necessary:

> ... a perfect priesthood is absolutely necessary because the priesthood is the soul of the entire legislation. All of the arrangements of the Law, the entire administration of the people, involves the priesthood. If there is a failure in the priesthood, the whole system breaks down. The Old Covenant was at the first entered into by sacrifice and could only be maintained by a renewal of sacrifice. The priesthood stood out as the essential part of the whole Jewish economy. Without the priesthood there was no approach to God. To change the priesthood is to change all.[114]

The key to understanding this is Hebrews 7:11-12. If one understands these verses, he understands the eschatological and apocalyptic relationship between the Old Covenant and the New Testament and/or Covenant. He understands why the Old Covenant was inferior and why the New Covenant is superior. He understands why the author so seriously warns the Hebrew readers not to go back to the old outdated ways. If the Old Covenant priesthood was inferior, therefore the entire Mosaic legislation is inferior. The Old Covenent Law could not provide perfection. It could only point to a better eschatological reality, the Order of Melchizedek. Furthermore, the prediction of the Melchizedekian order proves the abrogation of the entire Old Covenant system, both its priesthood and laws, "Now if perfection was through the Levitical priesthood (*for on the basis of it the people received the Law*), what further need was there for another priest to arise according to the Order of Melchizedek, and not designated according to the order of Aaron? For when the priesthood is changed, of necessity there takes place a change of law also (Heb 7:11-12)."

---

[112] Westcott, p. 180.
[113] Lane, p. 197.
[114] Dods, p. 311.

Notice especially the interesting phrase in parenthesis, "for on the basis of the priesthood the people received the Law." This is a rather remarkable parenthesis. Here the author asserts the Exodus generation did not receive the Mosaic Law directly, but through the priesthood. This means that even the Old Covenant was mediated through the priesthood. It is generally thought that God gave Israel the Law first and then later on instituted the priesthood. However, this widespread opinion is done away with in Hebrews 7:11. Not only does this understanding contradict Hebrews 7:11, but also the historical record itself in Exodus. Even in Exodus, the priesthood was the basis or foundation for the Mosaic Law.

Exodus 19-20 shows that while the provisions of the Mosaic Law were declared through the fiery smoke of Mt. Sinai, the people did not enter into the Old Covenant itself until chapter 24, *after Moses had sprinkled all the people and the book with blood*, "For when every commandment had been spoken by Moses to all the people according to the Law, he took the blood of calves and the goats, with water and scarlet wool and hyssop, and sprinkled both the book itself and all the people, saying, ' *this is the blood of the covenant which God commanded you* (Heb 9:19-20)." Moses therefore spoke of the *blood* of the Old Covenant, which is actually a reference to the priesthood of the Old Covenant, and the people did not enter into the covenant until after the sprinkling of blood, "Therefore even the first covenant was not inaugurated without blood … and according to Law, one may almost say, all things are cleansed with blood, and without shedding of blood there is no forgiveness (Heb 9:18, 22)."

In Exodus 19, the people could not approach God. They are told to keep their distance lest they die. After this, God gave them the 10 commandments (Exo 20:1-17). More commandments were then given in chapters 21-23, but the people themselves did not enter into covenant until Exodus 24. In fact, at Mt. Sinai, they had to keep their distance while the commandments were being given. However, in Exodus 24, they finally did enter into the Old Covenant with God, and this is where Moses sprinkled them with blood and water, "So Moses took the blood and sprinkled it on the people and said, ' Behold the blood of the covenant, which the Lord has made with you in accordance with all these words (Ex 24:8)." After this, "the elders of Israel ate and drank with God, and the sons of Israel saw the glory of God on Mt. Sinai (Ex 24:9-18)." It is also no coincidence that immediately following this event, God gave the commandments concerning the tabernacle, from which the practices of the Levitical priesthood were based on (Ex 25-31).

Thus, when the author of Hebrews says that on the basis of the priesthood the people received the Mosaic Law (Heb 7:11), he is referring to the history of Exodus 19-24. The Exodus generation entered into the Old Covenant through the sprinkling of blood. In other words, through the priesthood they received the Old Covenant. Now obviously, the Levitical priesthood had not yet been set up when Moses sprinkled the people with the blood, but Moses was still a Levite. Moreover, the priests at that time were the first-born sons of Israel. It was not until later that God transferred the job of the priest from the first-born sons to the tribe of Levi (Num 3:1-51). The priesthood did therefore exist when Moses sprinkled everyone with the blood. Later the Levites became the priests, not by changing the priesthood, but by exchanging them through redemption (Num 3:12-13; 45). So in this sense, the Exodus generation entered into the Old Covenant on the basis of the priesthood. Even with the Old Covenant, there was still blood.

Exodus 19-24 and Hebrews 7:11-12 clarifies the relationship between the Old Covenant and the inauguration of the New Covenant. Since the priesthood is the basis for the Old Covenant, this means "when the priesthood is changed, of necessity there takes place a change of law also (Heb 7:12)." *Law* here in this context is a synonymn for *covenant*. For the Hebrew readers, this means that since there has been a change of the priesthood, from that of the Levitical to the Melchizedekian, then there must be a change of covenants as well, i.e., from the Old Covenant to the New Covenant.

In addition, this also means the New Testament church has a spiritual application of the New Covenant on the basis of the Melchizedekian Priesthood, and why it is no longer under the Mosaic Law. The church has a new high priest in Jesus Christ, and therefore a New Testament and/or Covenant. This is precisely why the author of Hebrews spends so much time talking about the priesthood. He understands that everything stands or falls on the priesthood. Furthermore, if he can properly teach them about the priesthood, they will understand why they can no longer remain under the authority of the Old Covenent Law. Since the priesthood has changed, the covenant must also change. Therefore, one cannot go back to the Old Covenant, and the Order of Melchizedek explains why this is the case. Hebrews 7:17 even strongly affirms that God will not repent with regard to the transition from the old and new priesthoods. This is backed up by the unusual solemnity of the oath given in Psalm 110 that the Messiah will be an eternal king-priest forever. There is thus no going back to the old system.

Not surprisingly, Hebrews 8 then introduces the New Covenant. In Hebrews 7, the whole discussion is about the priesthood, and this leads to the discussion of the New Covenant in Hebrews 8. The strong implication of Hebrews 7-8 is that the New Covenant is founded upon the Melchizedekian Priesthoood of Christ. What's more, the very words, "New Covenant," antiquate the Mosaic Law, "When He said,' a New Covenant,' He has made the first one obsolete. But whatever is becoming obsolete and growing old is ready to disappear (Heb 8:13)." The Order of Melchizedek clears the way for the inauguration of the New Covenant, which supersedes the Old Covenent Law, and makes it obsolete.

Now having a spiritual application of the New Covenant under the grace of the New Testament does not mean that one can live a lawless life, "for this is the covenant that I will make with the house of Israel after those days says the Lord: *I will put My laws into their minds, and I write them on their hearts* (Heb 8:10)." The Hebrew readers may not be under the Old Testament Law, but they *are* under authority of grace in the New Testament, and none of God's holy standards have been compromised in the changeover from the Old Testament Law to New Testament grace. While the New Covenant is a total replacement of the Old Covenant, this does not mean that God's holy standards have somehow been forgotten along the way. Nine out of the ten commandments are repeated in the New Testament, along with a host of many other commands consistent with the demands of a holy God. Many of the Old Covenant principles are the same and even carry over into the New Testament. Nonetheless, the New Covenant still stands on its own as a complete system which does not need to be supplemented by the Old Covenant. To try and fulfill both covenants at the same time would, in the end, compromise both.

Jeremiah the prophet categorically states the New Covenant will be different from the old one, "*Not like the covenant* which I made with their fathers in the day that I took them out of Egypt (Jer 31:31)." Ezekiel the prophet then adds the New Covenant will be a covenant characterized by the universal ministry of the Holy Spirit in the hearts and minds of God's people, "I will put My Spirit within you and cause you to walk in My statutes, and you will be careful to observe My ordinances (Ezk 36:27)." As such, not only will the New Covenant be different than the Old Covenant, it will also give supernatural spiritual provisions largely absent from the Old Covenant, and these supernatural provisions will enable God's people to live godly lives.

In addition, since Hebrews 7-8 connects the Order of Melchizedek with the New Covenant, this provides believers with resurrection life from the heavenly tabernacle to help them overcome sin and temptation. As such, the eternal divine laws of God have not been abrogated in the process of changing covenants. There are many commands under New Testament grace too. Hebrews 13 is full of ethical injunctions which God requires of His worshipers (Heb 13:1-17). As a matter of fact, a higher standard of living of supernatural character is actually required of the New Testament saint. With higher spiritual privileges comes higher spiritual responsibilities. Hence the warnings that are seen in the book of Hebrews.

While many decry disrespect for the laws of the Old Covenant, few decry the basic disrespect for the holy integrity of New Testament grace. Many, much like the Hebrew readers themselves, have presumed the New Testament is inadequate of itself to sanctify the saints, that the Old Covenent Law is still necessary to make God's people holy. This is essentially an attitude of unbelief in the new system, not much different than the unbelief of the Hebrew readers, in which the sufficiency of the New Testament grace is being questioned and doubted. Why is it that so many think that the New Testament is somehow lax and therefore needs to be supplemented by the Old Covenent Law? The book of Hebrews teaches that it is actually most dangerous to doubt the sufficiency of New Testament grace. To suggest that the Old Covenant is needed to enhance the holiness of New Testament grace is insulting to the Spirit of grace (Heb 10:29). It is the Holy Spirit who makes God's people holy, one of the great provisions of the New Covenant, not the Old Covenent Law. Worse, this attitude is disrespectful to the high priestly work of Christ, both with regard to His work on the cross, and His high priestly session in heaven at the right hand of God, according to the Order of Melchizedek.

The Old Testament Tabernacle Worship System Was Only Ritual – 9:1-28

That the Old Testament tabernacle was not heaven is the big thought of Hebrews 9. It was only a copy of the true tabernacle in heaven. The very fact the Old Testament tabernacle was on the earth proves the transitory nature of the entire Old Covenant. If the Old Testament priesthood is an earthly one, then so also is the entire Old Testament Law, and while this is clearly taught in Hebrews 7 and 8, it is even further emphasized in Hebrews 9. To discuss the difference between the Old Covenant worship system and the New Testament worship system is really to talk about the difference between the earth and heaven. The Old Covenant was an earthly worldly order, whereas the New Testament is distinctly a heavenly order. 9:1-14 distinguishes between the earthly priesthood and the heavenly priesthood, between the Old Testament tabernacle and the New Testament tabernacle, between the house of Moses and the house of Christ. 9:15-22 then teaches the reason why there has been a great transition between these two systems is because Jesus Christ died for sins once for all as a heavenly high priest. Under the Old Covenant, sacrifices were repeated again and again. Not so under the New Covenant. The once for all death of Christ has put an end to the worldly repetitive sacrifices of the Old Covenant.

This emphasis upon the worldliness of the Old Covenant order is stressed immediately in chapter nine, the first verse. In the original Greek, Old Testament sanctuary is explicitly called **worldly** here. The author flatly declares that the Old Covenant tabernacle was a **worldly** sanctuary. The meaning of this is not that there is anything wrong with it, but that it was built by human hands, and is therefore fleshly (Heb 9:11, 24). **Worldly** and *fleshly* in this context does not mean sinful, but rather limited and weak, and if the Old Testament tabernacle and priesthood were weak, then so is the entire Old Covenant. Whatever is true of the priesthood and tabernacle must also be true of the entire Old Covenent Law as well. The Mosaic Law is a reflection of the priesthood, and so if the Old Covenant priesthood is worldly, then so is the Old Covenant. Moreover, if the Old Covenent Law is worldly, then by definition it is also transitory, "The Mosaic tabernacle partook of the nature of the world and therefore was essentially transitory."[115] This, of course, would be very difficult for any Jew to accept, Christian or not. Even for many Christians this is very difficult to accept.

Now does this mean the Old Testament tabernacle and priesthood were worthless? The answer is no. In its time, it had great value. Since it was a copy of heaven, it taught the Jewish people what heaven was really like. More importantly, it pointed to the necessity of the coming Messiah, which is the entire argument of Hebrews 9. The value of the Old Testament tabernacle is not in itself, but in that it points to Messiah. This is why it is so tragically ironic that these Hebrew readers would rather have the earthly Old Covenant system itself rather than the Messiah, even though the entire Old Covenant worship system pointed to Messiah. They missed the whole point of what the Old Covenant priesthood and tabernacle were all about. Even Jesus tried to teach this to the Jews when He was on the earth. He taught them that He Himself was the Temple, something which the Jewish people simply could not understand (John 2:16-21). As Paul writes in Galatians 3:24-27, the Old Covenant was a temporary and provisional order to lead them to Christ, and once Christ has come, the old order is no longer necessary. This is the great theme of Hebrews 9.

In Hebrews 9:1-5, the sacred writer briefly describes the physical characteristics of the Old Testament tabernacle. He cannot speak in great detail about these things because of lack of time (Heb 9:5). However, the main point is the Old Testament tabernacle points to the future reality of the coming of Christ. In other words, the worldly tabernacle prepared the Jews for the eschatological reality, i.e, for heaven itself. This was the great value of the Old Covenant tabernacle and priesthood. It was like an elementary school to teach the Jewish people about what the coming of their Messiah will be like. For its time, therefore, it was exactly what the Jews needed. The Old Testament tabernacle was a type of heaven and so it fleshly illustrated what heaven was like. It portrayed symbolically what already existed in heaven (Heb 8:5; 9:9). God told Moses to make the tabernacle according to the pattern of heaven and showed him how to design it (Heb 8:5).

---

[115]   Westcott, p. 244.

The Old Testament tabernacle was a life size toy modelled after the pattern of heaven itself. Moreover, like all models, they are great for kids, but when they mature they can have the real thing. Here in Hebrews however, since the readers are so immature, they would rather have the toy model than the real thing. This makes no sense, something which the writer is trying to desperately make clear.

Now while Hebrews 9:1-5 the author discusses the arrangement of the tabernacle furniture, in 9:6-10 he briefly discusses how the tabernacle worship system operated. With interest, 9:1-5 emphasizes the difference between the outer holy place and the holy of holies, but with most of the attention focused on the holy of holies itself (Heb 9:3-5). The emphasis on the holy of holies prepares the Hebrew readers for the argument in 9:6-10 concerning the great significance of the Day of Atonement. While the Levitical priests are continually worshipping in the holy place (Heb 9:6), only the high priest is allowed into the holy of holies once a year on the Day of Atonement (Heb 9:7).

The Day of Atonement was the climax of the entire year on the Jewish worship calendar. On this day, once the high priest performed all the necessary sacrifices both for himself and for the people, he was allowed to enter into God's presence within the holy of holies. So on this day, through the representative of the high priest, the people were allowed contact with God. However, the encounter was very brief and only representative, surrounded with a myriad of necessary rituals of blood and water. There was no direct personal encounter with God with the exception of the high priest. Even his encounter was very brief, and then a whole year had to pass by before the encounter could be repeated. Thus, all of this pointed to the limitations of the Old Covenant tabernacle system, "The author's description here emphasizes the limited access to God through the Old Testament offerings."[116]

> The people themselves had no way into the holy place which was open to the priests only, and the priests had no way into the holy of holies which was only open to the high priest alone.[117]

---

[116]　Lane, p. 217.
[117]　Westcott, p. 252.

In reality, rather than open up access, the old sanctuary consisted of a system of barriers between the worshipper and God.[118]

With great irony, even though the gifts and sacrifices were required by Law for the people of Israel to approach God, in the end, these same gifts and sacrifices could not provide the decisive cleansing necessary for direct access to God, "They were very limited in nature as to what they could do."[119] The Old Testament offerings could only wash the flesh (Heb 9:10). They could not wash the conscience (Heb 9:10-14; 10:1-4). In short, the primary weakness of the Levitical system was that it simply could not perfect the worshiper, and this lack of perfection placed great limits on access to God. Without perfection, there can be no right of entry to God's Person. As such, under the Old Covenent Law, God could not be approached (Heb 9:8). As long as the worshiper was imperfect, direct access to God was impossible. The people of Israel were allowed to approach God only through sacrificial ritual provisions, and then only very briefly, and then only representatively.

This lack of direct access to God was to remain in force until the New Covenant time of reformation (Heb 9:10). From an Old Testament perspective, the times of the New Covenant were eschatological and/or apocalyptic. The author of Hebrews calls such days **the time of reformation** (Heb 9:10), **the good things to come** (Heb 9:11), and **the consummation of the ages** (Heb 9:26). However, while the apocalyptic days of the New Covenant have not been fulfilled to the nation of Israel, the eschatological days of the New Testament church have already come. In this sense, while the New Covenant has been inaugurated with the death and resurrection of the Messiah, it has not yet been fulfilled relative to its promises given to national Israel. This delay between the inauguration of the New Covenant and its fulfillment left the door wide open for the New Testament Church to come into existence and enjoy many heavenly benefits ahead of time even though the Messianic Kingdom itself has been temporarily placed into abeyance.

The author makes clear that the supernatural event of the cross, the once for all sacrifice of Christ, has thus brought about the inauguration of these prophesied New Covenant days of spiritual reformation (Heb 9:11-14). It is the sacrifice of Christ which cleanses the conscience, not

---

[118]   Lane, p. 226.
[119]   Ibid, p. 217.

animal sacrifices (Heb 9:14). His once for all sacrifice has decisively purged the worshiper so he can freely approach God. The eschatological reality of the death of Christ has replaced the models and types of the old economy. Genuine cleansing has actually occurred rather than ritual cleansing. Christ has died, and there is now no going back to the old system, the great theme of Hebrews 7-10. Even though the times of the New Covenant kingdom has not been fulfilled as required by many Old Testament prophecies, in great contrast to the limitations of the Mosaic Law, the heavenly truths of the New Testament Church must still be accepted and implemented into the lives of the saints.

The tabernacle ministry of the Old Testament (Heb 9:1-10) provides the necessary background to understand the heavenly ministry of Christ in the heavenly tabernacle (Heb 9:11-14), and this focus is sustained all the way through 10:18.[120] In 9:1-10, the action of the Jewish high priest on the Day of Atonement was the climax of the Old Covenant.[121] However, in 9:11-14, the high priesthood of Christ is now contrasted with it. The work of Christ is so magnificent it can only be understood in terms of contrast. His work on the cross was far more than an earthly event. It was also a supernatural heavenly event which can cleanse the worshiper's conscience, "How much more will the blood of Christ, who through the eternal Spirit offered Himself without blemish to God, cleanse your conscience from dead works to serve the living God (Heb 9:14)?" Here the author of Hebrews emphasizes the spiritual judgment of the death of Christ on the cross. Even though Jesus died physically in Jerusalem on the earth, more than that, He also died spiritually in the heavenly tabernacle offering His own life as a priestly sacrifice according to the Order of Melchizedek. If this was merely an earthly act, He could not be an Aaronic priest according to the Mosaic Law (Heb 8:4), but this does not preclude Him from being a Melchizedekian priest in heaven itself. As the great heavenly high priest according to the Order of Melchizedek, Christ died eschatologically once for all (Heb 9:11-14). It was this great spiritual sacrifice in the heavenly tabernacle which offers direct access to God, not the Old Covenant sacrifices. God is in heaven, and He cannot be propitiated by ritual earthly sacrifices. He can only be propitiated by a real spiritual sacrifice in the heavens, and this once for

---

[120] Ibid., p. 218.
[121] Westcott, p. 255.

all sacrifice is not merely climax of the old Jewish system, but in fact the climax of all history (Heb 9:26). The decisive once for all death of Christ in the heavenly sanctuary has inaugurated an entirely New Covenant and therefore an entirely new age (Heb 9:11-22).

Though mentioned only briefly in previous verses (Heb 1:3; 2:17; 7:27; 8:3), the sacred author now connects the death of Christ with the Melchizedekian Priesthood, "Prior to this point in the book of Hebrews, the emphasis upon the Melchizedekian Priesthood focuses almost entirely upon Christ's present activity in heaven as a heavenly intercessor."[122] The death of Christ too, not just His resurrection, must also be a part of His priesthood. The writer has been anticipating this argument here in chapter nine all along, but as of yet, had not got around to teaching it as a principle. The reference in 8:3, "Every high priest is appointed to offer both gifts and sacrifices; hence it is necessary that this high priest also have something to offer," is left undeveloped until Hebrews 9, "Here, the author finally directs attention to Christ as the sacrificial victim on the cross in connection with His priesthood."[123]

This emphasis upon the death of Christ in relation to the Melchizedekian Priesthood is entirely different than the previous references of Hebrews (Heb 4:14-16; 5:8-10; 7:24-25). These other verses focus on the relation between His resurrection and priesthood. That Jesus ever lives to make intercession for the saints is a question of resurrection life being made available to them for their spiritual sanctification. The salvation in view in these verses is sanctification salvation which is a process, not justification salvation which can occur only once. Sanctification is a daily process whereas justification is instantaneous. The author has been focusing on sanctification up to this point, because this was where they were faltering. Though they had already been justified as saints, they were not persevering in their sanctification. As such, the resurrection power of the Melchizedekian Priesthood is held before them to spur them onto spiritual maturity. The reason why the Hebrew readers are not spiritually growing is because they are still erroneously holding that sanctification is somehow connected to the old system.

The sacred author must correct this false thinking. So now, here in Hebrews 9, he points out the death of Christ has ended the old earthly

---

[122]   Lane, p. 235.
[123]   Ibid.

priesthood and covenant to bring about a new heavenly covenant and priesthood (Heb 9:11-22). If they rightly understand that the once for all death of Christ according to the Order of Melchizedek has ushered in a brand new spiritual priesthood far superior to the fleshly one, then they will turn to their messianic priest in heaven for their sanctification (Heb 3:1; 4:14-16; 10:19-25; 12:1-3), "The writer's primary concern here is no longer with the subjective salvation experience of the Christian, but with the objective salvation of Christ's death on the cross."[124]

The Order of Melchizedek provides two phases of salvation, i.e, one which was objectively accomplished once for all on the cross, and one which can be subjectively experienced by the Christian after his salvation. In other words, the Order of Melchizedek provides for both justification and sanctification. Up to now, the author has been focusing on sanctification. Now, he will begin to focus on justification, and this emphasis carries all the way through 10:18. Moreover, the primary reason why they are not doing well with regard to sanctification is precisely because they have not understood their once for all justification.

There is one big reason why the Old Testament tabernacle system has been outdated. It is precisely because Jesus Christ died once for all. His sacrificial death was both objective and final. It is objective in the sense that it occurred not in the Old Testament tabernacle *model* made with human hands, but in heaven itself, the greater and more perfect tabernacle (Heb 9:11). Animal sacrifices cannot objectively cleanse sin, but the *real* sacrifice of Jesus Christ Himself can (Heb 9:11-14). His death is also final in the sense that it is once for all (Heb 9:11). This means His death is an unrepeatable difference. What has been accomplished once for all bespeaks of total fulfillment with regard to the crosswork of Christ. It is an act which cannot be repeated. It is done.

The saying that a woman's work is never done, which means it must be done over and over again, does not apply to the death of Christ. His work was perfected on the cross. By definition work is repetitious. Life itself is repetitious, and all of this speaks of its vanity and imperfection. If someone must keep on doing something over and over again, it means that it was not done perfectly or completely in the first place. This was precisely what the Levitical priests did all the time. They repeated their work over and over again. This actually speaks of its imperfection and

---

124   Ibid., p. 251.

weakness. Their constant repetitious work proved its own inadequacy. However, there is one place where the work is all done, the death of Christ, and His death cannot be repeated precisely because He has done it perfectly and completely once for all. Christ died finally, completely, and perfectly. This is the force of once for all (Heb 9:11; 9:26-28; 10:10-14). More importantly, to the Hebrew readers, this means the repetitions of the Old Covenant priesthood and tabernacle are now outdated. The one time death of Christ has fulfilled the entire Old Covenant finally and completely (Heb 9:15-22).

Now, this does not mean that the other Old Testament Covenants, i.e., the Abrahamic, the Palestinian, the Davidic, and the New have been completely fulfilled. However, it does certainly mean the Mosaic Covenant has been fulfilled in Christ. Therefore, to go back to the Old Covenent Law is to act as if Christ did nothing at all. It is actually an act of high treason because it does not recognize or take seriously the force of once for all. It is an act of unbelief in all that Christ has done on the cross. Not only is this a failure to hold fast the Christian confession (Heb 3:6; 3:14; 10:22-25), but it is also to trample underfoot the Son of God, to treat common the blood of the covenant, and to insult the Spirit of grace (Heb 10:29). In other words, it is an act of apostasy.

The Hebrew readers faulty view on their once for all justification is leading them into apostasy. What's more, they were going down this trail not by being outwardly immoral, but by being religious, by hanging onto the Old Covenent Law, a perfectly good thing to do, properly understood, in its day. The problem is those days are no longer around. The good old days have passed. They are old. As such, the author of Hebrews makes it very clear that one cannot have it both ways. Jesus even spoke a parable on this with regard to new and old wineskins (Matt 9:15-17). It is impossible to have the Old Covenant and the New Covenant at the same time precisely because the New Covenant is a total replacement of the Old Covenant. This is the whole point of the New Covenant. Why is it called new except for the express purpose of replacing the old. Christ died once for all. Thus, it is either Christ or the Old Covenant. Which does one want?

The readers have lost sight of their objective salvation at the point of the cross, and this has led them away from Christianity back into the religious system of Judaism. Their confidence is also shrinking (Heb

4:14-16; 10:19-23; 10:35) because they have not believed that Christ has really paid the price for their sins once for all. Animal sacrifices could only cleanse the physical flesh (Heb 9:10), and like all baths they had to be repeated over and over again. Physical rituals simply cannot spiritually cleanse or sanctify. However, since the death of Christ is both objective and final, one can have his conscience *cleansed from dead works*, and this cleansing will be just as complete and final as the death of Christ. If they look at Christ's once for all death on the cross, this should give them great confidence to approach and worship God, recognizing that God has dealt with sin once for all.

Dead works here is related to the animal sacrifices of the Old Covenant system and are synonymous with rituals.[125] The Greek word *to serve* here is the word to worship. As such, the author is really saying the death of Christ can cleanse their conscience from the dead works of the Levitical system, so that they can worship God freely, something which they could never do under the Old Covenant. The Levitical offerings are mere rituals and cannot cleanse anybody of anything, "For it is impossible for the blood of bulls and goats to take away sins (Heb 10:4)." In fact, all the Levitical offerings do is remind the worshiper of his sins, rather than take them away (Heb 10:3).

The author peculiarly writes in 9:22, "And according to Law, one may *almost* say, all things are cleansed with blood, and without shedding of blood there is no forgiveness." Here the author teaches the importance of sacrificial substitution as God's only method for forgiving sin. What the worshiper deserves because of sin, i.e., death, the innocent animal receives instead. The animal dies in place of the worshiper, and since the penalty has been paid by death, God is now free to forgive sin. This principle was taught to the Hebrew worshipers every time they came to the tabernacle or temple to offer their sacrifices. However, while the sacred writer affirms the principle of sacrificial substitution, he further adds something unusual in 9:18. He says that one can *almost* say that the blood cleanses sinners, but not quite:

> The total argument centers on the potency of blood. In the course of the exposition the writer refers to the daily sacrifices (9:23), to the rites of purification involving the ashes of the red

---

[125]   See Hebrews 10:1-4.

heifer (9:13), to the sacrifices by which the covenant of Sinai was ratified (9:18-21), and to the ceremonies associated with the annual Day of Atonement (9:7). The elements that all of these occasions share in common are the presence of the blood and a profound religious conviction concerning the potency of blood to provide access to God, to consecrate, to cleanse, to inaugurate covenant, and to achieve purgation from defilement. In each case the *material character of the blood is not in view* but blood as a symbolic medium of power. *The writer's own religious understanding of blood is expressed most clearly when the sacrificial blood of animals is juxtaposed to the blood of Christ.*[126]

The author affirms to his readers that while ritualistic physical blood is helpful to teach the principle of substitution, it still cannot cleanse. Only the sacrifice of Christ as their messianic substitute can cleanse sin precisely because the cross was far more than a geographical physical event. Jesus offered Himself as a sacrifice in the heavenly tabernacle **through the eternal Spirit**. This speaks of the great spiritual power of the sacrifice of Christ, and its wide-ranging ability to cleanse sin. While the cross was certainly a necessary, excruciating and painful physical event, it was the judgment of God during the last three hours on the cross that provided men with salvation. Lots of men suffered on crosses, but only one died for the sins of the entire world as a sacrificial substitute.

Now the main thrust of the following paragraph (Heb 9:15-22) is that the once for all death of Christ means that the Hebrew saints are no longer under the authority of the Old Covenant, "for this reason He is the mediator of a New Covenant, in order that since a death has taken place for the redemption of the transgressions that were committed under the first covenant, those who have been called may receive the promise of the eternal inheritance (Heb 9:15)." **For this reason** (Heb 9:15) goes back to the previous verse (9:14), which emphasizes the once for all death of Christ. Since Christ has died once for all, He has redeemed them from the transgressions committed under the Old Covenant. What's more, the significance of the finality of His death is emphasized further, "For where a covenant is, there must of necessity be the death of the one who made it. For a covenant is valid only when men are dead, for it is never

---

[126]   Lane, p. 252.

in force while the one who made it lives (Heb 9:16-17)." The finality of His death means the change toward the New Covenant away from the Old Covenant is permanent, "Because He has already died, Jesus has deprived himself of all further power of choice or movement. While the victim still lives, he possesses the full power of action and freedom to change."[127] This explains why the New Covenant could not have been given to the original Jewish worshipers. The Messiah had not yet died for them, but now He has, and since He has done it, the New Covenant has been inaugurated.

The ritual sacrifices of the Old Covenant were fine for the earthly model to teach the principle of messianic substitution (Heb 9:18-22), but they will not work in heaven (Heb 9:24). Here Hebrews also mysteriously teaches that the heavenly tabernacle must also be cleansed. Sin began in heaven with Satan, who was originally the highest Cherub (Isa 14:12-14; Ezk 28:14-15). After he sinned, he brought sin with him into heaven itself. While the author of Hebrews does not elaborate, Christ is also the solution to the presence of sin in the heavens. His once for all sacrifice has great heavenly repercussions, something which no Levitical priest could ever bring about.

The author of Hebrews again greatly contrasts the weakness of the Old Covenant priesthood with the eternal priesthood of Christ (Heb 9:24-28), and the difference between them is nothing less than eschatological:

> For Christ did not enter a holy place made with hands, a mere copy of the true one, but into heaven itself, now to appear in the presence of God for us; nor was it that He should offer Himself often, as the high priest enters the holy place year by year with blood not his own. Otherwise, He would have needed to suffer since the foundation of the world; but now ***once*** at the consummation of the ages He has been manifested to put away sin by the sacrifice of Himself (Heb 9:24-26).

The once for all death of Christ, in contrast to the repetitious animal sacrifices, has not only inaugurated the New Covenant, but also has inaugurated the consummation of the ages (Heb 9:26). More to the point, His once for all death on the cross now looks forward to His

---

127   Westcott, p. 265.

apocalyptic second appearing, which will finally fulfill all of the conditions prophesied in the New Covenant (Heb 9:28). What is left in the meantime between the first and second comings of Christ is an interim period in which the New Covenant has a special limited application of the Holy Spirit within the New Testament church. The fulfillment of the prophecy of the New Covenant to the house of Judah and to Israel will not be until after Christ comes back to the earth to set up the Davidic Kingdom during the Millennium.

In short, here in Hebrews 9, "The securing of salvation can be described in terms of a forward movement into the presence of God. Under the Old Covenant, such movement was severely restricted."[128] Against this background, the writer contrasts the effectiveness of the unrepeatable sacrifice of Jesus Christ. His one time sacrifice is so great that it has eschatological results, eschatological results which are permanent and enduring. Even God will not repent on this. It was these eschatological results that the Hebrew readers were having such a hard time accepting.

Once Upon a Time & Eternal Security

While one must always be careful of building doctrine with mere words, the Greek word *Efapax* is intensive in Hebrews 9-10. It is an emphatic compound adverb. It occurs in loaded theological passages and is translated *once for all* in the sense of once forever. The preposition *epi*, meaning *upon*, has been compounded to the adverb *apax,*, meaning *once*, and the nature of its force is nothing less than total climactic fulfillment. The whole point here is that it is to be deeply contrasted with the repetitions of the Old Covenant worship system. When Jesus Christ died *Efapax*, i.e., *upon once*, He fulfilled completely the Old Covenant sacrificial system. Here in Hebrews, what Jesus Christ accomplished *upon once*, namely his crucifixion, but not to exclude His resurrection, cannot be repeated, "For it was fitting that we should have such a high priest, holy, innocent, undefiled, separated from sinners and exalted above the heavens; who does not need daily, like those high priests, to offer up sacrifices, first for His own sins, and then for the sins of the people, because this He did *once for all* when he offered up Himself (Heb 7:26-27)." *Upon once* is an historical event which is at the same time the end

---

128   Lane, p. 251.

of the Old Covenant era, "A final event can only happen once. A final decision is made once, or it is not made at all. The serious nature of the decision can be gauged by the fact that inevitably the decisive event takes place once for all, and once only."[129] *Efapax* speaks of an unqualified, non-repeatable event that is historically incomparable relative to the Old Testament.

Because of perfected fulfillment, the sacrifice of Jesus Christ is best understood through contrast, and when that contrast is set against the repetitious nature of the sacrificial system of the Old Testament (7:11-28; 9:1-28), the most superior of all religious worship systems, it can only mean that Christianity cannot be matched by anyone or anything outside of God Himself. The unparalleled superiority of Christianity rests on the basic fact that it cannot be repeated. The one-time salvation work of Jesus Christ (6:4-6; 7:26-27; 9:11-12; 9:25-28; 10:10-14; 10:18; 10:26) belongs to the category of unrivaled uniqueness. It represents nothing other than the consummation of the ages (9:26), which looks forward to the apocalyptic end of all history (Heb 9:28). This **upon once** fulfillment is the key theological thrust of the book of Hebrews. Jesus Christ died once. The Christian is saved once, "By this will we have been sanctified through the offering of the body of Jesus Christ **once for all** (Heb 10:10)."

Now the argument of 10:1-18 consists of three major paragraphs which consistently contrast the repetitious Old Covenant sacrifices with the once for all sacrifice of Jesus Christ. In 10:1-4, the sacrifices of the Law are inadequate to perfect the worshiper, "For the Law, since it is only a shadow of the good things to come and not the very form of things, can never by the same sacrifices year by year, which they offer continually, make perfect those who draw near. Otherwise, would they not have ceased to be offered (10:1-2a)?" In 10:5-14, the oft-repeated sacrifices of the Law have been superseded by the one sacrifice of Christ, "And every high priest stands daily ministering and offering time after time the same sacrifices, which can never take away sins; but He, having offered one sacrifice for sins for all time, sat down at the right hand of God … For by one offering He has perfected for all time those who are sanctified (10:11-14)."

---

129   Brunner, Emil. *The Mediator* (Lutterworth Press: London, 1934), pp. 26-27.

The concluding paragraph in 10:15-18 answers to the situation described in the initial paragraph in 10:1-4.[130] Here the eschatological arrival of the New Covenant answers perfectly to the inadequacies of the Old Covenant, "And the Holy Spirit also bears witness to us; for after saying,' This is the covenant that I will make with them, after those days, says the Lord: I will put My laws upon their heart, and upon their mind I will write them,' He then says,' And their sins and their lawless deeds I will remember no more.' Now where there is forgiveness of these things, there is no longer any offering for sin (10:15-18)." The New Covenant sacrifice therefore corresponds perfectly to the limitations of the Old Covenant, "This entailed the repudiation of the many sacrifices prescribed by the Law in favor of the one offering of the body of Jesus (10:5-10) and the rejection of the ineffective ministry of the Levitical priests in favor of the effective eschatological priest enthroned in the presence of God (10:11-14). The argument serves to sharpen an appreciation of the ultimate character of Christ's single, personal sacrifice for sins. It also establishes a context for defining the blessings of New Testament grace that were secured through his death."[131]

Hebrews 10:10-14 makes the strongest assertion of the doctrine of eternal security found anywhere in the New Testament:

> By this will we have been sanctified through the offering of the body of Jesus Christ once for all. And every high priest stands daily ministering and offering time after time the same sacrifices, which can never take away sins; but He, having offered one sacrifice for sins for all time, sat down at the right hand of God, waiting from that time forward until His enemies be made a footstool for His feet. For by one offering He has perfected for all time those who are sanctified (10:10-14).

The author says these most remarkable statements in spite of the spiritual condition of the Hebrew readers. He is not afraid to call these apostasizing believers once for all saved, and not just once, but twice (10:10; 10:14). The writer is confident that his readers are once for all saved, not by looking at their spiritual behavior, but by looking at their

---

[130]   Lane, p. 258.
[131]   Ibid., p. 259.

faithful high priest who died for their sins once for all. Unlike his Hebrew readers, and unlike many Christians today, the author understands the great value of the cross. He understands that once Christ has died for sins once for all, that's it. Once someone becomes a Christian through the sacrifice of Christ, there are no strings attached with regard to his salvation. The author clearly says with the strongest Greek possible that these Hebrew readers have been once for all sanctified (10:10), and then once for all perfected (10:14). Both of these statements are made in the perfect tense in the Greek, and this means that though the sacrifice of Christ has been completed, it will still have lasting or enduring results.

Thus the author most definitely is not talking about the spiritual experience of the readers here. In fact, he has spent an enormous amount of energy throughout the book explaining that they do not measure up in their Christians experience. However, this lack of Christian spirituality still does not take away the fact that they have been once for all sanctified and perfected. Moreover, these two assertions here are both parallel to the concept of justification as put forth in Romans 4 and Galatians 2. The author uses the word "sanctification" here not in the theological sense, but in the priestly sense of consecration and holiness. In Romans and Galatians, Paul uses the word justification in the judicial sense. The writer of Hebrews uses the word sanctification in a priestly sense, but the meanings are identical. Just as Paul uses the word justification in an absolute objective sense, so here the sacred author uses the word sanctification in the same way.

The writer of Hebrews simply cannot be talking about something subjective in their Christian experience. How can one say at the same time that the same people who are on the verge of committing apostasy are still nonetheless once for all perfect? Only the doctrine of eternal security can explain such a scenario. Here the writer is talking about something which human experience cannot remove. This may not look pretty, but the author of Hebrews strongly asserts that those who are about to lose their inheritance-rest through apostasy are still once for all sanctified and perfected. Their once for all sanctification and perfection is absolute, perfect, and is untouchable as far as human experience goes. Just as one cannot do any works to get justified from one's sins, so there is nothing one can do to lose that justification. It is the most secure privilege in all of life, and the reason why is not because of what people do, but because of what Christ did once for all.

Unless the meaning of *once for all* is changed here, the same people who are about to throw it all away, are still once for all saved. They may not be considered God's house (Heb 3:6). They may not be a partaker with Christ (Heb 3:14). They may come short of entering God's rest (Heb 4:1-11). They may not hold fast their confession (Heb 4:14). God may not permit them to grow up spiritually (Heb 6:3). They may not even be able to see the Lord in the eschatological future (Heb 12:14). Nonetheless, the author of Hebrews still calls them once for all saved. This is the import of the once for all sacrifice of Jesus Christ. No matter how contradictory and ugly this may appear to many, it is still the teaching of Hebrews, and it must be accepted by faith. Moreover, these are actually not contradictory because one is related to Christian experience while the other is not. Those things which may be lost are related to Christian spiritual experience. They are therefore conditional and dependent upon faithful obedience. However, here in chapter 10, there is one thing that is unconditional, and therefore cannot be lost, precisely because it is not dependent upon human works, but upon the once for all death of Christ which has already historically and objectively taken place. Christ was already obedient to God's will (Heb 10:5-14) with regard to salvation. As such, it is not necessary to repeat in one's life that which Christ has already done finally and forever. *By this will*, i.e., by the sacrifice of Christ (Heb 10:10) and not by the perseverance of the Hebrew readers, they have already been sanctified and perfected forever irrespective of what happens later.

No matter what happens in the Christian way of life, the ultimate cause of salvation is the cross of Christ plus nothing else. The Christian's ultimate salvation is not dependent upon the life that one lives, but strictly upon the cross. Now the great question of the Christian way of life is whether or not God's people really believe this. A negative answer can only be an expression of unbelief in what Christ has done finally and perfectly forever. The Hebrew readers, many a Christian in general, simply do not really believe that Jesus Christ did enough on the cross to save someone from the penalty of sin totally and perfectly forever. Did Jesus Christ really do enough on the cross to save a soul from his sins? Well, Hebrews 10 emphatically declares yes, and it says so in spite of the spiritual condition of the people he is writing to, one of the worst groups found anywhere in the New Testament. This means at once that while, "Jesus' saving action was performed in history, it possesses a validity that transcends both history and human experience."[132]

The Order of Melchizedek as a Rich Spiritual Experience – 10:19-25

Because the conscience of the Hebrew readers has been once for all cleansed (Heb 10:2), because they have been sanctified once for all (Heb 10:10), because Christ died once (Heb 10:12), because the Hebrew readers have been perfected once for all (10:14), because God will no longer remember their sins (Heb 10:17), because the readers have been forgiven (Heb 10:18), and because there is no longer any more offerings for sin (Heb 10:18), the Hebrew readers have confidence to enter the heavenly holy place through the blood of Jesus (Heb 10:19). This is the force of **therefore** found in 10:19, referring back to the previous part of the chapter. When the author of Hebrews uses the word **therefore** here, he marks the beginning of great transition away from theological argument into daily spiritual practice, and this emphasis carries all the way through to the end of the book. Here the author turns away from the objective once for all death of Christ and shifts to the results which the Hebrew readers are to enjoy:

> Since therefore, brethren, we have confidence to enter the holy place by the blood of Jesus, by a new and living way which He inaugurated through the veil, that is, His flesh, and since we have a great high priest over the house of God, let us draw near with a sincere heart in full assurance of faith, having our hearts sprinkled clean from an evil conscience and our bodies washed with pure water. Let us hold fast the confession of our hope without wavering, for He who promised is faithful; and let us consider how to stimulate one another to love and good deeds, not forsaking our own assembling together, as is the habit of some, but encouraging one another, and all the more, as you see the day drawing hear (Heb 10:19-25).

---

[132] Ibid., p. 270.

Here, the Hebrew readers are told that they can personally experience the great privileges of the Order of Melchizedek – even though it is not visible to the naked eye. The sacred author exhorts them to live by faith so they can experience their heavenly priesthood in their souls right now. Just as the Levitical priesthood provided ritual cleansing, so the Order of Melchizedek offers spiritual sanctification. The Hebrew readers have complete free access into the heavenly holy of holies, and this is most certainly not because they are spiritual giants, but strictly because Christ died for their sins once for all, and that Christ continues to be their great high priest, representing them in heaven. All of the merit here lies in the greatness of Christ, not in the Hebrew readers. In spite of their current woeful spiritual condition, they still have free access into the holiest of all places. From God's perspective, they have been already been sanctified and perfected by the blood of Jesus. This allows them entrance into the holiest of all, into heaven itself, and they can do so freely without any performance of any ritual whatsoever.

In contrast to the old Levitical way of offering dead rituals before God, the Hebrew readers are to enter the heavenly holy of holies *by a new and living way*. The *new* and *living way* according to the Order of Melchizedek is in contrast to the old and dead works of the Levitical worship system. This new living way is based on a superior covenant (Heb 10:15-18) and therefore a superior priesthood (Heb 10:21). What's more, the difference between them is nothing less than the eschatological difference between the earthly tabernacle and the heavenly tabernacle, between a mere model and the real thing, between mere physical life and resurrection life. Through the resurrection power of the Order of Melchizedek, the Hebrew readers have access to resurrection life within the heavenly holy of holies.

This is what Christian worship is supposed to be all about. Though they are physically on the earth, by faith the readers can worship God in heaven right now (Heb 10:19-22). This is because the priesthood of Christ confers resurrection life to His worshipers. For the first time ever, there is now a Man who permanently dwells within the heavenly holy of holies. He is the Great High Priest of heaven, and He represents Christians before the very presence of God (Heb 4:14-16; 7:27; 9:24; 10:21). This high priestly representation allows bold and confident entrance for Christian believers to enter within the veil of the heavenly holy of holies.

Moreover, the author of Hebrews adds that the veil into the holy of holies is the sacrificial flesh of Jesus (Heb 10:20). Here the writer recalls that when Jesus died on the cross, the veil of the temple was torn in two, signifying free access into the holy of holies (Luke 23:44-45). The Old Testament type, i.e., the veil, prefigured the sacrificial flesh of Jesus which gives access to God. The barrier of the veil has been removed once and for all, and the readers desperately need to believe this in order to progress spiritually.

The great problem is that the Order of Melchizedek is an invisible priesthood which can only be experienced by faith, "Let us draw near with a sincere heart in *full assurance of faith* ... (Heb 10:22a)." Mere rituals cannot provide this rich spiritual experience. Christ has already fulfilled the meaning of all the Old Covenant rituals. Yet, the readers are not too sure of this. They are wavering on this great issue. The readers wanted something they could sense with their senses. They somehow did not really understand that, "God is Spirit, and those who worship Him must worship in Spirit and truth (John 4:24)." Just as the Samaritan woman was sidetracked by the proper physical location of God's Temple, so the readers were being sidetracked by the physical Old Covenant priesthood. They did not understand that Christian worship is based on resurrection life and takes place in heaven, and through their unbelief, they were missing out on this great spiritual privilege. In this sense, they were not God's house (Heb 3:6).

The writer of Hebrews exhorts his readers to do three spiritual things in light of the fact that Jesus is their great high priest over the house of God (Heb 10:21-25). Number one, they are to draw near with a sincere heart with full assurance of faith since they have already been cleansed from their sins (Heb 10:22). Number two, they are to hold fast their Christian confession of hope (Heb 10:23). In other words, they are to continue to persevere in New Testament faith and doctrine, especially with regard to the priesthood of Christ. Number three, they are to encourage one another in love and good works, not forsaking the assembly of the church as some were doing (Heb 10:24-25). Moreover, they are to do all of these things with an apocalyptic mindset, "As you see the Day drawing near (Heb 10:25)." They are to worship God spiritually in heaven right now by doing these three things, because one day soon, heavenly reality will overtake everything.

The Lord is coming, and they need to be prepared for His coming. If they continue to persevere by faith in this priestly ministry, they will be richly rewarded because, "He who promised is faithful (Heb 10:23). However, if they do not persevere in this priestly ministry, there is yet another warning (Heb 10:26-31). Some people had already stopped going to church (10:25). They were not persevering as required. Others were being tempted to follow suit. As such, the author hopes to arrest this problem by giving them yet another warning, the most severe yet to be found the book of Hebrews.

CHAPTER NINE

THE DANGER OF PERSISTENT SIN – 10:26-31

The Parallel Relationship Between Hebrews 6 & 10

The great discussion on the Order of Melchizedek occurs between the two great warnings of Hebrews 6 and 10. As stated earlier, this makes the Order of Melchizedek integral to the warnings. The author is giving his readers an ultimatum to either grow up in the Melchizedekian Priesthood of Christ or suffer God's judgment. More than that, it also ties together very strongly Hebrews 6 and 10. The author first warns his readers very severely in Hebrews 6:1-8. Immediately following this, he then encourages them about the great privileges of the Order of Melchizedek, the New Covenant, and the heavenly tabernacle (Heb 6:9-10:25). Then, he warns his readers very severely yet again (Heb 10:26-31), almost re-stating the same warning all over again, just using different words and phrases. The parallel warnings between Hebrews 6 and 10 are so remarkable, that not only do they complement one another, but they also explain each other. What may be difficult to understand in Hebrews 6 can be understood more clearly by looking at Hebrews 10, and vice-versa. The strong parallel connection between Hebrews 6 and 10 can be proven by the following illustrated chart:

WARNING	6:4-8	10:26-31
Description of the Apostasy	Fallen away (6:6); re-crucifying the Son of God (6:6); exposing Him to open shame (6:6)	Deliberately persist in sin (10:26); trample upon the Son of God (10:29); treat the blood of the covenant as common (10:29); insult the Spirit of grace (10:29)
Prior Salvation Experience	Once for all enlightened (6:4); have experienced the heavenly gift (6:4); have become partakers of the Holy Spirit (6:4); have experienced the good Word of God and the coming age (6:5)	Have received a full knowledge of the truth (10:26); sanctified by means of the blood of the covenant (10:29)
Impossibility of Recovery	It is impossible ... to renew them to repentance (6:4,6)	No longer any sacrifice for sin (10:26)
The Judgment	Loss (6:6); close to being cursed (6:8); burning (6:8)	Terrifying expectation of judgment (10:27); raging fire (10:27); severer punishment (10:29); dread (10:31)

133

The Continuing Defiant Sin – 10:26-27

Fallen away in 6:6 is called **deliberately** or **willfully persisting in sin** in 10:26. It is also parallel to the **apostasy** of the Exodus generation (3:12). Although it does not mean final apostasy so as to lose salvation, it is still no ordinary sin being described here. The falling away and deliberately persisting in sin is qualified by other rather striking phrases like, "re-crucifying the Son of God," and, "exposing Him to public shame" in 6:6, and then, "trampling underfoot the Son of God," and "treating the blood of the covenant as defiled," not to mention, "insulting to the Spirit of grace," in 10:29. The author simply cannot be describing a typical everyday sin. While certainly all sin is an outrage to the holiness of God, the author of Hebrews here is going to great lengths to describe the gravity of this particular sin. These very descriptive phrases are unique in the New Testament, and only the sin of apostasy against the meaning of the cross, seen in a very narrow understanding, can account for such descriptions. Moreover, the gravity of the sin, in contrast to other sins, is brought about not just by these descriptive phrases, but by the author's emphasis that it is impossible to recover from this sin if committed (3:7-4:13; 6:5-6; 12:16-17). The author is therefore talking about a most serious sin:

---

133   This chart is borrowed from Lane's commentary. Lane also demonstrates with a similar chart that the encouragements following the warnings in both chapters six and ten are identical as well, pp. 296-97, volume 2.

For if we go on sinning willfully after receiving the knowledge of the truth, there no longer remains a sacrifice for sins, but a terrifying expectation of judgment and the fury of fire which will consume the adversaries. Anyone who has set aside the Law of Moses dies without mercy on the testimony of two or three witnesses. How much severer judgment do you think he will deserve who has regarded as unclean the blood of the covenant by which he was sanctified, and has insulted the Spirit of grace? For we know Him who said, "Vengeance is Mine, I will repay." And again, "the Lord will judge His people." It is a terrifying thing to fall into the hands of the living God (10:26-31)

In the Greek, the word **willingly** is emphatically placed at the beginning of the sentence, "to sin **willfully** is to sin not under the constraining force of sudden temptation acting upon the weaknesses of the mortal nature, but as without cause, that is by free choice and will."[134] Here the author is stating a general principle. Anyone who continues to sin willfully or wantonly can only expect the "fury of a fire which will consume the adversaries."

Specifically, this particular apostasy was that of denying the finality of the cross, relapsing back into some form of Judaism. However, it is rather apparent that any continuous apostasy merits the fury of God's wrath, not just this specific apostasy of the Hebrew readers. The author is clearly taking a general principle from the teaching of Scripture and applying to the situation at hand. The conditional participial construction, "for if we go on sinning," is in the present tense, intensifying the character of the willful sin. This sin is therefore a persistent sin. It is a "habit of life which the present tense describes."[135] Such a person is also considered to be an **enemy** of God which merits his wrath (10:27).

This willful sin or apostasy can obviously be committed by believers because the author includes himself in the warning by adding the word **we** in the participial construction. That this sin can be committed by a believer is clarified even further by the following phrase, "after receiving a full knowledge of the truth (10:27)." The Greek word **epignwsij** is here employed, referring to a **full experiential knowledge**, rather than to

---

134   Vaughn, C.J. *The Epistle to the Hebrews*, p. 202.
135   Dunham, *The Danger of Disregard*, p. 2.

a simple mental assent to some knowledgeable facts. "We may speak of a false *gnwsij* but not of a false or unusual *epignwsij*. The sacred writer, therefore, intimates by the very choice of the word that it is not a mere outward and historical knowledge of which he is here speaking, but an inward, quickening, believing apprehension of revealed thought."[136]

That this is equivalent to salvation is underscored much more strongly in 10:29. There the author strongly asserts, right in the middle of three most horrific descriptions of their apostasy, that they have already been sanctified[137] by the blood of the cross. This is also exactly parallel to 6:4-5 where the author categorically states that those who have been, "*once* enlightened and have tasted of the heavenly gift and have been made partakers of the Holy Spirit, and have tasted the good word of God and the powers of the age to come," are also the same ones who are about to fall away. To deny the readers are Christians is to deny the natural and plain meaning of the text in favor of a particular theology which cannot take into account what the Scripture is actually saying.

The continually willful sin being warned of in 10:26 is an apostate attitude toward the significance of the finality of the cross. Hence, the sacred writer quickly adds, "there no longer remains a sacrifice for sins (10:26)." The author states yet again, this time right in the opening statement of the warning that Christ's sacrifice was final. In fact, this is the second time that the author has explicitly used this phrase in this chapter, "there is no longer any offering for sin (10:18)." 10:10, 12, 14 underscore the contextual emphasis of the once for all significance of the cross even further. As such, the readers desperately need to understand this most basic principle of Christianity, or drift back into the worldliness of Jewish rituals and religion.

Now, this means that they are denying the cross, not so much by outright rejection, but by spiritual practice. They are refusing to persevere in the heavenly realities of the Melchizedekian Priesthood. They are far more comfortable at home in the worldly model of the Levitical priesthood. In their low estimation of the meaning of the cross, they have also refused to place themselves under the complete authority of the New Testament priesthood (10:29). In fact, the author states that they have regarded the *blood* of the *New Covenant* as if it were something

---

[136]   Delitzsch, Franz. *The Epistle to the Hebrews*, volume 2, p. 184.
[137]   Aorist Passive Indicative.

common, as if it were ceremonially unclean. They have failed to connect the blood of the cross with the inauguration of the New Covenant. They have failed to grasp the great spiritual significance of the cross of Christ which redeems them out of the limitations of the Old Covenant and places them into the privileged spiritual riches of the New Covenant (9:15-28). As such, the comforts of Jewish earthly religion must be abandoned. To refuse to press onto the spiritual heights of the Melchizedekian Priest-hood under the authority of New Testament grace is to regard the cross of Christ with contempt.

The figure of speech **to trample underfoot the Son of God** shows the blatant disregard and disrespect for the person of Christ. As such, they are not merely offending the work of Christ, but His Person as well. **Insulting to the Spirit of grace** also shows that what they are doing is also most offensive to the gracious ministry of the Holy Spirit (10:29). The great sin of the Hebrew readers is thus characterized by a strong and persistent anti-grace attitude. They are insulting God by rejecting His most gracious New Covenant gift of the Holy Spirit, paid for by the greatest cost conceivable, the blood of Christ. Judgment is thus the only option remaining for those who continue to reject the privileged status of Christianity. Jesus expressly died to advance the Hebrew readers into the Melchizedekian riches of grace and great privilege. To stay back in the confines of Judaism is to make a complete mockery of everything Jesus did on the cross. It is to act as if Jesus died in vain, an insult to be sure.

With such heinous descriptions of the apostasy being warned of, it is not surprising that many have tried to compare this passage with blasphemy of the Holy Spirit, otherwise known as the unpardonable sin (Matt 12:22-32). This is highly unlikely however. The Pharisees who said that Jesus was doing miracles in the power of Satan were unbelievers, and so Jesus was clearly warning unbelievers of such an eternal sin. The Hebrew readers on the other hand, are here clearly said to be believers. Secondly, it is perhaps impossible for someone to even commit the unpardonable sin today:

> Sheer logic leads us to see that if in the days of Christ's presence on the earth – to attribute His miracles to the power of Satan rather than to the power of the Holy Spirit, was to commit the unpardonable sin, then conversely, his absence today makes it

impossible for us to commit the unpardonable sin and our position is entirely consistent with a "whosoever will" Gospel. [138]

More than likely *insulting the Spirit* is to be seen as a sinful advance upon both grieving the Holy Spirit (Eph 4:30) and quenching the Spirit (1 Thess 5:19). One can grieve the Spirit. One can quench the Spirit. In the case of the Hebrew readers, even worse, they are being warned about insulting the Spirit. Now the Spirit is added to the Son and the sacrifice for sin as the object of offense. The participle **enubrisaj** means *mocking* or *insulting*, "What an activity directed at the Third Person of the Holy Trinity."[139] Nonetheless, even if the word blasphemy was thrown into this context, it still would not change the overall thrust of the meaning of the warnings in the book of Hebrews. Nehemiah speaks of the fact the Exodus generation committed *blasphemies* out in the desert, yet God still forgave them (Neh 9:16-21). Again, if God forgave the blasphemies of the Exodus generation, will He do less for saints in the Church age?

Nonetheless, with such graphic language, many have refused to accept the apostasy being warned of could be committed by true believers. How can a true Christian treat Jesus and the cross with contempt, not to mention insult the Holy Spirit? While this may be troublesome theologically speaking, in practical terms, it perhaps can occur all too easily. The Exodus generation committed apostasy and blasphemy. They persisted in their unbelief over an extended period of time which finally culminated in the desire to return to Egypt by killing Moses, Aaron and Joshua in the process (Num 14:1-10). To this the Lord responded, "Surely all the men who have seen My glory and My signs which I performed in Egypt and in the wilderness, yet *have put Me to test these ten times* and have not listened to My voice, shall by no means see the land which I swore to their fathers, nor shall any of those who spurned Me see it … *how long* shall I bear with this evil congregation who are grumbling against Me (Num 14:22-23, 27)?"

If the Exodus generation, a generally redeemed people, persisted in sin, then so can anyone else. When theologians have difficulty explaining the practice of sin in the life of any believer, it goes without saying that something rather peculiar is taking place. In psychology it is called

---

138   McGee, Jay Vernon, *Moving Through Matthew*, p. 37.
139   Dunham, *The Danger of Disregard: Hebrews 10:26-39*, p. 7.

denial. In more simple language it is a blind spot which actually begins to overlook sin because it precludes in advance that a Christian could commit such an offense:

> But a further question must be faced: How much of a sin constitutes contempt and insulting of the Godhead? Very few words seem to have been written about sin from God's perspective. The theologies are careful to explain what it means to man. But Chafer notes: 'Beyond the offense which **sin** is to God's government …, it because of its immoral nature, **outrages** and **insults** the holy Person of God.' He also observes that God may "be injured and offended by man's rejection of His Person, insult to His character and rebellion against His holy will." One must agree with Chafer's comments, and add that very little that an unbeliever may do is impossible for a believer. Peter denied his Lord. David committed adultery and murder. Thomas doubted the resurrection. Abraham lied about his wife. When the old nature controls our actions, sin is the result. Is the sin of a blood-bought believer less insulting and outrageous to God than that of the grossest unbeliever? It is not. It is far more serious. A child insulting his father is more wounding than a neighbor child insulting the same man. The idea that there is something cleaner or less insulting about the sins of the saints is reprehensible.[140]

Anyone who commits willful sin is God's enemy (10:26-27), unbeliever or believer. Jesus called Peter **Satan** because of his worldly attitude about the cross (Matt 16:21-23), perhaps not too far removed from what is happening here in the book of Hebrews. **Satan** means **adversary**. If Jesus called Peter a satanic enemy for his carnal attitude about the cross, there is no reason why the author of Hebrews cannot call his own readers the same for their own carnal attitude toward the cross. After all, they have earned it with their continuing rejection of New Testament truth, something which even Peter did not do, but still was called Satan.

With respect to the cross, however, the Hebrew readers seem to be following Peter's worldliness here, albeit on a more continuous basis. As such they are at the point of being willful enemies of God in practice,

---

[140]   Ibid, p. 8.

even though they have already been sanctified once for all at the point
of the cross (10:10-14; 27, 29). No matter how serious the description
of this sin may be, no matter how troubling or ugly or terrible it may
sound, the author of Hebrews clearly indicates that it is possible for a
Christian to commit such an outrageous sin against the Godhead. Those
who think otherwise perhaps should beware. Again, take a good hard
look at the Exodus generation as Paul strongly warns the Corinthians,
"Now these things happened (the Exodus disaster) to them as an example,
and they are written for *our* instruction, upon whom the end of the ages
have come. *Therefore let him who think he stands take heed that he does
not fall* (1 Cor 10:11-12)."

In light of the Exodus generation debacle, the Old Covenant itself
actually had a clause dealing with such sinful occasions. In other words,
unlike many a Christian theologian who rules out ahead of time which
type of sins one of God's people can commit, the Old Covenant actually
anticipated ahead of time what to do in the case of especially defiant
sins. What is to be done in such a scenario? Rather than deny that such
a sin could ever take place, the Old Covenant anticipated the problem,
and explicitly spelled out what to do in such a situation, "but the person
who does anything defiantly, whether he is native or an alien, that one
is blaspheming the Lord and that person shall be cut off from among his
people. Because he has despised the word of the Lord and has broken
His commandment, that person shall be completely cut off; his guilt
will be on him (Num 15:30-31)." In the context of Numbers, to be cut
off from the assembly is to be put to death.[141] Physical death is thus the
punishment for apostasy or high-handed sinning under the Law of Moses.
More to the point, with the exception of the Day of Atonement wherein
all the sins were atoned for (Lev 16), the Law of Moses simply made no
provision for high-handed sins. With all other sins, sacrifices could be
made to ritually atone for sin (Num 15:22-29), but not for defiant sins
(Num 15:30-31). Even in Leviticus 4-5, every sin listed that could be
ritually atoned for are all said to be unintentional sins, i.e., sins which
were not continuously willful.

Now in 10:26-27, the author of Hebrews brings up this principle up
to date from the Old Covenant. He expressly reiterates this same truth
even under New Testament grace. What was true of the Old Testament

---

[141]   The Septuagint translates "cut off" as *put to death*.

Law is also true of New Testament grace. The New Testament makes no provision for high-handed sins either. This is the import of the phrase, "there no longer remains a sacrifice for sins (10:26)." Just as there was a sin in which an Old Covenant offering could not remove divine punishment, so there is a sin which the New Testament offering will not remove divine punishment either. Divine punishment and chastisement will be just as certain under the authority of the New Testament as it was under the Old Covenent Law. The New Testament therefore, like the Old Covenent Law before it, also anticipates what to do when a Christian persists in willful sin, "there no longer remains a sacrifice for sins but a certain terrifying expectation of judgment and the fury of fire which consumes the adversaries (10:26-27):"

> The reader familiar with the Old Testament would know that no provision was made for willful or high-handed sin. Now, lest they think that there is some softening in the attitude of God towards sin, or that the sacrifice of Christ did something that the Old Covenant did not, he provides this warning. It is not to say that they have sinned beyond the power of the sacrifice of Christ, but there is a limit to the applicability of that sacrifice but a God who hates sin with a perfect hatred.[142]

Any willful sin, regardless of the covenant, is fatally dangerous.

Again, as has been said numerous times, this is not to say that their sin cannot be forgiven in Christ. Christ may have certainly died for that sin (10:29), but God will still mete out divine punishment for that sin (10:26-27). Forgiveness of sin does not always mean that people will escape divine punishment. This is the whole point of Hebrews 10:26-29. Someone who has been sanctified once for all (10:29) can still willfully sin which will merit the wrath of God (10:26-27). The cross may sanctify a saint forever, but this does not mean that **all** divine punishment is removed in every case. God still maintains the right to discipline the saints as His children when they sin, and sometimes with great severity if necessary, and no offering of any kind, including the sacrifice of Christ, will prevent a sinful saint from meriting God's punishment.

---

[142]   Dunham, p. 4.

In other words, it is one thing to remove the eternal penalty for sin, i.e., hell, at the point of the cross. It is quite another to chastise a sinful saint with a divine penalty other than hell. God does not need hell to chastise His children. He can impute His righteousness to them freely at the point of the cross, but He still maintains the right to punish the sinning saint at His discretion with penalties other than hell. In Hebrews, God punishes the sinful saint with judgment in time and loss of eternal reward.

Seen in this light, it is not contradictory to say that it is impossible to renew a saint to repentance who has committed a willful sin. There can simply be no more repentant sacrifices for sins for someone who has been once enlightened and then continues willfully in it:

> The believer today who sins through ignorance and weakness is protected from temporal judgment in time by the blood of Christ. The blood of Christ however, will not protect the believer who sins willfully. He is in danger of judgment after the Old Testament pattern, a judgment in time that may include physical death or worse.[143]

The fury of God's fiery judgment is therefore the only alternative in the case of continual high-handed sinning. In the same way there is no second repentance after apostasy (6:1-6), so there is not another sacrifice for sin which can be offered to remedy the situation (10:26-27). Indeed, Christ has died finally and once for all. There is not going to be another sacrifice on the cross. While the Old Testament teaches that there is no offering for high handed sins at all, the New Testament says it another way from a New Testament perspective, "There no longer remains a sacrifice for sins (10:26)." This means the cross itself is an ultimatum. If the finality the death of Christ does not motivate the Hebrew readers to serve God faithfully, judgment is the only viable alternative.

To continue to sin willfully after salvation leaves God with only one alternative: fiery wrath and severe punishment. Like the Exodus generation before them, God will forgive their sin, but also like the Exodus generation, he will still discipline and punish them severely. In severe cases such as the Exodus generation, and with regard to the Hebrew

---

143   Ibid.

readers as well, both forgiveness and divine discipline can be experienced at the same time. Just because God is a forgiving God does not mean that God will still not punish sin. There does come a time when people must still live with the consequences of their decisions even though they have already been forgiven of all their sins – whether past, present, or future. The sacred author has just made it very clear they already do have forgiveness of sins (10:18), and that they have been once for all sanctified and perfected (10:10-14). To make this clear, the author affirms right in the middle of the description of their most heinous sin in 10:29 that they have already been sanctified by the cross. As such, the author is not threatening them with loss of salvation. They are already saved once for all. However, eternal security does not mean that one can sin with impunity, "The Lord will judge His people (10:30)."

Indeed, right after Israel committed apostasy by worshiping the golden calf, an evil deed in which Aaron even promoted by making the idol, we read these most solemn words in Exodus 34, "The Lord, the Lord God is a compassionate and gracious, slow to anger, and abounding in lovingkindness and truth, who keeps lovingkindness for thousands, who forgives iniquity, transgression and sin; yet He will by no means leave the guilty unpunished ... (Ex 34:6-7)." With even greater interest, when Moses interceded for the people for God to forgive them at the height of their persistent sin in Numbers 14, he used this very Scripture verse in his prayer, "The Lord is slow to anger and abundant in lovingkindness, forgiving iniquity and transgression, but He will by no means clear the guilty ... (Num 14:18)." In response, the faithful God of Abraham and Isaac and Jacob thus literally pronounced exactly as Moses prayed, "I have pardoned them according to your word; but indeed as long as I live, all the earth will be filled with glory of the Lord, surely all the men who have seen My glory and My signs which I performed in Egypt and in the wilderness, yet have put Me to test these ten times and have not listened to My voice, shall by no means see the land which I swore to their fathers, nor shall any of those who spurned Me see it (Num 14:20-22)."

God pardoned the Exodus generation, but He still did not clear the guilty of their sin as He will forbid them to enter His rest. They are a forgiven covenant people, but God still forced them to live with the consequences of their continual disobedience. There comes a point in time when continually forgiving sin without forcing people to live with the consequences of their decisions will not help them anymore. The Exodus generation finally crossed that line. The same is about to happen to the Hebrew readers as well. Seen in this light, there is no contradiction between the perfect sacrifice of Christ which removes all sin, but there may still be a divine punishment in connection with particular continuous sins.

Old Testament sacrifices were sometimes offered to show contrition of heart that would lead to a genuine repentance or change of heart and mind (Psalm 51:17). The word "sacrifice" in 10:26 appears to be very similar to this, precisely because it is directly parallel to the phrase in Hebrews 6:6, "it is impossible to renew them to repentance." In the mind of the author of the Hebrews, to say that "it is impossible to renew to repentance," is to say, "there no longer remains a sacrifice for sins." Thus just as no second repentance can recover what the Hebrew readers are about to lose, so likewise, no additional sacrifice can suffice either. The judgment of God will be inevitable regardless of contrition of heart, repentance or any other possible sacrifice for that matter. Such a course of action simply will not remove the impending punishment of God.

More to the point, in the New Testament church, there are simply no more **sacrifices for sins** to be offered at all anyway. God simply will not accept any more of them in relation to sin, precisely because of the once for all sacrifice of Christ. If the Old Testament sacrificial system was strict, the New Testament is stricter yet still, "There no longer remains a sacrifice for sins. (Heb 10:26)." It was this New Testament strictness that the Hebrew readers disregarded, perhaps assuming that this new Christian church was becoming too lax with regard to ritualistic liturgy. This reverse course back to Old Covenant liturgy however was a reverse course which abandoned the holy starkness of the cross of Christ.

Punishment Worse than the Sin unto Death – 10:28-31

Allusions to the Exodus generation continue. The author reminds his readers about what happens to those who set aside the Law of Moses (10:26-28). They die "without mercy on the testimony of two or of three witnesses (10:28)." In fact, the threat of physical death for certain sins is alluded to throughout much of the Old Covenant Law, i.e., for idolatry and working on the Sabbath just to name a few. Moreover, physical death does not always and necessarily demand spiritual or eternal death. Perhaps it often does, but again, the primary illustration of the Exodus generation here in Hebrews reinforces the notion that physical death alone is in view rather than spiritual or eternal death. An entire generation physically died in the desert for their sin. Their death may not have been immediate, but it was still death all the same. In fact, it was worse than death as they were forced to live a miserable 40 years walking in circles in a great desolate wilderness. Though God redeemed them out of Egypt, he killed them in the desert because of their disobedience. If this was true under the authority of the Old Testament, nothing less can be expected for a defiant sinner under the authority of the New Testament. "The natural fear of death, multiplied by the knowledge that God is taking one because he cannot be trusted with another minute on the earth would be fearful indeed."[144]

It is not just the Old Testament which teaches about the sin unto death. This doctrine is also taught in the New Testament as well. The book of 1 Corinthians warns of this possibility not once, but twice (1 Cor 5:5; 11:30-32). Moreover, these two passages of Scripture sharply distinguish sin unto death from loss of salvation. 1 Corinthians 5:5 is the passage where Paul has decided to excommunicate the man from the Corinthian Church who has been sleeping with his own mother-in-law, a sin so bad that even the Romans and Greeks did not practice it (1 Cor 5:1). As such, Paul strongly asserts, "I have decided to deliver such a one to Satan for the destruction of his flesh, so that his spirit may be saved in the day of the Lord Jesus (1 Cor 5:5)." Even with such a heinous sin, Paul does not threaten the man with loss of salvation, but with physical death in contrast to eternal death. Likewise, Paul states in 11:30 that some of the Corinthians have actually already died the sin unto death. Paul then clarifies the situation further, "But when we are judged, we are disciplined by the Lord so that we will not be condemned with the world (1 Cor 11:32)." As such, God may kill some of the Corinthians for their sins, but this in no way suggests loss of salvation.

The punishment of physical death could be experienced even if the particular sin being judged was not a persistent sin as we see with regard to the Exodus generation. Achan died immediately because he hid stolen treasures. Aaron's sons died immediately because they offered strange

---

[144] Dunham., p. 9.

fire in the tabernacle. Ananias and Saphira died because they lied. None of these occasions point to a pattern of a sinful life. By the sovereignty of God, they died, even though others, who may have sinned worse and more excessively, lived. David committed adultery and murder and yet lived. Solomon fell into persistent idolatry with all of his foreign wives, yet still lived. King Saul persistently disobeyed the Lord, but still lived – but he was disinherited like the Exodus generation. The Exodus generation may have lived, but their experience of the sin unto death was prolonged over a miserable 40 years. The apostle John asserts there is a sin leading to death, but he does not specifically identify what that particular sin is (1 John 5:16).

Perhaps even more striking, Israel seldom practiced the death penalty as strictly required by the Mosaic Law. Furthermore, "the use of witnesses, the necessity for trial, and carrying out the penalty by the people, made some sins difficult to punish."[145] In addition, even though God demanded the death of an idolator according to the Mosaic Law, He continually commands the Israelites throughout her history to repent of her idolatry. This suggests that even though idolatry merited the sin unto death, it was not a sin which could not be recovered from like we see here with regard to the Exodus generation and the book of Hebrews. In fact, after the Exodus generation committed idolatry in the desert, though God still punished them, they still recovered, unlike the incident at Numbers 14, which was their Waterloo. Regardless of the apparent inconsistency that is seen in the Bible with regard to application of the sin unto death, Hebrews 10:28-31 suggests there is something even worse than physical death. This, the author intimates in 10:28-29, "Anyone who sets aside the Law of Moses dies without mercy on the testimony of two or three witnesses. *How much severer punishment do you think he will deserve* who has trampled underfoot the Son of God, and has regarded as unclean the blood of the covenant by which he was sanctified, and has insulted the Spirit of grace?"

Here, the author contrasts the sin unto death under the Old Covenant with the greater deserved punishment of the continuing willful sin under the authority of the New Testament. If the Hebrew readers continue to sin willfully, they will merit a more severe punishment than the sin unto death as specified under the Old Covenant. The readers have far

---

[145]   Ibid, p. 10.

greater privileges than anything the Old Covenant saints ever had. Instead of Moses they have Christ. Instead of the partial nature of the Old Testament, they have the completeness of the New Testament. Instead of the earthly priesthood of Aaron, they have the heavenly priesthood of Christ. Instead of rituals, they have spiritual reality. They also have the Holy Spirit, something which was never universal in the Old Testament. This being so, the sacred writer here applies the spiritual principle to whom has been given much, much is required.

The fact of the matter is, if the Hebrew readers continue in their current trajectory, they will merit a judgment worse than even the Exodus generation suffered. Their sin is greater precisely because their spiritual privileges are greater. As such, the author describes their sin in a most ignominious way. By neglecting their so great salvation, they are about to outrage the holy Godhead which can only merit a most furious judgment. God will repay with vengeance according to their deeds without any partiality. The reason for this is the penetrating witness of the Word of God (4:12-13) is far more able to judge the intentions of the heart than the required two or three witnesses of the Mosaic Law (10:28).

What can be greater than physical death? How about living in a spiritual wilderness of a wasted life as the Exodus generation suffered for 40 years? Indeed, the Exodus generation even complained they wished they had died in Egypt or in the wilderness (Num 14:2) when some of congregation underwent capital punishment because of their idolatry. In other words, they believed physical death was better than enduring the hardships of the desert. Closely connected to living a wasted life in the desert is loss of eternal reward.

The fiery judgments of Hebrews 10:26-31 is speaking of an eschatological judgment consistent with the judgment seat of Christ or God as is seen in 1 Corinthians 3:10-15 and Romans 14:10-12. Hebrews 6:8 is especially helpful to identify the nature of the judgment since it is directly parallel to Hebrews 10:28-31. There, the sacred writer warns his readers if they fall away, they will be *close* to being cursed, "If it yields thorns and thistles it is worthless and close to being cursed, and it ends up being burned." "Close to being cursed" rules out the possibility the author of Hebrews is warning of hellfire. Hebrews 6:8 is thus exactly parallel to 1 Corinthians 3:12-15 that warns of loss of eschatological reward, not loss of salvation. In fact, the reference to thorns and thistles in Hebrews 6:8

appears to be slightly worse than the mention of wood, hay and stubble in Corinthians 3:12. As such, anyone who has persisted in willful sin in this life can only expect great fear, suffering, and pain when he will give an account of himself before God at the judgment tribunal of Christ. Worse, in light of all the spiritual privileges he has been given under the New Testament, he will receive the strictest measure of judgment than other saints who lived in previous dispensations.

CHAPTER TEN

Perseverance of the Saints or Judgment – 10:32-12:29

Faithful Perseverance & Inheriting the Promises – 10:32-11:40

After giving a very severe warning in Hebrews 10, as is his habit, the sacred writer admonishes his readers to persevere in their faith. This emphasis upon perseverance begins in 10:32, and concludes at the final warning of the book in Hebrews 12. It is right in between these two chapters where is found the great section on the Old Testament heroes of the faith (Heb 11). In Hebrews 11, many Old Testament heroes of the faith are listed, and used as biblical examples and illustrations of faithfulness. The Hebrew readers themselves need to imitate the faith of the heroes of the past, "And we desire that each one of you show the same diligence so as to realize the full assurance of hope until the end, so that you will not become sluggish, but ***imitators*** of those who through faith and patience inherit the promises (6:11-12)."

In Hebrews 6:11-12, the sacred writer is anticipating Hebrews 11, the Old Testament hall of fame of faith. However, before he begins to discuss the Old Testament heroes of the faith, he first teaches them about the great significance of the Order of Melchizedek and the New Covenant, and then gives them yet another severe warning, before finally picking up on this thread again at the end of chapter 10, "Therefore, do not throw away your confidence which has great reward. For you have need of endurance so that when you have done the will of God, you may receive what was promised (10:35-36)." From here, the author now begins to give his readers many biblical examples of faithful Old Testament saints who persevered in their faith. The Hebrew readers need to imitate their faith so they can inherit the promise of entering God's rest. The whole thrust of Hebrews is that the readers must firmly hold fast their confession of faith (3:6, 14; 4:14; 6:11-12; 10:23, 35-39). So now in chapter 11, the author gives them a list of Old Testament faithful heroes to follow. Even more remarkable with regard to the Old Testament saints is that even though they could never experience the results of God's promises, they still believed in God's promises (11:39). They persevered by continuing to believe God's promises in spite of their difficult circumstances (11:32-39). This is precisely what faith is all about, and such faith is worthy of imitation.

What is so striking in Hebrews 11 is the author does not tell his readers how to get saved through faith, but how to live by faith after salvation. He everywhere assumes they are already saved (3:1; 10:10-14; 6:4-5; 10:26, 29; 12:22-24). Getting saved is nowhere said to be the problem in the book of Hebrews. The problem is over their post salvation experience with regard to spiritual perseverance. He therefore commands them throughout the letter what to do after their salvation, i.e., to persevere by faith, to endure by faith, to live by faith. It would be a waste of time to warn an unbeliever, or even a mere professor of faith, to persevere in the faith. The necessity to persevere only makes sense if it is already assumed the readers are already saved. Old Testament heroes of the faith simply cannot be imitated by unbelievers.

In chapter 11 the author over and over again speaks about how the faith of the Old Testament heroes led them to *do* divinely acceptably works (11:4-39). This means, at once, the faith he is emphasizing cannot be saving faith, but rather faith related to their sanctification. Saving faith is apart from works. Sanctification faith is with works. The only way to have saving faith is apart from works. The only way to have sanctification faith is to demonstrate its spiritual fruits with works. Here in Hebrews 11, the author is stressing the latter. The examples of faith listed here shows that by faith, the Old Testament hero *did* something. This being so, the author is talking about a faith which leads to good works, a faith which leads to a positive divine testimony (11:2, 39), a faith which is pleasing to God (11:6), a faith which God will richly reward (11:6), a faith which will inherit the promises (6:11-12), a faith which will enter God's rest (4:1-11). The job of the Christian after his salvation is therefore to persevere and endure in faith by doing good works in the process. This first of all results in sanctification, and then, if and only if there is sanctification, God will reward the faithful with a great spiritual inheritance both in this life and especially in the life to come, "Therefore do not throw away your confidence, which has a great reward. For you have need of endurance, so that when you have done the will of God you may receive what was promised (10:35-36)."

With this in mind, the examples of faith here are not parallel to Romans 4, i.e., how to get justified by faith apart from works, but how to be justified by both faith and works as in James 2. In fact, in Hebrews 11:17, the author quotes the same historical occurrence in Genesis 22 as James does when Abraham offered up his son on the altar, "By faith Abraham, **when he was tested**, offered up Isaac (11:17; James 2:21-24)." Here, when Abraham's faith was **tested**, James says that Abraham was justified by both faith and works (James 2:24). Abraham therefore passed the test and received a great reward of being called the friend of God (James 2:23). Closely connected, it was at this point in Abraham's life when the author of Hebrews earlier reminded his readers that Abraham inherited the promise (6:9-15). Because of his faithful perseverance under trial, God made an additional oath to Abraham, swearing by His own holy character that, "I will surely bless you and I will surely multiply you (Gen 22:17; Heb 6:14)." In this way, the divine oath confirmed that Abraham will indeed be heir of the promise because of his obedience to God. This is in great contrast to the historical occurrence of Genesis 15 and the doctrinal explanation of it in Romans 4 when Abraham was justified apart from his works. In Romans 4, Abraham has no works to boast about before God (Rom 4:2).

As such, justification by faith apart from works (Gen 15:6; Rom 4:1-8), precedes justification by faith and works under spiritual testing (Gen 22; James 2:21-24). Some 25 years or more separate these two great historical events in the life of Abraham. What began in Genesis 15, Abraham's justification by faith without works, was perfected in Genesis 22 by faith and works (James 2:21-24). As such, James writes, "And the Scripture was *fulfilled* which says, and Abraham believed God, and it was reckoned to him as righteousness, ***and he was called the friend of God*** (James 2:23)." What began as a righteousness imputed by God's grace apart from works in Genesis 15:6, was *fulfilled* many years later by Abraham when he obediently offered up Isaac on the altar, "And as a result of works his faith was *perfected* (James 2:22)."

In other words, Genesis 15:6 is God's imputed righteousness, a divine act in which God justifies the ungodly apart from works. This was credited to Abraham's account in spite of his pagan background and character when he first trusted in the Lord. However, in Genesis 22, James demands of his readers that this imputed righteousness should later lead to a godly life of righteousness demonstrated by good works. As such, imputed righteousness is designed by God to lead to a spiritual life which shows righteousness, and so James calls this is a *fulfillment* of imputed righteousness (James 2:23-24). Imputed justification at the point of salvation is designed to lead to a sanctification justification in which the believer does divinely acceptable works – works which God will accept, works which God will justify. More to the point, having perfected or finished his initial faith, Abraham received a great reward. He was then called the friend of God. Thus the issue in James 2, as well as in Hebrews 11, is the perfecting of faith, not the beginning of faith.

To justify simply means to be declared righteous. Context will determine in what way and why a man is justified. In Genesis 15 Abraham was justified apart from his works for initial salvation (Rom 4:1-8: Gal 3:1-14), but in Genesis 22, he was justified by his works when God tested him with regard to his sanctification (James 2:21-24; Heb 11:17-19). Seen in this light, and only in this light, can it be said that a man is justified by works, and not by faith alone (James 2:24). Here, the point is not that Abraham's ultimate salvation before God is based on both faith and works, but that works, though not a necessary condition of salvation, are a demanded consequence of salvation. Just because the condition of salvation is without works in no way implies that good works are not necessary. On the contrary, it is precisely because they are saved that believers need to do good works (Eph 2:8-10; Titus 3:5-8). God demands good works of faithful obedience in the life of the believer, and Abraham is a prime example of exactly what God expects.

However, demanding spiritual obedience is one thing, and fulfilling spiritual obedience is quite another. This is the whole point of not only the book of James, but the entire book of Hebrews as well. In both James and Hebrews there are too many brothers in the church who lack faithful obedience. As such, both writers write blistering letters against them, some of the most convicting found anywhere in the New Testament. However, neither James of the author of Hebrews ever questions the salvation of their readers. In both letters, their readers are called brothers.

In sanctification, a man is justified by faith and works, but sanctification is never seen as a condition of salvation, but always the consequence of salvation. More to the point, perseverant faith in sanctification leads to justification by works. It is precisely this kind of perseverant faith the author of Hebrews wants to see in his readers, a faithful obedience which inherits the promises and enters God's rest (Heb 4:1-11; 6:11-12; 10:35-36). Paul wrote something very similar in Colossians 1:22-23, "Yet He has now reconciled you in His fleshly body through death (justification by faith without works), in order to present you before Him *holy and blameless and beyond reproach* (justification by works) *IF indeed you continue in the faith firmly established and steadfast, and not moved away from the hope of the gospel that you have heard.*" Even Jude chimes in with such sentiments when he writes, "Now to Him who is able to keep you from stumbling, and to make you stand in presence of His glory *blameless* with great joy (Jude 1:24)."

Jesus is the Supreme Winner to Follow – 12:1-3

Now in Hebrews 12, the author gives his readers the best example of faithful perseverance of all – that of Jesus Himself (12:1-3). The emphasis upon faithful perseverance therefore continues. Only this time, instead of using Old Testament saints as examples to imitate as in chapter 11, the author uses Jesus Himself as the supreme example of all. Here, the author turns away from the Old Testament heroes of the faith to Christ Himself as *the* hero of the faith. At the same time, the author also returns to his usual method of exhortation. In other words, Hebrews 11 was a history lesson, but then in chapter 12, he is back to exhortation and warning akin to Hebrews 10:32-39. In fact, in 12:1-3, the sacred writer is elaborating further the fact his readers have **need** *of endurance.*[146] Chapter 11 interrupted the exhortation of chapter 10 to bring in many concrete Old Testament examples to follow. However, the best example of all cannot be the saints under the Old Covenant, but Jesus Himself, the supreme example of persevering faith.[147] In short, the author resumes his admonition by pointing his readers to the life of Christ as the premier example to follow (10:32-12:3).

Jesus is Himself is the prime example of a man who lived by faith. As such, He is called the champion and perfecter of faith (12:2), "The champion and perfecter who exercised faith like no one else ever has.[148] Jesus continued to trust God in spite of all adversity, in spite of the shame of the cross, and in spite of the hostility of people (12:1-3). Then the sacred writer states the reason why Jesus persevered in spite of such great adversity, "Who for the joy set before Him endured the cross, despising the shame, and has sat down at the right hand of the throne of God (12:2)." In other words, Jesus did what He did to obtain the great reward of sitting down at the right hand of God. This joy to sit down at the right hand of God, i.e., to enter God's rest, Jesus desired greatly, and so He endured the shame and suffering of this earthly life. Jesus was willing to do everything He did because of the great glorious joy that would follow. In the same way, the Hebrew readers need to do likewise. They need to side with the shame and starkness of the cross in spite of religious peer pressure not to do so. They need to get their eyes off of the their old religious system and look forward to the glorious joy of the eschatological future. If they do so, they can survive the fiery trials of life as Jesus did.

This is why the sacred writer uses the illustration of a runner at a race (12:1). Athletes suffer greatly in training, not because they love suffering, nor because they enjoy making themselves miserable, but for the joy of winning the prize. To win is the greatest fulfillment in life. Nevertheless, to win also demands faithful endurance. If people want the prize, they need to have a winning attitude. They cannot behave as the Exodus generation did who complained continually and yet still expected to enter rest. No, they must have a winning attitude as Joshua or Caleb did, or even better yet, as Jesus did. Otherwise, they will suffer the same consequences as the Exodus generation. Winning and losing

---

[146]   Lane, p. 404.
[147]   Ibid, pp. 406-07.
[148]   Ibid., pp. 412-13.

are therefore inherently part of the whole Christian experience, and Christians need to prepare themselves so as to win, or suffer great loss at God's judgment.

Jesus endured, and so inherited the prize to sit down at the right hand of God. He completed His work of salvation on the cross, and so has entered God's rest. He now sits as ruler over all. Because of His suffering obedience, He will now reign forever from the right hand of God. The Hebrew readers also need to persevere in their faith if they want to be heirs with Christ in this great eschatological world to come at the right hand of God (Heb 1:1-3:14). Otherwise, they will not enter God's rest just as the Exodus generation failed to do so. As such, they need to lay aside every encumbrance and besetting sin (12:1). They need to run with endurance the race that is set before them (12:1). Moreover, they can do this only insofar as they occupy themselves with the trials and glories of Christ Himself.

Divine Discipline and Forfeiture of Seeing the Lord − 12:12-15

The theme of Hebrews 12:1-11 is occupation with Christ in the midst of divine discipline, and this is quickly followed by the last severe warning of the book in 12:12-29. As such, if the Hebrew readers are not willing to endure divine discipline by focusing on the Lord (12:1-11), then God's judgment will come upon them (12:12-29), really the last resort in divine discipline. As such, the sacred writer says **therefore** in Hebrews 12:12. Because of the victory of Christ (12:1-3), because of divine discipline (12:4-11), because God's discipline shows His love for them (12:6), because divine discipline leads to spiritual character (12:7-11), therefore, because of all of these things, the Hebrew readers are commanded to, "strengthen the hands that are weak and the knees that are feeble, and make straight paths for your feet so that limb which is lame may not be put out of joint, but rather be healed (12:12-13)."

Here, the author of Hebrews commands them to strengthen themselves with all of the glories of Christianity in the previous chapters that the author has been discussing, or suffer judgment. The problem is that his readers are characterized as being weak handed with feeble knees. In such a condition, they simply cannot walk along the crooked paths of false doctrine without becoming injured, "so that limb which is lame may not put out of joint (12:13)." The bumps and holes along the trails of false doctrine will leave them injured and stranded in the wilderness without chance of any recovery. They therefore need to get back on the straight path of Christian truth if they want to recover their spiritual health. The sacred writer says it another way in Hebrews 13:9, "Do not be carried away by varied and strange teachings; for it is good for the heart to be strengthened by grace, not by foods, through which those who were so occupied were not benefited." The Hebrew readers need to be strengthened by the teachings of grace, not the varied and strange teachings of liturgy and ritualism which cannot provide any spiritual benefit to those who practice them. Worse, if they do not strengthen themselves through grace teaching, they will come up short of the grace of God, and like Esau, be disinherited (12:14-17). Just as Esau lost his inheritance rights through disobedience, so the same can also happen to the Hebrew readers.

Now at this juncture, the sacred writer intimates just how serious this disinheritance will be. Those who fall short of God's sanctification grace will not be able to see the Lord (12:14). Here, the sacred writer in no uncertain terms presents that a future heavenly vision of the Lord requires faithful obedience in this life. Seeing the Lord is clearly presented here as a reward for faithful obedience. It is therefore not something automatically presented to all, but only to those, who by faith and patience, inherit the promises, "Pursue peace with all men, and the sanctification, without which no one will see the Lord (12:14)." Seeing the Lord in the heavenly future is thus conditioned upon perseverance in sanctification. This is also consistent with the beatitudes, "Blessed are the pure in heart, for they shall see God (Matt 5:8)."

Many have suggested here again in Hebrews 12:14 that the sacred author is warning his readers about loss of salvation. Not seeing the Lord is a very serious consequence, one which on the surface seems to imply loss of salvation. However, there is nothing in this context which demands this worst-case scenario, especially in light of everything that has already been discussed throughout the book of Hebrews. Moreover, if only those who pursue sanctification can enter heaven, then the author of Hebrews is teaching a form of salvation by works, not too far removed from Roman Catholic teaching. In light of this, and in keeping with theological consistency throughout the book, it is best to see this vision of the Lord as a special future heavenly reward for obedience, closely connected with the idea of entering God's rest. Those who have been faithful on the earth, will enjoy a unique and special intimacy with the Lord that will not be permitted to others, "The idea of going to *see* someone is commonly used, and in it is resident the concept of fellowship with him."[149] Indeed, even when Jesus was on the earth, it was not everyone who had special intimacy with the Lord. It was the disciple John who was Jesus' best friend. Then there was the three: John, James, and Peter. Then there were the 12, and beyond the disciples there was Lazarus and his family, so on down the line until the crowds at large, with increasing distance of concentric circles. There is no reason to think that this relationship will be any different in heaven. Not all will have special intimacy with the Lord even in heaven. Here the author of Hebrews promises a special beatific vision of the Lord if they faithfully pursue sanctification.

That the author of Hebrews must be talking about a special vision of the Lord perhaps goes without saying. The fact of the matter is that at the revelation of Christ, "Every eye will *see* Him, even those who pierced Him; and all the tribes of the earth will mourn over Him (Rev 1:7)." Here the apostle John describes the glorious Second Advent of Christ which *all* will see, both believer and unbeliever. At the revelation of Christ, all will see the glory of the Lord coming with the clouds of heaven. The apostle John also writes in 1 John that every believer will see the Lord, "Beloved, now we are children of God, and it has not yet appeared as yet what we will be. We know that when He appears, we will be like Him, because we will *see* Him just as He is (1 John 3:2)." However, with great interest, John also speaks of those who will not be ready for the coming of Christ, "Now little children, abide in Him, so that when He appears, we may have confidence and not shrink away from Him in shame at His coming (1 John 2:28)." John here intimates that some believers will shrink away from the Lord at His appearance precisely because they have not consistently been faithful to Him. It is these believers who will be denied special intimacy with the Lord in heaven. They will not be able to intimately see the Lord in heaven. As their intimacy with the Lord was much to be desired on the earth, this will be no less true in

---

[149]   Dunham, *The Danger of Disaffection*, p. 2.

heaven. Moreover, this loss will not merely be temporary, but for all of eternity.

Likewise, though a redeemed generation, only a few from the Exodus generation were allowed to see the glory of the Lord, and then only Moses was given a close-up glimpse on Mt. Sinai, a mountain which the author will soon refer to (12:22). After the Exodus generation entered into the Old Covenant with the sprinkling of the blood (Ex 24:1-8), Moses, Aaron, Nadub, Abihu, and 70 elders of Israel, "saw the God of Israel; and under His feet there appeared to be a pavement of sapphire, as clear as the sky itself. Yet He did not stretch out His hand against the nobles of the sons of Israel; and they saw God, and they ate and drank (Ex 24:9)." Though Nadub and Abihu saw the God of Israel, they later died the sin unto death when they offered strange fire to the Lord (Lev 10:1-6). It was only Moses, however, who was given the most intimate revelation of the Lord. On the other hand, even Moses could not be exposed to the full glory of God:

> But He said, "You cannot see My face, for no man can see Me and live." Then the Lord said, "Behold, there is a place by Me, and you shall stand there on the rock; and it will come about, while My glory is passing by, that I will put you in the cleft of the rock and cover you with My hand until I have passed by. Then I will take My hand away and you shall see My back, but My face shall not be seen (Ex 33:20-23)."

Paul later teaches Timothy that the Lord, "dwells in unapproachable light, whom no man has seen or can see (1 Tim 6:16)." In light of this, there is nothing to say that the Lord can deny many a Christian the possibility of seeing Him in a special unique vision. If the Christian wants to intimately see the Lord in eternity, he must live a life of perseverant sanctification while still on the earth. This the author of Hebrews flatly declares. This, of course, is great motivation in and of itself to pursue sanctification.

Failure to Inherit the First-Born Blessing – 12:16-17

Esau is given only a few verses in chapter 12, and so is not the primary biblical example like the Exodus generation. Nonetheless, the issues are again almost identical. Esau, like the Exodus generation, lost his inheritance blessing through disobedience.[150] Esau also committed a sin which was irreparable, and because of it, he lost his first born status. Furthermore, this illustration does not support loss of salvation. Esau did not lose family status. He was still Isaac's physical son. He lost his first-born status. The firstborn received a double portion of the estate, while the other sons single and equal portions. This being so, the loss of first-born eminence in no way means a loss of family status, but it does mean that one has lost his right to be the spiritual ruler of the family. The double portion of his father's estate was forbidden Esau because he bargained it away for a single meal (12:16).

Esau actually despised his birthright (Gen 25:34), and so lost his right to be the spiritual priest-leader of the family. This was what was specifically lost. Isaac refused to give it back to him because of his apostasy (12:17; Gen 28:33-37). The author of Hebrews states that after he sold his birthright to Jacob, Esau sought to *inherit* his first-born blessing through loud and crying tears. However, Esau "found no opportunity for repentance." In other words, Isaac would not change his mind. His decision was final. Esau was thus not able to recover his birthright which he foolishly forfeited.[151]

Esau had little regard for his birthright and so hastily sold it to Jacob. He sold his birthright to Jacob because of *one* unsuccessful hunting trip (Gen 25:29-34). Esau was a hunter and lived off of the land (Gen 25:27-28). He apparently was no farmer like Jacob (Gen 25:27). As such, one day he came home famished after an unsuccessful hunting trip.

---

[150] With some interest, there is one contrast between Esau and the Exodus generation worthy of note. Whereas countless passages portray the Exodus generation as *redeemed*, the Biblical witness is silent with regard to Esau's salvation. Many suggest that Romans 9:10-13 indicates that Esau was unsaved, but the passage does not necessarily teach this. The issue at hand in Romans 9:10-13 is God's gracious choice of Jacob over Esau. God decided that Esau would serve his younger brother Jacob before they were even born. In other words, God decided who would receive the first-born status, not who was to be saved, "the older will serve the younger (Rom 9:10-13)." Furthermore, this choice by God (Rom 9:10-13) in no way contradicts the outcome that Esau deserved to lose his first-born status because of his disobedience (Heb 12:15-17). Moreover, Isaac still did bless Esau, but not with his birthright (Gen 28:39-40; Heb 11:6).

[151] Reuben also lost his first-born status in Jacob's family through disobedience, i.e., he slept with his father's concubine, another act of apostasy (Gen 49:3-4).

Apparently, he was at the mercy of Jacob for food, and so Esau asked Jacob for some. Jacob asked Esau to sell him his birthright in exchange for the food (Gen 25:31). It was here that Esau committed his apostasy, despising his birthright (25:34), "Behold, I am about to die; so of what use then is the birthright to me (Gen 25:32)?"

This horizontal viewpoint of Esau, "I am about to die and so what use is the birthright to me?" cost him his birthright. The author of Hebrews here calls Esau both immoral and secular, nay even godless (Heb 12:16). These are, of course, synonyms for an apostate attitude, the opposite of holy.[152] Esau had little regard for his spiritual birthright and so committed an act of apostasy by selling it for the immediate gratification of the flesh. Moreover, his decision was irreversible. Once he gave it up, he could not get it back. There was no opportunity to regain what he hastily gave up. Isaac even refused to repent on the matter, "Behold, I have made him (Jacob) your master, and all his relatives I have given to him as servants; and with grain and new wine I have sustained him. Now as for you (Esau) then, what can I do, my son (Gen 28:37)?" The author of Hebrews summarizes, "For you know that even afterwards when he desired to inherit the blessing, he was rejected, for he found no place for repentance, though he sought it with tears (Heb 12:17)."

Esau could not recover from his apostasy, much like the Exodus generation many centuries later, and not too far removed from the Hebrew readers who are about to follow suit. Hebrews 6 clearly teaches it will be impossible to renew the Hebrew readers again to repentance if they fall away (6:4-6). Like Isaac, God will not grant them repentance to get back what they forfeited, and like the Exodus generation, they will die in a spiritual desert without any rest or any hope of recovery to regain what was lost. There comes a time when it becomes impossible to start over again after having given it up, and Esau is just another example of this.

Esau's emotional cry, parallel to the Exodus' generation cry after God sentenced them to die in the wilderness (Num 14:39), shows that he was not completely devoid of spiritual orientation:

> In spite of his impulsive disregard for divine things Esau still retained some sense of God's promise. And so he sought to secure

---

[152] Lane, p. 455.

what naturally belonged to him. He asserted the prerogative of his birthright even though he recklessly surrendered it.[153]

Emotional tears still could not bring back what was lost, however. Esau may have been very sorry, but as the old adage goes, "Sorry does not get it done."

It must finally be remembered that the judgment in view in Hebrews chapter 12 refers to loss of first-born status just like Esau, not loss of salvation. What's more, assuming the warnings are consistent throughout the book of Hebrews, and they most certainly are, then loss of first-born blessing is a result of being cut off from God's House (3:6), of not being a partaker with Christ (3:14). Without this it will be impossible to enter God's eschatological rest (4:1-11), and thus be able to see the Lord (12:14).[154] Being God's house, a partaker with Christ, entering rest, and seeing the Lord are closely related to each other. They are part and parcel of the church's inheritance rights, but these can all be lost through apostasy just like the Exodus and just like Esau lost them.

The Final Warning – 12:25-29

Hebrews 12:25-29 is the final warning. After the tragic failure of Esau is illustrated (12:15-17), Mt. Zion is then used as a strong encouragement to get the readers minds off their circumstances and onto the glories of heaven (12:18-24), and then the final warning itself is given in 12:25-29. As such, if the Hebrew readers fail to strengthen themselves at this point, if they do not pursue sanctification, if they fall short of the grace of God, if they do not appreciate the great heavenly glories of Mt. Zion and the Order of Melchizedek, they may fall under the same judgment as Esau, i.e., disinheritance.

Hebrews 12:26-27 then adds another illustration to emphasize the seriousness of the judgment at hand. In these verses, the sacred writer speaks of a fearful and future eschatological earthquake which will shake away everything not based on eternal principles, "Yet once more I will shake not only the earth, but also heaven. This expression, *yet once more,*

---

153   Westcott, p. 408.
154   With great interest 1 John 2:28-3:2 speaks of those who will shrink back, and thus look down in shame and not see the Lord, because of disobedience at Jesus' coming when all will see Him as He really is.

denotes the removing of those things which can be shaken, as of created things, so that those things which cannot be shaken may remain (12:26-27)." The author then concludes, "Our God is a consuming fire (12:29)." Earthquake and fire are therefore used as parallel illustrations to teach the fearfulness of the judgment seat of Christ

Hebrews 12:25 recalls yet once again the great comparison between the failure of the Exodus generation and the readers' own spiritual plight, "See to it that you do not refuse Him who is speaking. *For if those did not escape* when they refused Him who warned them on the earth, *much less will we escape* who turn away from Him who warns from heaven (12:25)." *Those* is a reference to the Exodus generation. They, of course, did not escape the judgment at Kadesh-Barnea (Num 14:1-38). Though they tried to repent after God laid down the judgment, it was too late (Num 14:39-45). Like Esau they found no opportunity for repentance in order to inherit the promise (Heb 12:15-17). As such, the author recalls yet once again the Exodus generation did not escape the judgments of the Old Covenent Law which were pronounced at Mt. Sinai. As he has been warning all along, neither will the Hebrew readers escape God's judgment under the authority of the New Covenant spoken from Mt. Zion, if they continue along the same lines.

Mt. Zion is called the heavenly Jerusalem (Heb 12:22). Mt. Zion is the coming millennial Kingdom of God promised throughout the Old Testament in which the Messiah and Israel will rule the world in righteousness, prosperity, and peace (Isa 2:1-4; Mic 4:1-8). It is directly parallel to the eschatological world to come mentioned in Hebrews 2, and God's rest in Hebrews 4. In this coming kingdom, the Messiah will "judge between many peoples, and render decisions for mighty distant nations (Isa 2:4; Mic 4:3)." This great judgment will then give way to the millennial kingdom of Messianic peace, "Then they will hammer their swords into plowshares, and their spears into pruning hooks; Nation will not lift up sword against nation, and never again will they train for war (Isa 2:4; Mic 4:3)." The world will thus be at rest, "Each of them will sit under his own vine and under his fig tree, with no one to make them afraid, for the mouth of the Lord of hosts has spoken (Mic 4:4)."

David adds further, "The Lord has chosen *Zion*; He has desired it for His habitation. This is My resting place forever; Here I will dwell, for I have desired it. I will abundantly bless her provision; I will satisfy her needy with bread (Ps 132:13-150)." This clearly associates Zion with the promised Messianic kingdom of rest found in many places throughout the Old Testament (Psalm 48; 50; 65). [155] Psalm 69 concludes, "Let heaven and earth praise Him, the seas and everything that moves in them. For God will save **Zion** and build the cities of Judah, that they may dwell there and possess it. The descendants of His servants will *inherit* it, and those who love His name will dwell in it (Ps 69:34-36)."

David sounds here very similar to the sacred writer of Hebrews. David writes, "Those who love His name will dwell in" Mt. Zion, which in this context means to *"inherit"* Mt. Zion, or inherit the Kingdom of God, or enter rest. In this particular psalm, David anticipates that future resurrected saints who love the Lord will *inherit Mt. Zion.* In other words, those who love the Lord will share in governing the eschatological world to come, perfectly consistent with the teaching of the book of Hebrews. Mt. Zion, i.e., heaven on earth, will be an unprecedented time wherein both resurrected saints and mortal men and women will live together at the same time. Those peoples and nations, including the saved remnant of Israel, who survive the great judgments of the Great Tribulation, will enter the Millennial kingdom of justice and peace in which both resurrected Old Testament and New Testament saints will also participate in (Isa 9:1-7; 11:1-10; 65-66; Dan 12:1-3; Rev 20:1-10). It will certainly be the most exciting time of history in which to experience, but in order to enjoy it in the future, David adds the condition of *love* for the Lord today.

While it may be true that Hebrew readers have *already come to Mt. Zion* (Heb 12:22), they have not yet inherited Mt. Zion as a prize to be taken by faithful perseverance to the end. The Hebrew readers thus need to love the Lord in light of their Mt. Zion privileges and responsibilities. They simply cannot afford to, "refuse Him who is speaking (12:25)." The author, therefore, commands them to *watch out*. It is almost as if one was walking across the street and heard a shout behind him, "Look out!"[156] In addition, the imperative is in the present tense, demanding that

---

[155] It also must be remembered that the prophet Isaiah and the apostle John envision that the millennial kingdom of peace on the earth will be transformed into a new heavens and a new earth (Isa 65-66; Rev 20-22). Thus millennial inheritance or reward will also have eternal repercussions.

[156] Ibid, p. 4.

the vigilance to watch out should be constant.[157] More to the point, they are to be vigilant to pay close attention to the Word of God which the author is giving them, "Watch out that you do not refuse Him who is speaking (12:25)." This is directly parallel to the first warning in the book where the author warns them to pay close attention to the Word which they heard from the apostles (2:1-4). Here, the author recognizes the Scriptural authority of his own letter as being the very Word of God, "Do not refuse Him who is speaking (12:25)." The author is giving them the very Word of God, and his readers need to watch out lest they fall into judgment.

Careful attention to the Word of God is required to avoid God's fatal judgment. His readers need to adjust themselves to the teachings of New Testament truth as depicted here in the book of Hebrews. They can only refuse listening to the Word of God at their peril. In a word, to refuse the divine authority of the Scriptures is to personally turn away from God Himself. The Hebrew readers need to pay close attention to the Word which they have heard, or suffer judgment like the Exodus generation (2:2-4). Applying New Testament doctrine into the spiritual life is therefore not an option. It is a requirement which can be avoided only at risk of great judgment.

At this point, the author of Hebrews intimates the judgment of Mt. Zion will be worse than the judgment of Mt. Sinai. The sacred writer teaches the warning of Mt. Zion is a heavenly warning, rather than merely an earthly warning like Mt. Sinai. Its judgments will therefore be eternally permanent. As such, the primary difference in Hebrews 12 compared to the other warnings is the eschatological repercussions are emphasized. Here, the author is clearly stressing the eschatological consequences of apostasy. Not only will they not be permitted to spiritually grow up in this life (Heb 5:11-6:8), neither will they be able to inherit God's Sabbath rest in the eschatological world to come (Heb 1:14-2:8; 3-4; 12:25-29). They will have lost their eternal reward, beginning with the millennium and extending to the new heavens and the new earth.

The author then goes on to illustrate the impending fearfulness of God's judgment. He uses the example of an earthquake to indicate how God will judge them. Just as there was a fearful earthquake at Mt. Sinai during the Exodus generation, so there will be an eschatological earthquake at Mt. Zion for Christians. This will most certainly occur since it

---

[157]   Ibid.

has been promised by God, "And His voice shook the earth then, but now He has **promised** saying, Yet once more I will shake not only the earth, but also the heavens (12:26)." Earthquakes always occur without notice, and once they begin, the sooner they end the better. It is a fearful thing to feel the solid ground shake like a leaf, "The Lord reigns, let the peoples **tremble**; He is enthroned above the cherubim, let the earth **shake**. The Lord is great in **Zion**, and He is exalted above all the peoples (Ps 99:1-2)." Furthermore, earthquakes show the quality of that which is built. Poorly built structures quickly cave in and crumble while well-built structures can endure with only minimal damage. Sometimes there is considerable damage to a building, but it still remains intact. Something parallel to this will happen at the judgment seat of Christ when every believer will have to pass through the test of God's eschatological earthquake.

Whatever the Hebrew readers did in this life will all be evaluated by this fearful eschatological earthquake. There will be no escape from this judgment. Everything they did not do in accordance with the eternal word of God will be shaken away and removed, "This expression, yet once more, denotes the removing of things which can be shaken, as of created things, so that those things which cannot be shaken may remain (12:27)." This earthquake will be far more fearful than the earthquake at Mt. Sinai which the Exodus generation experience. This eschatological earthquake will shake away the entire created universe, and every work of the flesh throughout history. As such, the Hebrew readers must learn to use the eternal principles of the Word of God in their lives on a consistent persevering basis if they want to survive this great earthquake. Anything less will crumble under the pressure of God's judgment. This great eschatological earthquake will reveal everything which has lasting value, and destroy everything that does not.

In the Sermon on the Mount, a sermon given by Jesus which has much to say about blessing and eternal reward in the Kingdom of heaven, Jesus Himself concluded with a severe warning, "Everyone who **hears** these words of Mine and does not do them, will be like a foolish man who built his house upon the sand. The rain fell, and the floods came, and the winds blew and slammed against that house, and it fell, and great was its fall (Matt 7:26-27)." Jesus here warns His own followers (Matt 5:1-2) that merely hearing the Word of God (Matt 7:26) will not prevent disaster when judgment comes. They must act on His word, and thus be compared to a man who built his house upon the rock (Matt 7:24). Such a man's house will survive the great floods of judgment. The man who built his own upon the sand will lose his house when the great floods of judgment come. Moreover, what is lost was not the man, but his house, i.e., what he built. Even Paul sharply warns the Corinthians with regard to all the divisions in the church, "But each man must be careful how *he builds* (1 Cor 3:10)." Paul then immediately warns them of loss of eternal reward, not loss of salvation (1 Cor 3:14-15). Wood, hay and stubble will not survive the fiery flames of God's judgment, only gold, silver and precious stones (1 Cor 3:12). So in the same way, if Jesus' disciples want to build something which has eternal value, they must hear the Word of God and act upon it, "For no man can lay a foundation other than the one which is laid, which is Jesus Christ (1 Cor 3:11)." The same principle also applies here in Hebrews 12:25-29. The great eschatological earthquake will remove everything worthless.

In light of this great eschatological earthquake, the author of Hebrews concludes the warning, "Therefore, since we have a kingdom which cannot be shaken, let us show gratitude, by which we may offer to God an acceptable service with reverence and awe. For our God is a consuming fire (12:28-29)." It is often stated that salvation is grace, and ethics is gratitude. This is exactly what the sacred writer of Hebrews is stating here. His readers already have an unshakeable kingdom. It is theirs by the free grace of God. This gracious gift naturally leads into a life of gratitude, service and thanksgiving to God. The Greek word *to serve* here is the word used to worshipfully serve the Lord in the tabernacle ministry.

However, instead of serving the Lord according to the old ritualistic system of the Old Covenant, the Hebrew readers need to worshipfully serve the Lord according to the Order of Melchizedek under the authority of the New Testament. This order is an eternal order which will reward the Hebrew readers with the eternal inheritance of God's rest at the right hand of God. To fail to worshipfully serve the Lord in this awesome manner is to invite the fires of God's judgment (12:29). As such, while the Order of Melchizedek is full of grace, it also demands reverence and awe, "For our God is a consuming fire (12:29)."

Though again it is very serious indeed, the fire mentioned in this verse nowhere calls into question the salvation of his readers. The author is warning his readers here, who are about to commit apostasy, that they have already come to Mt. Zion (12:22). **Have already come** is strong in the Greek being a perfect tense. The Greek perfect tense speaks of a past completed action which has enduring results.[158] The author is, therefore, not suggesting his readers will somehow lose their salvation. They have already come to Mt. Zion, and will remain there. Moreover, the author uses another perfect tense in 12:23, "having been **enrolled** in heaven." The permanency of this enrollment is thus underlined here.

At the same time, this does not mean that they are out of danger. Again, with great privilege comes great responsibility. New Testament privilege calls for allegiance and obedience.[159] A failure to pay close attention to New Testament truth can only be catastrophic in light of the great privileges they have already been given. The doctrine of eternal security nowhere implies that a Christian will get away with sin. All sin will be judged by a holy impartial God at the judgment seat of Christ, "For we must all appear before the judgment seat of Christ, so that each one may be recompensed for his deeds done in the body, according to what he has done, **whether good or bad** (2 Cor 5:10)."

The warning of 12:25-29, in light of the previous context, is also threatening his readers with something akin to the loss of firstborn status like Esau. In the Old Testament, the firstborn was the ruler-priest of the family, which privilege Esau carelessly bargained away (12:15-17). As such, with the failure of Esau in mind, it is no coincidence that author adds another description of the nature of the church, calling it the **church of the Firstborn** (12:23). While the exact title the **church of the firstborn** is unusual, the thought is not. Jesus Himself is called the **firstborn** in several places (Rom 8:29; Col 1:15, 18; Heb 1:6). This does not mean that He is literally the firstborn, but that He is the King of all creation, including the church. It therefore follows that those who are faithful to Him and who have been also partakers with Christ on the earth, will share in His first-born rights over all creation (Heb 3:14) in Mt. Zion. This is also consistent with entering God's rest, i.e., to rule over the created universe. Even the apostle John calls Jesus the firstborn (Rev 1:5-6). This is quickly followed up with a reference to the privileges of the church in light of this divine designation, "And He has made us to be

---

[158]   The perfect tenses of 10:10-14 indicating eternal security and the subsequent warning of 10:26-31 parallel the perfect tenses of 12:18-24 and the warning of 12:25-29.
[159]   Lane, p. 490.

a kingdom, priests to His God and Father (Rev 1:6)." Just like the Order
of Melchizedek in Hebrews, the apostle John calls the saints in the church
a kingdom of priests. John even adds that this was something that Jesus
Himself did, "He **made us** to be a kingdom of priests (Rev 1:6)." This is
certainly a strong allusion to the Order of Melchizedek as described in
the book of Hebrews. The Church has been designated by God to share
in the firstborn rights of the Son in kingdom of God. This means they
are to be eternal kings and priests.

Being called the ***church of the Firstborn***, it appears that this is a special blessing specifically given to the Church. In contrast to the saints
of the past, they will treated as the first-born of God's inheritance rest.
The relationship between the Church and Israel may very well be that
the Church will be treated as the first-born. The author of Hebrews
mentions another great group of people in contrast to the Church of the
first-born, "The spirits of righteous men made perfect (12:23)." This is
generally held to be a reference to Old Testament saints. If this is the
case, then in some sense, the Church shall receive a double portion of
God's estate in contrast to Israel.

Therefore, the reference to the ***church of the first-born*** (12:25) is an
allusion to the inheritance rights which may be lost through disobedience. Compared to Israel, and just like Esau and Jacob, even though
the Church came second, it will be given the inheritance rights of the
first-born. They will share in the same first-born sonship rights of
Jesus Christ (Rom 8:29; Col 1:15-18; Heb 1:6; Rev 1:5). Although they
came later in history, the church shall receive a double portion of God's
estate being treated like the firstborn. As in the case of Esau and Jacob,
though Israel is older, they shall serve the younger, the Church. However, also like Esau though too, is that this first-born inheritance can be
lost through apostasy. Reuben was another Old Testament example of a
son who lost his firstborn status through disobedience. Because he slept
with his father's concubine, Jacob gave the firstborn inheritance rights
to Joseph (Gen 49:3-4, 22-26; 1 Chron 5:1). Thus even in this instance,
comparable to Esau, what is being warned of is not loss of family status,
i.e., salvation, but the right to be the spiritual ruler in the family. The
Hebrew readers might barter away their blessings as firstborn in the
Church for the religious bells and whistles of Judaism.[160]

---

160   Ibid.

The right to function as the firstborn, to enter God's inheritance rest, must be earned by spiritual obedience. Indeed, even Jesus promised the disciples that they would sit as judges over the 12 tribes of Israel because of their perseverance (Matt 19:28), "You are those who have stood by Me in My trials; and just as My Father has granted Me a kingdom, I grant you that you may eat and drink at My table in My kingdom, and you will sit on thrones judging the 12 tribes of Israel (Luke 22:30)." This will be their great inheritance. They will be great kings and priests pronouncing great judgments in the eschatological world to come. They will also have close intimacy with Jesus in His kingdom, eating and drinking with Him. They will thus certainly *see the Lord* as they share in His inheritance rest, "Everyone who has left houses or brothers or sisters or fathers or mother or children or farms for My name's sake, will *receive many times as much*, and will *inherit eternal life* (Matt 19:29-30)." Receiving abundant eternal life is clearly equated with inheriting eternal life, not unlike inheriting rest here in Hebrews. Jesus promises those who faithfully obey Him that they shall receive or inherit abundant eternal life. They will enter God's inheritance rest, and there they will share great intimacy with the Lord, and rule in this so great eschatological world to come. The right to rule in God's inheritance is clearly conditioned upon faithful obedience. The alternative to this is frightening (12:29). Without obedience, they will not inherit rest, but rather inherit the consuming wrathful fire of God.

As such, the author of Hebrews sums up all of his warning and admonition very tersely, "For our God is a consuming fire (12:29)." Here we have a parallel passage to the burning of 6:8, and the fury of fire seen in 10:27. Here again, many quickly resort to the fires of hell as the only viable interpretation in keeping with the severity of the warning. However, this conclusion is outright denied by the great Lawgiver Moses himself in Deuteronomy 4:21-24. In Deuteronomy 4, the Exodus generation has finally died off after a long 40 years in the desert, and so Moses is now exhorting their children, the conquest generation of Joshua, to take possession of the land, i.e., to enter rest.

In Deuteronomy 4:21-22, Moses reminds them that God did not allow even him to enter the promised-land, "Now the Lord was angry with me on your account, and swore that I would not cross the Jordan, and that I would not enter the good land which the Lord your God is giving you as an inheritance. For I will die in this land, I shall not cross the Jordan, but you shall cross and take possession of the good land (4:22)." After using himself as a negative example of sin unto death, Moses then warns the conquest generation to be very careful themselves in 4:23, only to conclude with a most remarkable reason given in 4:24, "For the Lord your God is a consuming fire (4:24)." While this is not an exact quotation of Hebrews 12:29 since the sacred writer replaces *your* with *our*, it is so close, that it cannot be denied he is warning his own readers with the same warning that Moses warned Joshua's generation of some 1500 years before. In Deuteronomy 4:24, Moses specifically applies the consuming fire passage to himself and puts it out as a warning against the conquest generation. Moses was denied the inheritance rest because of the consuming fire of God's judgment. The same may also happen to Joshua's generation if they are not careful. This nails it down even more that the consuming fire of judgment in Hebrews is directed against God's own people, i.e., to believers rather than unbelievers, and that the consequences are not hellfire and brimstone, but loss of inheritance and reward.

CHAPTER ELEVEN

WORSHIP AND CHRISTIAN ETHICS – 13:1-25

The great thrust of the book of Hebrews is on how to worship God in the age of New Testament grace. The Hebrew readers had lost respect for Christian worship because of the lack of outward display so characteristic of pure Old Testament religion (and of course their own contemporary Judaism). As such, the sacred author his sermon to correct their faulty views of Christian worship. Here he shows his readers that even though Christian worship is invisible, it is awesome. It is far more spectacular than anything the Levitical priests ever did on the earth. In fact, because of the Messiah's one time sacrifice for sins, Christians can actually worship God in heaven right now through the power of the resurrection, ascension, and priesthood of Jesus. They can worship God confidently and boldly through Christ within the heavenly holy of holies. The author, therefore, spends an enormous amount of time contrasting Old Testament worship with the New Testament worship.

Moreover, New Testament worship is better in every way conceivable, precisely because it is the real thing as opposed to mere model. The problem is the Hebrew readers were being tempted to go back to the old model at the expense of the real thing. The author thus exhorts his readers – that is, he both severely warns, but also encourages them, to experience the greatness of the New Testament worship, according to the Order of Melchizedek, in heaven itself, inside the veil. The book of Hebrews is essentially an exhortation, nay even a warning, on how to worship God acceptably, "Therefore since we receive a kingdom which cannot be shaken, let us show gratitude, by which *we may offer to God an acceptable service* with reverence and awe (12:28)." Earlier, the sacred writer asserted, "How much more will the blood of Christ, who through the eternal Spirit offered Himself without blemish to God, cleanse your conscience from dead works *to serve the living God* (9:14)."

Christian worship today is an awesome experience. It is a heavenly experience. However, this heavenly experience can only be experienced through the exercise of faith, not through the fleshly senses. This is why the author of Hebrews constantly exhorts his readers to believe God throughout the book. He is warning them to believe God so they can acceptably worship Him. There is only one way to worship God, through faith. Without faith, it is *impossible* to please God (Heb 11:6). As such, by faith in the heavenly Order of Melchizedek, the readers can experience the reality of their heavenly priesthood right now, far above the Levitical priesthood, even though they are still physically alive on the earth. Moreover, this magnificent priesthood is not just given to a select few, but to all, to every saint, assuming they persevere in faithful obedience to God. Thus through faith, the readers can have this heavenly perspective which is so necessary to vital worship. Without this faith, they will end up with mediocre worldly religion.

The recipients of the letter to the Hebrews need to understand that Christianity is awesome. They have already come to Mt. Zion, the heavenly city of God (12:22-24), and this heavenly city is to be their spiritual focus, not the worldly religion of the Old Testament. Christianity is the most spectacular accomplishment that God has yet to bring forth, and the Hebrew readers desperately need to understand this basic truth. The sacred author, therefore, writes one of the most outstanding books found anywhere in ancient literature to describe the lofty heights of supernatural Christianity. The great problem, however, is the awesomeness of Christianity can only be seen by the eyes of faith, and without this, there can be no genuine worship from within the church. Worldly religion will inevitably take over and cloud the great glories of Christian worship. This is essentially what the book of Hebrews is all about, to get people beyond the worldly religious system to experience real supernatural living by faith. A church is far more than a religious social club, and the book of Hebrews describes why this is so.

And so having established the supernatural foundations of Christianity, now at the end of the book in Hebrews 13, the author finally begins to blend Christian worship with Christian ethics. Here the sacred writer avoids the spiritual trap of many who first emphasize biblical ethics before first establishing a theological foundation. As such, Christian morality does not show up until the end of the book, i.e., chapter 13. Here is finally seen a do and don't list with regard to Christian worship. In other words, after 12 chapters of very difficult theological explanation and warning, the author finally gets around to Christian ethics. The author clearly understands that without theology, without sound bible doctrine, there can be no spiritual life acceptable to God. Hence theology comes first, and then ethics. Ethics without theology is bare religion full of humanistic ideals, void of supernatural life.

As such on 13:1, the sacred writer demands of his readers to let brotherly love continue. Closely related, they are not to neglect showing hospitality to strangers, and to remember the imprisoned and ill-treated who are suffering for their Christian testimony (13:2-3). This of course suggests that the Hebrew Church is under some form of civil pressure. In 13:4, the readers are commanded to honor the marriage bed. God will judge both adulterers and fornicators. Likewise, they are to be free from the love of money. They need to be content with what they have (13:5). Though God may discipline them, the fact is God will never forsake them (13:5), "The Lord is my helper, I will not be afraid. What will man do to me (13:6)?" Again, there is a strong sense of persecution in the air as the author tries to encourage his readers.

In 13:7, the Hebrew readers are to follow their spiritual leaders who spoke the word of God to them. This means they are to imitate their faith. In contrast to their teachers who taught them the Word of God, they are not to be carried away by various and strange teachings which are opposed to grace (13:9). Anti-grace teaching is generally a sign of false doctrine. The fact of the matter is that New Testament grace affords his readers a most prestigious altar which other religious teachings cannot copy or replace (13:10). They can experience the Melchizedekian Priesthood within their very souls, far above any religious system of rituals on the earth. However, in order to experience this, they must be willing to suffer outside the gate of religious culture like Jesus did. The Hebrew readers must make a decision between religion and Christ. They cannot have both at the same time.

In 13:15, they are to continually offer up a sacrifice of praise to God. They are not to neglect doing good, sharing with fellow believers (13:16). They are also to obey, and submit to their leaders. In 13:18-19, the author requests that his readers pray for himself and for his companions as they are certain that they have behaved honorably in all things. They appear to be on the defense here. Again this suggests that they under some form of public or civil scrutiny of some kind. After a closing benediction in 13:20-21, the author urges them to bear "this word of exhortation (13:22)." The author clearly recognizes his sermon will be difficult for many to listen to. Then in 13:23, he reminds them that Timothy has been released, and that if he comes, then the author will be able to see his readers. The author then concludes his sermon with greetings and the final, "Grace be with you all (13:25)."

As such, what is being discussed by the sacred writer is not a typical religious ethic. He is talking about an ethics according to grace, ethics according to heavenly New Testament principles, ethics according to supernatural realities, not according to human religious culture. The foundation for Christian ethics is the grace of God as embodied in the New Testament. Hebrews 8:10 makes it clear the New Testament ethic will be a supernatural ethic produced by the power of God Himself in the life of the believer. In this way, it will be fundamentally different than the Old Covenant, "Not like the covenant which I made with their fathers … (8:9)."

In the New Covenant, God is the One who takes initiative. *He* will put *His* laws into their minds *He* will write them upon their hearts. *He* will be their God and they shall be His people. Thus, the Christian ethic list given in Hebrews 13 comes out of God's activity with regard to the establishment of the New Covenant. According to the supernatural grace principles of the New Covenant, God will prescribe spiritual laws which believers will abide by in contrast to the Old Covenant. In so doing, giving up the Old Covenant is not to embrace antinomianism or lawlessness. The New Covenant is not a lawless way of life, but a supernatural heavenly life within the holy of holies where God provides spiritual resources so that His people can do His will, "Now the God of peace, who brought up from the dead the great Shepherd of the Sheep through the blood of the ***eternal covenant***, even Jesus our Lord, equip you in every good thing to do His will, working in us that which is pleasing in His sight, through Jesus Christ, to whom the glory forever and ever. Amen (13:20-21)."

THE PUN ON CALVINISM

The most famous sermon in North American colonial history was delivered by Jonathan Edwards, perhaps the greatest American theologian of all time. The title of his well-known sermon was, "Sinners in the hands of an angry God." Although this sermon was delivered in a church setting, with great interest and very consistent with Calvinistic views on perseverance, he presumed the many of his congregation were not saved. As such, he warned many people in his congregation about the dangers of hellfire. The title therefore, "Sinners in the hands of an angry God," reflects how Calvinists characteristically use the church to warn sinners who really do not comprise the church, a somewhat odd state of affairs. In other words, in this very graphic sermon, Jonathan Edwards was not warning saints in his church, but sinners who were outside the church, though they attended the church. He was sure that a very large part of his congregation was unsaved.

In colonial days however, this should not be surprising. Going to church was something that the American colonialists simply did even though they were not necessarily Christians. It was a way of life due largely to the fact that cultural religious peer pressure was very strong. Under such conditions, religious nominalism actually flourished. This in turn left colonial churches with a religious cultural moralism, sometimes even associated with deistic views, rather than with a genuine supernatural spiritual life.[161] This was especially true with regard to Jonathan Edward's church. Jonathan Edwards inherited a church which believed that participation in the Lord's Supper was a means by which God imparts saving grace. The church also followed the Congregationalist tradition in New England of the Half-Way Covenant where they practiced infant baptism, even if the parents were unbelievers. In addition to this, Half-Way Covenant churches also allowed both believers and unbelievers to participate in the Lord's Supper. As such, these types of church traditions were largely responsible for creating and promoting a nominal Christian atmosphere wherein pews were filled with believer and unbeliever alike. Thus Jonathan Edwards preached fire and brimstone messages to his church to awaken the spiritual slumber of those who were regular parishioners, but very nominal in their faith.

While this certainly was a real problem in colonial churches, and is also very evident today as well, it also reflects an attitude which Calvinists have typically foisted upon the New Testament church. The nominal faith atmosphere of Colonial America is far removed from the beginning of the New Testament church. In turn, this has clouded their interpretation of the New Testament in general, especially with regard to the warning passages. When Jonathan Edwards and other Puritan Calvinists interpreted the New Testament, they always assume that there were many people in the New Testament church who were not saved, exactly like the churches of their own day. In short, they presume the religious cultural problems of their own day, i.e., that since churches were full of a mixed multitude of believers and unbelievers, this must have also been true of the early New Testament church as well. This, of course, is not a good starting point for exegesis. Current human religious experience becomes the basis for interpreting Scripture rather than the other way around. In this way, the behavior of nominal Christians of their own day leads to a rather peculiar understanding of the warning passages of the New Testament. *Sola Scriptura*, the hallmark of the Reformed faith, has been left behind because of the present activities of nominal Christians. Worse, nominal Christian experiences became the basis upon which the word of God was interpreted, rather than the text itself. In a word, in

---

161 Deism was fairly strong in colonial America at this time. Deists like Benjamin Franklin attended church regularly for moral purposes, but rejected the supernaturalism of the Bible.

the same way that bad cases make bad laws, so bad experiences make bad interpretations.

This has actually led to dubious exegesis on the part of many a Calvinist. Warnings in the New Testament, most notably in the book of Hebrews, and most especially in Hebrews 6, are acutely misinterpreted. While nominalism is certainly an important issue to grapple with in any church, the book of Hebrews was not written to warn so-called nominal believers, but saints who had experienced a once for all conversion (3:1-4:13; 6:1-8; 10:10-31). More to the point, in typical Calvinistic interpretation, even other warnings in the New Testament, which are clearly directed against believers, are conveniently redirected and become leveled against unbelievers instead. Thus almost every time a most serious warning shows up on the pages of the New Testament, the nominal Christian is plucked out of the proverbial hat, even though the New Testament letters have very little to say about such people. Paul and other New Testament authors wrote to the *saints*, not to professing saints. In fact, the only place where Paul clearly talks about nominal Christians is in 2 Timothy, and even there, he stays out of the arena of judgment, "The Lord knows who are His (2 Tim 2:19)." While Paul clearly delineates in this passage that, "Everyone who names the name of the Lord is to abstain from wickedness," he does enter judgment to determine whether people under Timothy's care are unsaved or not. This Paul clearly leaves in the hands of the Lord. Moreover, throughout the New Testament, Paul gives his congregations the benefit of the doubt with regard to their salvation. As such, he simply warns them as Christians, not as fakes who have a strange ill-defined inadequate faith of some sort. These kinds of discussions simply do not exist on the pages of the New Testament, and one will search in vain looking for passages where authors of Scripture assume that many people in their churches were unsaved. The fact of the matter is that the warnings passages found in the New Testament, especially in Hebrews, are directed against the saints, not to professing unbelievers.

"*Saints* in the hands of an angry God" is far more synonymous with New Testament teaching than "sinners in the hands of an angry God." As such, this teaching needs to be revived in the modern church, especially in an age where warning and seriousness is almost always disparaged as something out of touch with the hearts of people, and out of touch with the psychological spirit of the age. With great irony, Calvinists themselves, who are suppose to be known for their spiritual discipline, have played a large role in contributing to the present sloth of modern churches for the simple reason that they never really warn Christians. In essence, New Testament warnings are simply dropped in favor of their pet doctrine, the perseverance of the saints. The so-called real saints are never warned therefore, because of course, real saints are incapable of committing the kinds of continual sins which merit God's wrath. So-called "real" Christians thus go on with their spiritual lives without ever really getting warned, assuming that these warnings are for unbelievers, rather than for themselves. As such, application of these warnings are sorely lacking in the modern church. The result is that a spiritual indolence has replaced sharp spiritual thinking.

In fact, Calvinism has yet to counter the Catholic and Arminian charge that their once saved, always saved teaching leads to antinomian behavior. Their doctrine of the perseverance of the saints only has confused the issue further, which has resulted in less and less application of these warnings into the church over the last several centuries. How can one teach eternal security and yet still warn the saints? How can one give comfort to the Christian, and yet at the same time warn him of abusing that same comfort? The perseverance of the saints is an inadequate doctrine to handle this most acute problem. By placing the onus on the unbeliever rather than upon the believer, they have essentially created an easy free atmosphere in the church where serious warning is seldom a topic of discussion anymore. Christians simply assume that this or that particular warning is for someone else. After all, all real Christians persevere. The fact of the matter is that the perseverance of the saints is a pat theological answer to very difficult questions and problems that should have been discarded long ago. While it is good that the Calvinism brought back to the church grace concepts like eternal security, it has come with a hidden cost that real Christians never get warned. Ministers of the word of God must learn to teach eternal security and warn the saints about taking advantage of this great privilege at the same time. This is a most difficult balancing act which few seem to really appreciate today. In the end, the doctrine of the perseverance of the saints actually removes the pressure of this tightrope walking.

Such luxury, the sacred writer of the epistle to the Hebrews never entertains. The author of Hebrews knows how to walk a theological tightrope, comforting his readers with eternal security (7:25-28; 10:10-14; 12:22), yet at the same time severely warning them of their spiritual indolence (2:1-4; 3:7-4:13; 6:1-8; 10:19-39; 12:4-29). And this the author of Hebrews does very carefully, using the sure history of the Old Testament as a basis for his New Testament doctrines about salvation and warning. The author of Hebrews extensively uses Old Testament historical types throughout his book to exhort and warn his readers, and he most assuredly does not use the doctrine of the inevitable perseverance of the saints to straighten out his readers.

In the book of Hebrews, New Testament interpreters must be far more sensitive to the history of the Old Testament than they are to their textbook theology answers. The historicity of the Exodus generation, the person of Melchizedek, and Esau go a long way in explaining the great difficulties and perplexities of the book of Hebrews. The negative example of the Exodus generation shows how God judges a saved people with loss of inheritance rest, not loss of salvation. From Genesis 14, from the authority of the Pentateuch itself, the historical existence of the king-priest Melchizedek demonstrates there is another authoritative priestly line, not derived from the Mosaic Law, which is not only before the Levitical priesthood, but also superior to it. The author then builds his case throughout Hebrews 7 showing how Melchizedek is clearly a historical type of Christ, and as such, foreshadows a future priesthood far above the earthly Levitical priesthood.

By putting together both Genesis 14 and Psalm 110, the sacred writer strongly asserts to his Jewish audience that they should have expected and known that there would be another priestly Messianic line superior to their Old Covenant priesthood, i.e., the Melchizedekian line, and that this superior priesthood would also entail a change of covenants from the old to the new (Hebews 8). The sacred writer then shows that this decisive change of covenants in based upon the one time offering of Jesus Christ on the cross (Hebrews 9-10). The offering of the Melchizedekian priest, therefore, is a decisive sacrifice which has irreversible consequences, that the Hebrew readers can only ignore at their peril (10:26-31). The historical type of Esau is then used at the end of the book as the final example of warning. Esau forfeited his first-born inheritance rights through disobedience, but this does not mean that he stopped being a son of Isaac, or a brother to Jacob. Thus again, like the Exodus generation after him, the example of Esau shows how it is possible to be in the family of God, and yet lose inheritance rights because of divine discipline, the great thrust of Hebrews 12. These historical types certainly go a long way in illustrating the distinctive doctrines of the book of Hebrews by placing controls on how Hebrews is to be interpreted. The historicity of these examples limits the Hebrew warning passages to mean severe divine discipline, rather than the perseverance of the saints, or hellfire or loss of salvation.

EPILOGUE

THE WARNING PASSAGES OF 1ST CORINTHIANS

1st Corinthians parallels the book of Hebrews in many important ways. Their sins may have been very different, i.e., Jewish sins vs. Gentile sins, but the parallels between these two books are remarkable. Just as Hebrews has five warnings (Heb 2:1-4; 3:7-4:13; 6:1-6; 10:26-31; 12:12-29), so does 1 Corinthians (1 Cor 3:10-17; 6:9-10; 9:24-10:13; 11:28-32; 16:22). Just as the Exodus generation warning is the longest in Hebrews (Heb 3:7-4:13), so this is also true in 1 Corinthians (1 Cor 9:24-10:13). Just as the author of Hebrews assumes the Exodus generation was saved (Heb 11:29), so Paul has no doubts about the matter either (1 Cor 10:1-4). Just as Hebrews warns of loss of inheritance, reward and rest, so 1 Corinthians warns of loss of reward (1 Cor 3:14-15), inheritance (1 Cor 6:9-10), and the prize (1 Cor 9:24-27). Just as Hebrews warns against sinning willfully (Heb 10:26-27), so 1 Corinthians warns against continual sin (1 Cor 6:9-10). Nonetheless, all this sinning does not call into question the salvation of the readers however. Just as the author of Hebrews assumes his readers are saved (Heb 3:1), so neither does Paul question the salvation of the Corinthians (1:1). In other words, neither the author of Hebrews nor the apostle Paul pulls out the doctrine of the perseverance of the saints to straighten everyone out. Rather, they warn their readers about losing their eternal reward, inheritance, or prize instead. Both authors also distinguish between having eternal life and entering rest or inheriting eternal reward.

The Corinthians were involved in many sins, and so the apostle Paul has to write a very severe letter to warn them. In 1 Corinthians 1-2, the church is full of divisions, as people have been pitting one apostle or Bible teacher against another. In 1 Corinthians 5, the church has taken no responsibility with regard to a man who was sleeping with his own mother-in-law. They were apparently looking the other way all the while the man was fellowshipping with them in church. In 1 Corinthians 6, the saints are suing each other in court, and some are committing fornication. In 1 Corinthians 8-9, they are abusing their spiritual liberty at the expense of weak believers. In 1 Corinthians 10, Paul compares their behavior to the Exodus generation. In chapter 11, there are problems with unruly women.

Perhaps worst of all, however, is that the communion table had been profaned. It was carried out in chaos, and some were actually getting drunk on communion wine. As such, God was in the process of disciplining the Corinthians. Some had become weak, others were sick, and still some others had even died. Then in 1 Corinthians 12-14, Paul rebukes them for abusing their spiritual gifts. Pride and arrogance over the gift of languages had left the church worship service in spiritual confusion. This in turn negatively affected their witness to the outside world (1 Cor 14:23). Finally, if all of this was not enough, some were following the unbelief of Thomas, doubting the reality of the resurrection. With all of this deplorable behavior, Paul therefore writes a blistering letter against the Corinthians. However, Paul never doubts they were Christians, nor threatens them with a loss of salvation. He does, however, threaten them with loss of eternal reward (1 Cor 3:14-15), with not inheriting the kingdom of God (1 Cor 6:9-10), with losing the prize (1 Cor 9:24-27), and the sin unto death (1 Cor 11:28), and finally of being treated as accursed (16:22).

In 3:10-17, Paul warns the Corinthians that God will judge each man's work by fire to test its quality at the judgment seat of Christ. This is in connection with all the divisions in the church where various people are pitting one apostle or Bible teacher against another. As such, Paul severely warns the Corinthians about losing their eschatological reward when God will judge them for their works (3:12-15). Paul also warns them that God may indeed destroy them (3:17). Paralleling loss of reward, in 6:9-10 Paul threatens them with disinheritance just like Hebrews 3-4. Those whose lives are characterized by habitual sin, i.e., those who continue to sin willfully, will in no way inherit the kingdom of God. Not surprisingly, Paul then brings up the disaster of the Exodus generation at the beginning of chapter 10 (10:1-13) after warning them a third time about forfeiting their prize by abusing their spiritual liberty (9:24-27). In 1 Corinthians 11:26-32, Paul warns them of God's judgment for the fourth time, this time relating it to sickness, weakness and the sin unto death with regard to the abuse of the communion table. Not unlike the phraseology of the warning in Hebrews 10:29, 1 Corinthians 11:27 reads, "Therefore whoever eats the bread or drinks the cup of the Lord in an unworthy manner, **shall be guilty of the body and blood of the Lord.**" This is not too far removed from trampling underfoot the Son of God and regarding common the blood of the covenant (Heb 10:29). The last warning in 1 Corinthians is given very briefly, yet very starkly, at the end of the book, "If anyone does not love the Lord, he is to be accursed (16:22)." Just as many Old Testament people, including the saints, experienced the curse of the Old Covenant Law for their disobedience, there is also a cursing placed on believers in the Lord Jesus for not loving Him. This cursing cannot be an eternal curse, but is a form of divine discipline and judgment that may indeed threaten their future retirement in heaven so to speak.

Paul's usage of the Exodus generation illustration is very striking in the book of 1 Corinthians. This strongly ties together the warning passages found in Hebrews with the warnings that are found in 1 Corinthians. As such, the warning passages found in 1 Corinthians can help explain the warnings in Hebrews and vice-versa. Like the author of Hebrews, Paul includes himself in the warning about the possibility of being disqualified from the prize (9:24-27). He then slides right into the example of the Exodus generation debacle (10:1-13), an example to avoid at all costs. What this means is that obtaining the prize in 9:24-27, which Paul says can only be obtained by spiritual discipline, is parallel to entering rest as we see in Hebrews 3-4. This, in turn, also means that the disqualification from the prize is also parallel to the loss of eschatological reward in 3:10-15. Furthermore, losing the prize or reward, or even losing rest, is also distinct from losing salvation. As such, it is highly unlikely that 6:9-10 is threatening the Corinthians with loss of salvation, but rather with loss of rest, inheritance, the prize, or eschatological reward just like Hebrews 3-4. After all, Paul calls the reward an inheritance in Colossians 3:24, another parallel warning passage. As such, when he warns his readers that they will not inherit the kingdom of God if their lives are characterized by habitual sin, this is to be seen far more likely as a loss of eschatological reward rather than loss of salvation. Hebrews 12:14 says it yet another way, "Pursue peace with all men and the sanctification, without which no one shall see the Lord." Receiving a reward, entering rest, inheriting the Kingdom, obtaining the prize, and seeing the Lord are all based upon spiritual obedience. As such, they cannot be discussing salvation in the ultimate sense, but eschatological reward to be determined at the judgment seat of Christ.

When these warnings are compared together in context, rather than in isolation from each other, it presents a strong case for the doctrine of eternal security, rather than the typical Calvinistic or Arminian approach. Both the Calvinists and the Arminians have much to be desired when it comes to interpreting the warning passages of the New Testament. The warning passages found in Scripture are actually the Achilles heel of both systems. The Calvinist is all too ready to deny that a real Christian can commit terrible acts of apostasy in spite of the biblical evidence suggesting otherwise. It simply cannot explain the defeat and failure of God's people precisely because the doctrine of perseverance precludes this as a possibility in advance. It therefore uses forced exegesis to maintain its sacred theological cow. Many assumptions not found in the text suddenly come out of nowhere to the rescue.

On the other hand, Arminians are too quick to throw people into hell. Neither the book of Hebrews nor 1 Corinthians threatens that God will cast the readers of these epistles into hell. The Calvinists are right in their desire to make sure that this cannot happen, but have done violence to Scripture in order to maintain their theological system. Contrary to popular opinion, eternal security is the best approach precisely because it maintains both the certainty of salvation and the severity of the warning passages all at the same time. The Bible teaches in more than a few places that a Christian cannot lose his salvation. The Bible also teaches in many places that a Christian can lose his reward. As such, one must teach both at the same time according to the demands of Scripture.

As such, though not a perfect theological system to be sure, Eternal Security is still the best theological explanation. It can take into account most of the Scriptures with the fewest number of problems. It may present theological conclusions which may not look pretty, and which are painfully realistic, and so will never be politically or religiously popular, but it is still far more biblical. Nevertheless, popularity is not the standard for biblical interpretation. In addition, eternal security, though certainly emphasizing grace, in no way takes sin lightly, demanding the judgment of God, "The Lord, the Lord God, compassionate and gracious, slow to anger, and abounding in lovingkindness and truth, who keeps lovingkindness for thousands, who forgives iniquity, transgression and sin; yet He will by no means leave the guilty unpunished ... (Ex 34:6-7)."

Grace is not leniency. If more understood this principle, they would teach grace more consistently and with greater boldness, recognizing that the grace of God, while completely free, in no way compromises the holy justice of a righteous God who demands punishment of sin. Such is the great theme of the books of Hebrews and 1 Corinthians.

BIBLIOGRAPHY

Bruce. F.F. _Hebrews_. (William B. Eerdmans Publishing Company: Grand Rapids, Michigan, 1990), 426 pages.

Brunner, Emil. _The Mediator_ (The Lutterworth Press: London, 1934).

Clough, Charlie. Hebrews, sermon tapes series, Lubbock Bible Church (Lubbock, Texas 1973).

Delitzsch, Franz. _The Epistle to the Hebrews_, 2 volumes.

Dillow, Jody. _Reign of the Servant Kings_ (Schoettle Publishing Company: Hayesville, NC, 1992), 649 pages.

Dods, Marcus. _Hebrews_, from the Expositor's Greek New Testament (Eerdmans Publishing: Grand Rapids, Michigan, 1990), edited by W. Robertson Nicholl.

Dunham, Duane. _Doctoral Dissertation on the Hebrew Warning Passages._

Erickson, Millard. _Christian Theology_ (Baker Book House; Grand Rapids, Michigan, 1983).

Geisler, Norman L. _A Popular Survey of the Old Testament_ (Baker Book House: Grand Rapids, Michigan, 1977).

Kistemaker, Simon J. _Hebrews_ (Baker Book House: Grand Rapids, Michigan, 1984).

Lane, William. _Hebrews_ (Word Publishers: Dallas, Texas, 1991), 2 volumes.

McGee. Jay Vernon. _Moving Through Matthew._

Niemala, John. _No More Sacrifice_ (Chafer Theological Seminary Journal: Fountain Valley, CA, 1998-99).

Pink, Arthur. _Eternal Security_. (Guardian Press: Grand Rapids, Michigan, 1974), 126 pages.

Robinson, A.T. _Redating the New Testament._

Ross, Allen P. _Creation and Blessing: A Guide to the Study and Exposition of Genesis_ (Baker Book House: Grand Rapids, Michigan, 1987), 744 pages.

Vaughn, C.J. _The Epistle to the Hebrews._

Vincent, Marvin R. *Word Studies in the New Testament* (William B. Eerdmans Publishing: Grand Rapids, Michigan, 1989).

Westcott, Brooke F. *Hebrews*.

Whitlock, *Dictionary of Theology*, (Baker Book House: Grand Rapids, Michigan), edited by Walter Elwell.

INDEX OF SCRIPTURE REFERENCES

Made in the USA
Middletown, DE
24 June 2017